Central Banking as Global Governance

Money is a social convention, but with what social consequences? In this innovative study, Rodney Bruce Hall argues that those who govern the parameters of money's creation, its destruction, and its valuation are responsible for the governance of international finance. The volume is an analysis of central banking as global governance, employing the institutional philosophy of John Searle as a theoretical basis for exploring the consequences of money as a social institution, and the social relations of credit and debt. While previous studies in this field have made forays into the political economy of monetary institutions, this book breaks new ground by offering a constructivist social analysis that identifies the mechanisms of governance as social rather than material processes. The volume will therefore be of great interest to a wide range of scholars and students, particularly those with an interest in international relations, international finance, and international political economy.

RODNEY BRUCE HALL is University Lecturer in International Political Economy at St. Cross College, Oxford University.

Cambridge Studies in International Relations: 109

Central Banking as Global Governance

Cambridge Studies in International Relations is a joint initiative of Cambridge University Press and the British International Studies Association (BISA). The series will include a wide range of material, from undergraduate textbooks and surveys to research-based monographs and collaborative volumes. The aim of the series is to publish the best new scholarship in International Studies from Europe, North America and the rest of the world.

Cambridge Studies in International Relations

Series list continued after index

Central Banking as Global Governance

Constructing Financial Credibility

RODNEY BRUCE HALL

St. Cross College, Oxford University

CAMBRIDGE UNIVERSITY PRESS
Cambridge, New York, Melbourne, Madrid, Cape Town, Singapore, São Paulo, Delhi

Cambridge University Press
The Edinburgh Building, Cambridge CB2 8RU, UK

Published in the United States of America by Cambridge University Press, New York

www.cambridge.org
Information on this title: www.cambridge.org/9780521727211

First published 2008

Printed in the United Kingdom at the University Press, Cambridge

A catalogue record for this publication is available from the British Library

Library of Congress Cataloguing in Publication data
Hall, Rodney Bruce, 1960–
Central banking as global governance : constructing financial credibility / Rodney
Bruce Hall.
    p.   cm. – (Cambridge studies in international relations ; 109)
Includes bibliographical references and index.
ISBN 978-0-521-89861-4 (hbk.)
1. Banks and banking, Central.   2. Corporate governance.   I. Title.
HG1811.H25   2008
332.1′1 – dc22   2008037731

ISBN 978-0-521-89861-4 hardback
ISBN 978-0-521-72721-1 paperback

For Joan Marie – still adventuring

. . . markets look more efficient from the banks of the Charles than from the banks of the Hudson.

Alan S. Blinder

Contents

Preface

This book arises out of my fascination with social theory, the ever-changing artifice of finance, and the question of how this artifice is constructed and reconstructed. Since leaving my native country in 2003 for Oxford's old stone walls I have been fascinated by economic differences between my native and adoptive countries. I have been fascinated by what money will and won't buy on either side of the Atlantic, and by the fact that the price of goods other than property and petrol has been relatively stable, though food prices and other commodity prices have also risen in recent years. Food, fuel, and housing are not accounted for in "core inflation" indices in either country. Presumably so long as one does not need a roof over one's head, to travel to work, or to eat, inflation is no great issue?

The past half decade or more saw people pay exorbitant prices for quite modest homes and count themselves wealthy and confident that "bricks and mortar" would assure their future wealth – with never a thought that they might be purchasing shockingly overpriced property with badly debased currency. In a financial world awash with liquidity, actors in the global bond markets have snapped up highly risky developing world sovereign debt issues, whose quite significant risks of default might relegate them to junk bond status, at trivial yield spreads above US Treasuries. Then within months of extending cheap credit to those with little chance of being able to repay in an economic downturn, UK banks were charging one another nearly 7 percent Libor rates for overnight loans when credit conditions worsened in the aftermath of the "subprime" credit crunch. Credit conditions nearly collapsed in late 2007 as financial institutions discovered to their consternation that they could not find a price in the market for their large positions in collateralized debt obligations (CDOs). We have seen all of this financial drama unfold because the world's central banks have printed an awful lot of money, and that money has been seeking a return and

generating the destructive asset bubbles that form the financial headlines of the day. We have seen the central bankers talk to the markets in
various attempts to tell them where their monetary policy was going,
and the markets have talked back, and told the central bankers, with
diverse and far from united voices, where they want monetary policy
to go.

Enormous tides of capital have been generated and swept away in
these discussions, and I have been struck by the similarities in the public
discussions between those central banks which have been granted independence from finance ministries, and actors in the bond and foreign
exchange markets. It is a highly social interaction, and the social relations of credit and debt that constitute global finance are articulated
in this exchange. We have seen global financial governance unfold in
these discussions, with enormous causal significance for the direction
of capital formation. The current offering is my effort to develop and
explain these highly social relations of credit and debt through which
the mechanisms of global financial governance are constructed.

In the era of fiat money, money (financial capital) is a social convention. Those who govern the parameters of its creation, its destruction,
its valuation, as well as the parameters of the valuation of the promises
upon which the social convention of money is constructed, are those
who govern global finance. The mechanisms of governance are social,
not material, processes. The literatures in monetary economics and
central banking are replete with quite explicit references to the social
nature of these mechanisms. Central banks must establish "credibility" to ensure price stability, we are told. The literature concerns itself
with inherently social concepts, and the social scientist can read there
the exertions of monetary economists and central bankers grasping for
an analytic lexicon, which the highly stylized language of neoclassical economics clearly fails to provide, that might deal with the real
problems that face them. These are inherently social problems. Their
resolution requires a genuinely social analysis. The current offering is
humbly offered as an attempt to help. It is high time for a constructivist book on money and central banking. In grasping for a socialized
lexicon with which to deal with many of their analytic problems the
literatures of specialists in these fields tell us it is time as well. I hope
others better suited to the task than me will follow up the beginning
proffered in these pages.

I am grateful to Rawi Abdelal, Mark Blyth, Louis Pauly, two anonymous Cambridge referees, and my students at Oxford in the postgraduate seminar on global financial governance for useful criticisms of earlier versions of this work. I am grateful to John Haslam at Cambridge University Press and to the editors of the series Cambridge Studies in International Relations for their interest in and support of the project. Thanks to the Oppenheimer Fund of Queen Elizabeth House for financing the book's index. And always my deepest gratitude is reserved for my wife, Joanie, who puts up with me while I play in my intellectual sandbox.

1 | *Central banking as governance*

Don't fight the Fed!

Wall Street aphorism

It is well enough that the people of the nation do not understand our banking and monetary system for, if they did, I believe there would be a revolution before tomorrow morning.

Henry Ford Sr.

Governance is thus a system of rule that is as dependent on intersubjective meanings as on formally sanctioned constitutions and charters.

James N. Rosenau

The literature on central banking is currently dominated by references to the need for, or attempts by central banks to attain, "credibility" with the financial markets. The vehicles by which central banks are to attain this credibility are typically identified by monetary economists and central bankers as "independence" and "transparency." Independent central banks have the authority to conduct monetary policy without interference or political pressure from the finance ministry or the government. This independence can be granted as full "operational independence" where the choice of the vehicles by which monetary policy is executed is left to the discretion of the central bank. It can also be granted in the form of "goal independence" where the level of domestic inflation to be tolerated as consistent with the mandate of the central bank to maintain "price stability" is also left to the discretion of the central bank.

Possession of either or both of these forms of independence leaves the central bank in command of enormous authority over, for example, the domestic money supply and the supply and price of short-term credit to the banking sector, as well as the price of money in the short-term money markets. It also permits central banks to delegate authority to other actors, including private actors in the financial markets.

The neoclassical literature on monetary economics and central banking tells us that this independence from government pressure to print money to monetize debt or to stimulate the domestic economy provides the central bank and its monetary policy with "credibility" with the financial markets, particularly with the foreign exchange (FOREX) and bond markets. An unfortunate source of confusion in this literature arises from the fact that the models from which the assertions that central banks are tempted to generate excess monetary stimulus are drawn are rational choice theoretic. However, the credibility that central banks require to resolve these problems can only result from the establishment of intersubjectively shared social understandings between central bankers and market actors.

Credibility is a social relationship as much as (or rather more than) an economic relationship. When we are "credible" we are trustworthy, and when we are trustworthy we can be relied upon to meet our commitments and to keep our promises. Central banks are entrusted with the guardianship of price stability. Central banks are "credible" when market actors and the public trust central bankers to act to uphold their promise to maintain the purchasing power of the money they issue. In our contemporary era of fiat money in which we lack a capacity to measure the value of money against an external standard – such as gold or some other valuable commodity in limited supply – all money is fiat money. Money's value is stipulated by fiat, and the central bank explicitly or implicitly pledges to maintain that fiat value. Thus money is a promise.

As a consequence of this social nature of money, the "rational expectations" of market actors cannot help them in making carefully calculated, rationally determined decisions regarding the credibility of the social understandings that they share intersubjectively with governors of central banks. The "utility" of "rationality" encounters severe limitations as a basis for market decisions in this context. Market actors have, then, to make a choice. They can either trust the central bank's promise of stable money – and thereby loan their own money to governments, commercial enterprises, or municipalities at a small premium – or they can decline to trust the promise of stable money and demand a high-risk premium to compensate them for the devaluation their own money might suffer while out on loan.

Market actors will consequently base their investment decisions on "intersubjective expectations"[1] rather than "rational expectations" and will look to central banks (and to one another) for signals of continuity of the validity of the promise that the money issued by the central bank represents.

Central banks, anxious to reinforce hard-earned intersubjective expectations of market trust in their money's credibility, will wish to avoid disappointing market actors lest their credibility be lost, and their reputations as trustworthy guardians of price stability suffer. Surprises will always disappoint market actors. Thus we see the contemporary move toward increasingly independent (thus ostensibly "credible") central banks, toward enhancing the "transparency" *vis-à-vis* market actors of central bank expectations regarding inflationary pressures in the economy, and the transparency of banks' monetary policy decision-making procedures. These moves toward enhanced transparency generate increasingly sophisticated central bank communications strategies that are directed toward market actors in the hope of steering their intersubjective expectations, shared with other market actors, of the future direction of monetary policy. In this way central bankers hope to enlist market actors in reinforcing the direction of central bank monetary policy *vis-à-vis* long-term interest rates. Market actors may thereby be enlisted as monetary policy force-multipliers, because these long-term rates are determined not by the central bank but by private actors with capital to lend in the disinter-mediated bond markets.

To the extent that independent central banks are successful in establishing "credible" intersubjective expectations with market actors that their monetary policy will maintain price stability – and to the extent that they are successful in establishing "transparent" intersubjective expectations with market actors who consequently trust that central bank signals will point them toward the future direction of monetary policy – then institutional convergence toward central bank independence and transparency constitutes an increasingly effective instrument of global financial governance.

---

[1] These are related to what Blyth calls "conventional expectations." See Mark Blyth, "The Political Power of Financial Ideas: Transparency, Risk, and Distribution in Global Finance" in Jonathan Kirshner (ed.) *Monetary Orders: Ambiguous Economics, Ubiquitous Politics* (Ithaca, NY and London: Cornell University Press, 2003), pp. 239–59.

Governance

This introductory chapter, while conceptually important and summative, is very brief. It introduces the notion that current trends toward institutional convergence in central banking – specifically recent moves toward increased central bank independence and transparency – are the bases for establishing a new system of monetary governance. This is developed as a system of multilevel governance, with contributions from financial and policy actors that have been allocated various forms of constituted authority that will later be developed as "deontic powers" in the system of governance.

In a growing literature on the topic of governance, the meaning which is most useful for the explication of the relations of global financial governance in general, and monetary governance in particular, is social and relational. The writings of Benjamin Cohen and James Rosenau provide a strong point of departure. While institutions are often implicated in social relations of governance, Benjamin Cohen points out that:

> Governance . . . does not necessarily demand the tangible institutions of government. It may not even call for the presence of explicit actors, whether state-sponsored or private, to take responsibility for rule-making or enforcement. To suffice, all that governance really needs is a valid social consensus on relevant rights and values.[2]

Governance is therefore an inherently social, relational phenomenon. While governance relations may develop institutional forms in practice, over time they need not rely on institutions of government. As Rosenau has developed the concept:

> Governance refers to activities backed by shared goals that may or may not derive from legal and formally prescribed responsibilities and that do not necessarily rely on police powers to overcome defiance and obtain compliance. Governance . . . is a more encompassing phenomenon than government. It embraces government institutions, but it also subsumes informal, non-governmental mechanisms . . . Governance is thus a system of rule that is as *dependent on intersubjective meanings* as on formally sanctioned constitutions and charters.[3]

[2] Benjamin J. Cohen, *The Geography of Money* (Ithaca, NY: Cornell University Press, 1998), p. 145.

[3] James N. Rosenau, "Governance, Order, and Change in World Politics" in James N. Rosenau and Ernst-Otto Czempiel (eds.) *Governance Without*

Global financial governance – and particularly monetary governance – is argued in this book to be a system of rule based on systems of distributed authority networks among both public and private actors that are strongly dependent upon intersubjectively shared meanings. As it is a system with multiple sites of authority, it is a decentralized system of multilevel governance.[4] As such, the sites, or locations, of authority are found at numerous levels of organization. I argue that authority over monetary governance is found at the national level, at the supranational level, and at both the public and private transnational levels.

At the national level, authority over monetary governance is found in the executive branch of many governments, particularly in the finance ministries and in central banks. Authority at the national level over monetary governance may be found in abundance particularly among central banks which have been granted independence by the government. A major argument of this book is that the emerging system of global monetary governance is designed to drive governance capacity down to the lowest possible level in a system of multilevel governance – namely the national level – through institutional convergence toward independent (and preferably "transparent") central banks. At the national level the system of governance is represented by increasingly independent, variably transparent central banks and their communications strategies, as well as foreign ministries, and national fiscal and political authorities. Central banks have been allocated an enormous range of "deontic powers" ascribed in this system of governance. These will be developed briefly later in this chapter, and described in considerable detail in chapter 3. For now, it should suffice to add that "deontic powers" are the result of "deontologies" and thus are forms of authority (or governance capacity) resulting from collective assignment of status functions.

At the public transnational level these actors include the International Monetary Fund (IMF) and the Bank for International Settlements (BIS) as foci of fiscal policy surveillance and enforcement, and of coordination of central bank policy respectively. While these

Government: Order and Change in World Politics (Cambridge: Cambridge University Press, 1992), p. 4, and quoted in Cohen, *The Geography of Money.* Emphasis added.

[4] For the etymology of this terminology from the literature on European integration see e.g. Lisbet Hooghe and Gary Marks, *Multilevel Governance and European Integration* (Lanham, MD: Rowman and Littlefield, 2001).

public transnational actors serve as sources of the neoliberal ideational infrastructure of the emerging system of monetary governance, and they are briefly discussed later in the book, the focus in this work is on explicit institutions and "institutional facts" rather than broad historical ideational changes that have prepared the way for the emerging system of financial and monetary governance. The important ideational transformations that have led to the eclipse of Keynesian economic ideas,[5] the collapse of the Bretton Woods gold-exchange standard,[6] and the transformation of the various public international financial institutions such as the IMF,[7] and even the BIS,[8] into public transnational champions of neoliberal ideas and prescriptions, have been well studied by others in an exciting and recently developing constructivist literature on international political economy. But the present work would suggest that while transformation of these public international institutions has been an important enabling condition for the emerging system of monetary governance, the major agencies and mechanisms of governance are located elsewhere. They are located largely at the national and private transnational levels of governance.

At the private transnational level the emerging system of governance includes financial market actors, particularly participants in the FOREX markets and the disintermediated bond markets. These actors are allocated authority to adjudicate the "credibility" of fiscal and monetary policy through market judgments – as well as private bond rating agencies like Moody's and Standard and Poor's who are allocated the deontic power to "grade" that credibility on a ranked scale for use by participants in the markets for sovereign, corporate, and municipal debt instruments.

---

[5] Mark Blyth, *Great Transformations: Economic Ideas and Institutional Change in the Twentieth Century* (Cambridge: Cambridge University Press, 2002) and Wesley W. Widmaier, "The Social Construction of the 'Impossible Trinity': The Intersubjective Bases of Monetary Cooperation" *International Studies Quarterly* 48 (2004): 433–53.

[6] Eric Helleiner, *States and the Reemergence of Global Finance: From Bretton Woods to the 1990s* (Ithaca, NY: Cornell University Press, 1994) and Jacqueline Best, *The Limits of Transparency: Ambiguity and the History of International Finance* (Ithaca, NY: Cornell University Press, 2005).

[7] Rawi Abdelal, *Capital Rules: The Construction of Global Finance* (Cambridge, MA: Harvard University Press, 2007).

[8] Ethan B. Kapstein, *Governing the Global Economy: International Finance and the State* (Cambridge, MA: Harvard University Press, 1984).

At the supranational level the emerging system of monetary governance includes a new supranational European Central Bank (ECB) and the ancillary system of national European central banks. The burgeoning use of the euro as a global reserve currency and as a vehicle for currency substitution introduces a supranational level of governance into the system, which does not, however, impact all actors equally. The ECB has a mandate enshrined in the Treaty of the European Union (EU) to ensure price stability and it operates procedurally in accordance with its supranational charter. This mandate can only be overturned by renegotiation of the treaty and ratification of a two-thirds majority of the members of the EU.

The success of this emerging global system of multilevel monetary governance relies on policy convergence as "best practice" as defined by epistemic communities of monetary economists and central bankers. The effect (and it is highly likely, the intent) of these efforts toward policy convergence is to drive the most critical governance structures down to the lowest possible, national, level of governance so that they may provide uniformly effective impetus toward price stability throughout the international monetary system. In the chapters to follow I emphasize the importance of establishing money as a social, institutional fact – rather than a brute or observational fact – for correctly specifying the power of central banking as a governance mechanism. The concluding chapter will sketch out the major forms of constituted authority (which will be developed as "deontic powers" in accordance with John Searle's institutional philosophy) that constitute the emerging system of global monetary governance in the era of fiat money and floating exchange-rate regimes. Central banks (monetary institutions at the national level of governance) have an important role to play in generating and institutionalizing this system of monetary governance.

Plan of the book

I will now proceed with the plan of the book. As I am developing a constructivist theory of monetary relations and monetary governance I will be required to equip the reader with the proper conceptual apparatus with which to apprehend monetary power relations as social relations. Thus the second and third chapters will critique orthodox monetary theory for its inadequacies in helping us to properly apprehend the social nature of money and monetary relations, and the nature of the institutional facts upon which all monetary relations and institutions are built. Subsequent chapters will build upon a fresh conceptual apparatus that is designed to flesh out the details of the emerging system of monetary relations based upon the authority relations constituted in no small measure by central bank "credibility" and "transparency" strategies.

Chapter 2 will develop the social character of money and central bank finance. I critique orthodox monetary theory's basis in the commodity theory of money and its quantity theory variant, as well as its view of money as a "neutral veil" in the "real economy." I will develop and critique the historical and intellectual antecedents of orthodox monetary theory's three "functions" of money as a "store of value," a "medium of exchange," and a "unit of account."

The deflationary monetary systems of the classical gold standard and monetarism will be demonstrated to spring from the "store of value" function of orthodox theory. The gold standard system arose from the assumptions of the commodity theory of money, and monetarism from the quantity theory of money. Orthodox theory's view of money as a medium of exchange impels the demand for money creation and empowers central banks to regulate its supply. The continued search for a new "nominal anchor" for the international monetary system – with the demise of metallic standards and the non-viability of monetarism in the light of monetary velocities and the proliferation of "near monies" – is developed as a major intellectual legacy resulting from the orthodox view of money as a unit of account.

Orthodox monetary theory misses several insights crucial to a proper understanding of the nature of money, not least that money's value in the era of modern central banking is an intersubjective scale of value. In this context, the value of money is constantly interpreted and reinterpreted. Thus in practice money's value is determined domestically by central bank fiat and internationally by negotiation of social relations of trust between central banks and market actors. Thus money's social character is developed as a promise between central banks, governments, and purchasers of government securities, as well as users of money among the general public. In later chapters this social character of money will be demonstrated to have enormous consequences for the construction of the social relations of governance of monetary orders.

Chapter 3 presents the major theoretical insights critical to the constructivist development of central banking as a social institution and the social character of money. I draw upon the institutional philosophy of John Searle in developing the international financial realm as a realm of social, institutional facts that is rigorously distinguishable from the realm of brute or observational facts. Searle's work illustrates how institutional facts are generated by the collective assignment of status functions to people, institutions, and objects that thereby acquire deontic powers (authority resulting from an institutional deontology) that are explicable only through a constitutive, rather than a causal, logic. These power and authority relations are institutional facts. Institutions are constructed from deontic powers ascribed by actors to other actors, by collective assignment of status functions (by fiat). They engender creation of constitutive rules. Searle demonstrates

The creation of an *institutional fact* is, thus, the collective assignment of a status function. The typical point of the creation of institutional facts by assigning status functions is *to create deontic powers* . . . we have created a situation in which we accept that a person S who stands in the appropriate relation to X is such that (S has power (S does A)).[9]

The concept of money as an institution will be developed with recourse to these foundational constructivist concepts that help us to understand the constitution of social kinds and their distinction from natural kinds. The theory is then applied to develop the deontic powers of central banks. These include (but are not limited to) the deontic powers of (1) money creation and destruction in the process of setting interest rates, (2) liquidity creation and risk socialization powers (lender of last resort functions), (3) powers to value and revalue the domestic product of the nation through exchange-rate and foreign reserves management, (4) the power to monetize government debt, and (5) powers of credit allocation via government directed lending and "window guidance." Each of these deontic powers of central banks is developed with recourse to the theory in some detail.

Chapter 3 concludes with a discussion of why we should trouble to develop a socialized view of central banking and international monetary systems. It matters because understanding money, credit, and

[9] John R. Searle, "What is an Institution?" *Journal of Institutional Economics* 1(1) (2005): 21–2. Emphasis added.

central banks as social institutions permits us to begin to discover
the monetary and economic realms as rule-governed spheres of social
action. It helps us to make an analytic cut into the rule-based architecture of international monetary affairs. This rule-based realm has
always been governed by an institutional logic of institutional practices in response to institutional facts and the constitutive rules that
arrange these into social reality, rather than by the wholly uncoordinated actions of means–ends instrumentally rational actors. We need
a "logic of appropriateness" intersubjectively shared between actors,
and not simply a "logic of instrumentalism" individually endogenized
by atomized rational individuals, to explain both central bank behavior
and market behavior in national and international monetary affairs.

Chapter 4 will analytically relate and contrast the notion of deontic power as developed from Searle's institutional philosophy to currently developing concepts of power in the extant constructivist literature in international relations, as well as to current developments in
the analysis of the notion of international monetary power. Deontic
power will be related to but distinguished from the useful taxonomy
of power developed within explicitly constructivist theories, and the
deontic powers of central banks developed within chapter 3 will be
further analyzed within this taxonomy in order to explore the constitutive power relations that central banks and their interaction partners
engender within monetary power relations more fully.

The international monetary order has always been rule based. Its
history is the history of the construction and demolition of rules: constitutive and regulative, explicit and tacit, substantive and procedural,
national and transnational. Bretton Woods was a rule-based monetary
system whose relatively recent demise in international monetary history has been a test-bed for many explanatory schools of thought. But
it has been well studied recently. Chapter 5 will instead focus on the
consequences of the continuing debates among monetary economists
and central bankers regarding the relative merits and problems of
rule-based vs. discretionary monetary orders. It applies the constructivist institutional theoretical framework to the distinctions between
the rule-based gold standard and the current "discretionary" system of
competitive floating exchange rates. The comparative deontic powers
of central banks are developed in each system.

In my analysis, rule-following behavior in both systems is found to be
discretionary and contingent. The "rules of the game" of the classical

gold standard are seen to have been sometimes observed in the breach. Both systems were also "contingent" in the sense that their rules could be suspended under well-defined contingencies. The chapter develops a major argument of the book, carried to its conclusion in chapter 7, that the current moves toward universalizing central bank independence and transparency (sophisticated central bank communications strategies) constitute an attempt to develop a new "nominal anchor" for the international monetary system in the era of "fiat money," to establish the value of money in the absence of the prior anchors of metallic standards.

I will argue that this new nominal anchor is intended to provide the benefits (price stability) of the gold standard without the consequences (deflation and periodic deep global recession). The new nominal anchor is to retain elements of discretion (instrument, and occasionally goal, independence of monetary policy by independent central banks) and contingency (independent central bankers may accommodate exogenous shocks and output gaps) but to provide the benefits of a rule-based system without the negative externalities associated with rigid, mechanical rules such as a metallic standard or monetary targeting. Constitutive and regulative rules generated by the deontic power of central banks in the developing and developed worlds are discussed in the chapter, and their functioning in various monetary operating systems associated with the choice of various exchange-rate regimes is described. The problems of this new nominal anchor in generating the desired combination of price stability and output in the "real economy" are developed as problems attending inadequate development of intersubjectively shared social understandings within central banks, and between central banks and markets.

Chapter 6 begins with a discussion of the historical and contemporary debates attending the benefits of rules vs. discretion in monetary policy, while emphasizing the requirement of nominal monetary anchors in the absence of rules to ensure price and financial stability. I trace key themes in the continuing debate to their origins that are so well developed in a famous Great Depression era essay on the topic by liberal Chicago School economist Herbert Simons. These themes have been picked up by contemporary monetary economist and central banker Otmar Issing, among other contemporary analysts. Writing seventy years apart, both appear to yearn for the benefits of price stability that some have believed to flow from simple mechanical rules, but recognize that the negative deflationary consequences for the economy are untenable for governments constituted by liberal, democratic polities. Simons[10] issued a plea for a simple mechanical rule in which we could trust "religiously" upon discovery, and Issing[11] abandons the search for such a rule and urges us to trust in independent central banks as a surrogate for a rule-based monetary mechanism.

The chapter develops theoretically and analytically the relationships between trust, authority, confidence, and governance in monetary affairs in the era of fiat money. Issing suggests that trust in central banks means trust in the expertise of central bankers, whose sanguine exercise of their authority is to be guaranteed by independence from governmental pressure to expand monetary stimulus to generate short-term domestic political benefits. The literature on monetary economics is replete with references to the importance of the "credibility" of central banks to ensure price stability at all costs. This chapter explores the network of social relations by which that credibility is constructed.

The chapter then explores the sources of this central bank authority, and the relationship between trust, authority, and confidence in independent central banks. The relationship between authority and governance in monetary affairs is then developed. The sources of authority and financial governance are found to be shared between governments, central banks, and financial markets. An institutional account of this governance structure is generated, employing the theoretical framework developed in chapter 3 in mapping out the allocation of deontic powers among these actors, and some resulting constitutive rules of monetary governance.

Chapter 7 describes the problems of intersubjectivity within central bank decision-making as well as the problems central banks face in attempting to establish systems of intersubjectively shared social meanings with financial market actors. The move to central bank "transparency" via mechanisms such as immediate release of monetary policy committee decisions on interest rates, establishment of inflation targeting regimes, release of central bank inflation reports, forecasts, and models are analyzed as "monetary policy force-multipliers" by central banks.

[10] Henry C. Simons, "Rules Versus Authorities in Monetary Policy" *Journal of Political Economy* 44(1) (1936): 1–30.
[11] Issing, Otmar, *Should We Have Faith in Central Banks?* (London: Institute for Economic Affairs, 2002).

Because central banks can directly control only very short-term interest rates in the money markets, they cannot through their own operations rely on transmission of their policy decisions efficiently throughout the economy. Long-term interest rates (the long end of the bond yield curve) on sovereign, corporate, and municipal debt issues are determined by the disintermediated bond markets. Miscommunication between central bank intentions and the understandings of financial market actors can result in a failure of market actors' perceptions and expectations of central bank intentions regarding the structure of long-term rates. These "intersubjective disconnects" can endanger the goal of price stability. Market actors are seen to rely upon "intersubjective expectations" rather than "rational expectations" to coordinate market action. Evidence is presented that the predictions of rational expectations theory regarding bond market behavior fail rather dramatically when tested empirically.

Thus central bank transparency and communications strategies emerge as critical components of the developing structure of monetary governance. Coupled with moves toward universalizing central bank independence, the move toward universalizing central bank transparency is a critical structural element of governance in generating this pair of institutional mechanisms as a new "nominal anchor" for the international monetary system in the era of fiat money and capital mobility. The emerging system of global financial governance is then outlined and summarized. I conclude the book by expressing skepticism of the ultimate success of the emerging governance structure to provide the stable nominal anchor that is intended for the system, given the limitations of convergence processes, and the tendency for the modern capitalist economy to generate financial innovations that defeat rules or anchors constructed to constrain it.

This system of global financial governance is required to replace now defunct systems based upon metallic standards as an external referent of value. As money is a promise and not a commodity in the era of fiat money, it is governance that must make this promise credible, and tangible. The institutions that generate this promise are consequently, and not surprisingly, the focus of the attempts of aspiring architects of international financial architectures to consolidate and homogenize this governance capacity.

2 | *The social character of money*

Men of business in England do not . . . like the currency question. They are perplexed to define accurately what money is: how to count they know, but what to count they do not know.

Walter Bagehot

Although economic theory has a good deal to say about the role the money plays in the economy, it remains uncomfortably vague about the appropriate definition of money.

Mervyn King

THE BUCK STARTS HERE

Plaque in the office of former US Fed Chairman Greenspan

Central banking has developed an enormous mystique in recent years in no small measure because central bankers are widely believed to have a monopoly of the power to create the money supply of the nation, "and ultimately the power to create is the power to destroy."[1] Once exclusively within the power of sovereigns, money is now created and destroyed by central banks, and the mechanisms by which they do so will be elaborated in this chapter. They do so largely with the assistance of two technical mechanisms whose social character will also be elaborated, as it is the social character of money, its generation, and its destruction, and the manner in which this generation and destruction arises from social processes, that interests us.

Contemporary economic thought on the nature of money, and to a significantly lesser extent contemporary practice within the central banking profession, subscribes to the commodity theory of money. In this view money is produced exogenously of social relations, and is

---

[1] Paul Volcker, foreword to Marjorie Deane and Robert Pringle, *The Central Banks* (London: Hamish Hamilton, 1994), p. viii.

introduced into the economy by central banks acting as the agents of governments. This view spawned the "monetarist revolution" within monetary economics, which gave credence to the thesis that as money is exogenously injected into the banking system, and from there into the economy through the unique money creation function of central banks, then central banks can ensure price stability by generating stable expectations regarding the supply of money. This was to be accomplished by careful accounting and control of monetary aggregates within the economy. Since central banks are, in this view, the sole source of money creation, then central banks, acting to monetize government debt and finance government fiscal imprudence, are the source of excess money in the economy. This excess money in the economy is, in the monetarist view, the sole source of price inflation, and these ideas constitute the basis of Milton Friedman's monetarist mantra, that "substantial inflation is always and everywhere a monetary phenomena."[2]

The monetarist experiment, led by the Volcker Federal Reserve (Fed), to crush the "Great Inflation" of the late 1960s through the early 1980s in the industrialized world, by targeting and restricting the money supply, was successful in changing expectations and restoring price stability. But it was successful at enormous social cost, and has since been abandoned, albeit subsequent to the restoration of relative price stability in the early 1980s. The consequences of the monetarist experiment for small businesses with high debt reliance were brutal, and the lesson learned from the experiment was that "money works, but it does not work miracles."[3] Here expectations were changed by restricting the supply, thus raising the cost of money, treating money like any other bulk commodity whose price is bound to rise in the face of restricted supply and constant or rising demand. Wild gyrations in interest rates (the cost of money) indeed resulted from a punishing restriction of supply. The social and economic costs of the maneuver climbed until society capitulated and was finally induced to believe that the central bank had gained the "credibility" that it would persist in restricting the supply of money and watching its cost spiral until the public changed its expectations and stopped bidding up commodity and consumer prices. This policy was pursued by the Volcker Fed

---

[2] Milton Friedman, *Money Mischief: Episodes in Monetary History* (New York: Harcourt Brace, 1994), p. 193.
[3] Deane and Pringle, *The Central Banks*, p. 118.

irrespective of the severe social and economic costs that it inflicted upon those who had continued to make economic decisions predicated on the very different assumptions regarding the supply and cost of money envisioned as a commodity.

What is money?

The question of what constitutes money arises early in monetary history. In debates over the 1844 Bank Charter Act (Peel's Act) by which Britain attempted to limit the supply of money in the banking system, the British Parliament only recognized specie, bank notes, and "cash in hand" as money, failing to recognize bank deposits (or "demand deposits") as such.[4]

Even under the restrictive, commoditized view of money dominant in neoclassical economics, particularly among monetarists, a more expansive definition of money was required as financial vehicles proliferated with the development of commerce and finance. Central banks, believing themselves to control the supply of money to the economy, found themselves devising means by which to measure this "commodity" in the forms into which it was proliferating. The US Federal Reserve, for example, when it considers monetary aggregates, considers various forms of money delimited by their liquidity, and thus by the likelihood that this form of money will be circulated within the economy.

The principal monetary aggregate, known as the M-1 money supply, is money that is immediately liquid, namely "the gross sum of all the currency and demand deposits held by every consumer and business."[5] This is a relatively small stock of money in an advanced industrialized state, as this stock of money will be circulated any number of times during the course of a year in routine transactions (e.g. in the terminology of monetary economics, it will have a high "velocity" of circulation). Money held in savings for longer terms at rates of interest which vary with the length of time it is "on deposit" with a financial institution is counted in the M-2 money supply. This includes all small savings accounts and time deposits at banks, credit unions, savings and loan societies, as well as in money market mutual funds. Funds held for periods of three to six months or longer in certificates of deposit

[4] *Ibid.*, p. 41.
[5] William Greider, *Secrets of the Temple: How the Federal Reserve Runs the Country* (New York: Touchstone, 1987), p. 57.

of large denominations of $100,000 or more (normally by firms or financial institutions) are counted in the M-3 money supply. And even less liquid types of investment readily convertible to spendable money are counted in a class designated "L" for total liquidity. This includes US Treasury bills, commercial bonds, US savings bonds and like debt instruments that can be readily converted to cash, even if at a slight discount in the markets for such instruments.[6]

Moves toward recognition that the banking system creates money in the form of bank credit, however, made it difficult by the late twentieth century to account for, let alone control, proliferating forms of monetary aggregates. The long-standing neoclassical tendency to view money as a commodity which could consequently be quantized, accounted for, and controlled by central banks, was demonstrated to be impractical in practice. Attempts to account for and to manage the money supply during monetarist episodes in central bank history resulted in a situation in which "myriad forms of credit-money had given rise to new measures of the money supply. M-2 led to M-3 and so on to M-17."[7]

Viewing money as a commodity, in orthodox monetary economics, has led to a trifunctional (with emphasis on the term functional) view of money as a "neutral veil" which serves three functions in the "real economy" of barter. In this view money serves as a "store of value," a "unit of account," and a "medium of exchange."[8] As a store of value, money was thought to consist of the precious metals that it contained. Bank notes had value to the extent that they represented the value of specie or bullion, and were convertible into these scarce commodities. Money as specie or its representation, then, was thought to store value that was strongly coupled to the cost of its production, in the medium to long term, and to only temporarily store value due to demand for money as a commodity in the short term.[9]

Money as a store of value in orthodox monetary theory

Historically there have been numerous problems with this hyper-commoditized view of a metallic standard for money, and gold has

---

[6] *Ibid.*, p. 58.   [7] Ingham, *Nature of Money*, p. 30.
[8] Deane and Pringle, *The Central Banks*, p. 107. See also Cohen, *The Geography of Money*, p. 11.
[9] Ingham, *Nature of Money*, p. 19.

been largely demonetized at this writing in no small measure as a consequence of these practical problems. As one observer has recently quipped, gold "has a future, of course – but mainly as jewelry" with the caveat that "[g]old also has a future as a store of value in parts of the world with primitive or unstable monetary financial systems" in the form of monetized gold reserves, held by central banks as part of a "nominal anchor" to defend a currency peg.[10] But as a store of value, gold has proven to be an increasingly poor inflation hedge, and has served as a better store of value during periods of deflation than inflation.[11] Moreover, the use of a gold standard for currency issue has been famously deflationary, with disastrous consequences[12] as the "rules of the game" of the gold standard required nations to "ship gold" when experiencing a balance of payments deficit, raising interest rates and restricting the money supply in order to attract it back again. The central bank was supposed to raise interest rates in response to gold outflows, restricting credit and holding down domestic prices relative to trading partners, thus enhancing the competitiveness of exports, and dampening demand for imports. Conversely, according to these "unwritten rules" the bank was supposed to lower domestic rates, reversing the economic incentives generated by tightening the rates, and encouraging gold outflows when the nation was experiencing a balance of payments surplus.

But the latter exercise in global trade-and-monetary-good-citizenship was more rarely executed,[13] and the "rules of the game" of the gold standard were often enough observed in the breach for the "equilibrating" effects of their exercise not invariably to be enjoyed. Moreover, the global money supply on the gold standard could only rise as rapidly as global gold production would permit. Such are the foibles of specieism, which can render the enthusiasm for a return of a gold standard by contemporary "gold bugs," whose numbers are reported to include former Federal Reserve chairman Alan Greenspan,[14] somewhat mystifying.

---

[10] Niall Ferguson, *The Cash Nexus: Money and Power in the World, 1700–2000* (New York: Basic Books, 2001), p. 325.

[11] *Ibid.*

[12] Barry Eichengreen, *Golden Fetters: The Gold Standard and the Great Depression 1919–1939* (Oxford: Oxford University Press, 1995).

[13] Ferguson, *Cash Nexus*, p. 153.

[14] Jerome Turccille, *Alan Shrugged: Alan Greenspan, the World's Most Powerful Banker* (New York: John Wiley&Sons, 2002), p. 243.

Yet this suggestion may be unfair, in light of the fact that the early discovery by sovereigns of the profits of seigniorage – taking the profits of the difference between the cost of minting coins and their value once issued – and subsequently of debasement of coin suggested a need to fix the value of coins in terms of some metallic standard. This standard nearly invariably involved gold or silver. This was particularly important at times when the price of gold relative to silver varied significantly on the open market. To this end, in his capacity as Master of the Mint, Sir Isaac Newton in 1717 fixed the Mint price of gold at £3 17s. 10½ d. per ounce, and paper money could then be issued which was backed by gold at a price fixed in sterling. This gold fixing generated remarkable price stability in Britain throughout the eighteenth century, until gold convertibility was suspended in 1797 at the start of Britain's entry into the Napoleonic Wars. This suspension led to a round of inflation that saw prices rising by 80 percent through 1818. Bouts of inflation had been seen to accompany all suspensions of gold convertibility of national currencies, not the least of which was the inflation attending the suspension of dollar convertibility by the United States in 1971. Yet cleavage to a gold standard has just as consistently exerted enormous deflationary pressures on national, regional, and global economies during times of sustained economic downturn.

Consistent with the commodity-based theory of money, however, central bankers and finance ministers throughout the world believed that the Great Depression had been prolonged by problems with the global distribution of monetary gold. They argued that these "maldistributions" had proven "disequilibrating" for the global economy, rather than blaming the inherent deflationary bias built into the gold standard by its tendency to prohibit the injection of monetary stimulus into a national economy. While ultimately nation after nation abandoned the gold standard during the Depression in favor of fiscal and monetary policies of national protection and autarky, their finance ministers and central bankers did so under protest and duress. When the UK suspended gold convertibility "temporarily" on 21 September 1931 the former Lord Privy Seal, Tom Johnson, was reported to have exclaimed in alarm that "[n]obody told us we could do that."[15] And

[15] Gianni Toniolo, *Central Bank Cooperation at the Bank for International Settlements, 1930–1973* (Cambridge: Cambridge University Press, 2005), p. 132.

economic historian Gianni Toliono reports that according to another
UK observer at the time the gold standard had "become a religion
for some Boards of Central Banks in Continental Europe, believed in
with an emotional fervor which makes them incapable of an unpreju-
diced and objective examination of possible alternatives."[16] The gold
bloc countries, particularly of Europe, abandoned the gold standard
only when forced off by the deflationary effects of maintaining it, and
then did so only in the face of defection from gold by major trading
partners.[17]

But as a valuable commodity whose price remains rather stable
over time, gold served as the basis of all reserves of central banks
for decades, and originally all reserves were held in gold, rather than
securities or foreign currencies. Gold shipments constituted the only
basis for payment in international settlements. By the mid-1990s total
official gold holdings in the vaults of the world's central banks constituted over 36,000 tons, or over 30 percent of all the gold estimated to
have been mined. In the period between 1948 and 1964, central banks
bought 44 percent of all the gold on offer on world markets. While
gold has retained a high level of price stability in real terms against all
national currencies since the United States "closed the gold window"
and suspended dollar–gold parity and convertibility, it retains the dis-
advantage to the holder that as a commodity – rather than a security
or contract – it does not pay interest. Nor is it particularly liquid as
an investment. No major holder of gold reserves could sell any very
significant amount of its holdings in a moderate period of time without
precipitating a significant price decline.[18]

The gold standard also provided a role highly prized by finance
ministers, central bankers, and participants in global financial markets
alike, by serving as a "commitment mechanism." Adherence to the
gold standard required fiscal discipline from governments wishing to
attract investment and to maintain the benefits of strong credit in the
form of low borrowing costs. Adherence to the gold standard as a
commitment mechanism accomplished this; "by removing exchange
rate risk and affirming a country's commitment to 'sound' fiscal and

[16] *Ibid.*
[17] Eric Helleiner, *States and the Reemergence of Global Finance: From Bretton
Woods to the 1990s* (Ithaca, NY: Cornell University Press, 1994), pp. 29–30.
[18] Deane and Pringle, *The Central Banks*, pp. 181–3.

monetary policies, it reduced the cost of international borrowing for countries that joined."[19]

With gold now removed as a transnational "nominal anchor" for "sound" money in an era of floating exchange rates, the post-Bretton Woods monetary order has cast about for a replacement anchor. The history of the international monetary system can be written as a history of a search for a new, viable, stable nominal anchor amid numerous failed experiments with a bewildering array of exchange-rate regimes, to restore the "credibility" and "confidence" in the value of money that gold parity had provided. Monetarism's "commitment" to a pre-determined growth in the money supply has been put forward, and then put away again, as another nominal anchor to replace gold.[20] But the practical difficulties of identifying and quantifying, let alone controlling, the money supply doomed monetarism's pretense to provide the panacea to anchor a return to "sound" money. The problem was fundamentally derivative of the commoditized theory of money's conceptual difficulties in identifying precisely what money is in the context of capitalist finance.

The bias of neoclassical economics toward a commoditized view of money as a store of value, reflecting the real value of a commodity that money represents, goes a long way toward accounting for this fervor of our contemporary "gold bugs." But geostrategic designs and power politics could also make a nation cleave to gold in a world in which gold anchored the international monetary system. And gold was brought out to once again anchor the international monetary system at Bretton Woods, which contracted a *de facto* dollar standard in which all other currencies were fixed at a specified exchange rate to the dollar. As the United States stood in possession of 70 percent of the world's monetary supply of gold at the end of the Second World War, it would ensure the gold anchor by promising to redeem, upon demand, dollars for gold at the fixed price of $35 per ounce of fine gold. Drawing upon archival evidence, Francis Gavin demonstrates that the United States went to extraordinary lengths to preserve the convertibility of the dollar into gold, as the inflationary pressures of US fiscal difficulties attending the Vietnam war, and Lyndon

---

[19] Ferguson, *Cash Nexus*, p. 332.
[20] W. Max Corden, *Too Sensational: On the Choice of Exchange Rate Regimes* (Cambridge, MA: MIT Press, 2002), p. 17.

Johnson's war on poverty, brought this convertibility under pressure in the 1960s:

US policy makers frantically worked to avoid ending dollar–gold convertibility and allowing the dollar to "float," and instead went to extraordinary lengths in a desperate attempt to maintain a system that was collapsing. Capital controls, trade restrictions, massive multilateral interventions to stymie currency markets, the creation of a new "international" money, troop withdrawals, and threats to end security commitments were all considered more attractive policies than allowing currency markets the power to determine the value of the dollar.[21]

The United States put enormous pressure on its European allies to stop cashing in their dollars for gold. It pressured the Federal Republic of Germany to redress its trade surpluses with the United States to ease speculative pressures on the dollar by reducing US trade deficits, and ultimately threatened to bring US troops home and suspend the US guarantee of the security of the Federal Republic of Germany against the Soviet Union.[22] Seemingly money can be something more than a store of value. Consistent with the "political economy" approach to monetary order, in this view, politics can be seen to drive economic policies, including the choice of monetary institutions, rather than the converse.[23] The role of ideology is crucially implicated in this process.[24]

As the United States faced a particularly severe balance of payments crisis in 1968, putting particular pressure on the credibility of the capacity of the US dollar–gold convertibility link, President Johnson received alarming, even hysterical, scenarios of the consequences of suspending convertibility from his advisors, who seemed to envision nearly unimaginable consequences, and clearly had no idea what suspension of convertibility could mean. Rostow warned Johnson that a "crisis of confidence" in the global financial system could "feed on itself much like a run on a bank. The end result could be a serious contraction of economic policies – at home and abroad – to preserve

---

[21] Francis Gavin, "Ideas, Power, and the Politics of US International Monetary Policy During the 1960s" in Kirshner, *Monetary Orders*, p. 198.

[22] *Ibid.*, pp. 205–12.

[23] William Bernhard, J. Lawrence Broz, and William Roberts Clark, "The Political Economy of Monetary Institutions" *International Organization* 56(4) (2002): 693–723.

[24] See Jonathan Kirshner, "The Inescapable Politics of Money" in Kirshner, *Monetary Orders*, pp. 3–24.

their gold holdings."[25] Nothing particularly spectacular did happen when President Nixon "temporarily" suspended gold convertibility in 1971, or when the illusion that the suspension was temporary was abandoned in 1973. By this time,

the last prop for the money illusion [that money represents a store of value of a tangible commodity] was kicked away ... Demand deposits had been backed by the same promise that applied to currency – any private citizen could, in theory, go to the bank and redeem his money in a quantity of gold.[26]

Today, even famous monetarists write blithely of the "metallist fallacy" in denying that money must be backed by a commodity with an intrinsic value for other purposes, while still pointing out that "[b]efore 1971, every major currency from time immemorial had been linked directly or indirectly to a commodity" except in "times of crisis."[27] But the same famous monetarists will simultaneously argue that the

abstract concept of money is clear: money is whatever is generally accepted in exchange for goods and services ... not to be consumed but as an object that represents *a temporary abode of purchasing power* to be used for buying still other goods and services.[28]

In other words, still entirely consistent with a commoditized version of money as now abstractly representing other goods, money is a temporary store of value, and it matters not that money has evolved from exchange of metallic specie, to notes redeemable for specie, to demand deposits transferable by check,[29] or to a plastic card. Orthodox monetary economics does not dwell on the fact that "it took generations for the public to overcome its natural distrust of checks"[30] as money. Nor do they dwell much on the social meaning of the fact that "commodity money was replaced with 'representative' money" which many of them "speak of contemptuously as 'fiat money.'" Still less do they dwell on the social meaning of the phenomena that "next the paper itself disappears. Money becomes truly invisible ... social trust is conferred upon plastic cards. The plastic is not itself money, only a coded key that gives access to money."[31]

[25] *Ibid.*, p. 214. [26] Greider, *Secrets of the Temple*, p. 228.
[27] Friedman, *Money Mischief*, pp. 14–15. [28] *Ibid.*, p. 16. Emphasis added.
[29] *Ibid.* [30] Greider, *Secrets of the Temple*, p. 228. [31] *Ibid.*, p. 229.

Instead, the view of money as a commodity, however ethereally man-ifested in modern finance and banking, subordinates the question of what money is, or how it is introduced into the economy, to questions of how much of it is in demand in the economy at any given time.[32] This question is in turn subordinated by the monetarists to the ques-tion of how much of it should be supplied to the economy at a given time. This commoditized vision of money has led orthodox monetary economists, therefore, to focus on the consequences rather than the causes of variations in the money supply.[33]

Milton Friedman's restatement of Irving Fischer's "equation of exchange," which expresses the orthodox quantity theory of money, is the basis for the monetarist revolution. As it expresses the quantity theory of money, it is a quintessential example of the persistence of the view of money as a commoditized "neutral veil." Monetarist thought distinguishes between the "nominal" quantity of money expressed in terms of the amount of currency in circulation, and the "real" quan-tity expressed in terms of the amount of goods and services that the nominal quantity will purchase. The former, Friedman argues, is deter-mined by the central bank, and the latter by the public.[34] The demand for money is in this view determined, consistent with classic rational utility maximizing behavioral assumptions, to result from a simple cost–benefit analysis. Demand for money is determined by its utility as a temporary store of value. Thus "separation of the act of sale from the act of purchase is the fundamental productive function of money" vs. the (inflationary and opportunity) cost of holding money in the form of cash.[35]

Monetarism becomes an exercise in attempting to demonstrate that the real demand for money cannot be increased over the long run by an increase in the nominal supply of money, and that the only result is to induce people to bid up the nominal (not the real) value of goods and services in the short term. Their bidding has long-term effects as people adjust their expectations to higher nominal prices.

The monetarist insistence that price inflation is fundamentally a monetary phenomenon finds famous expression in Irving Fischer's equation of exchange in which Fischer lays out the essentials of the quantity theory of money that provides the basis for modern

---

[32] Ingham, *Nature of Money*, p. 19.   [33] *Ibid.*, p. 20.
[34] Friedman, *Money Mischief*, p. 19.   [35] *Ibid.*, p. 22.

monetarism.[36] Fischer generated a simple algebraic equation that represented the balance of the quantity of money residing in notes, coin and checkable demand deposits against the price level of all transactions over the course of a year as follows:

$$MV + M^1 V^1 = \sum pQ = PT$$

where M represents all notes and coin, M^1 all checkable demand deposits, V and V^1 the respective velocities of circulation, p a specific price of a good or service, Q an individual transaction at that price, P the general price level, and T the aggregate of all transactions. Friedman presents a simplified version of this equation in a collection of essays on money intended to be accessible to the layperson, and declares that "Fischer's equation plays the same foundation-stone role in monetary theory that Einstein's $E = mc^2$ does in physics."[37] Friedman is a worthy successor to Fischer in that

all Fischer's efforts were directed toward demonstrating that causation could not run from prices to money, and as the equation was logically true, it had...to operate in the opposite direction. In short MV (money and its velocity of circulation) caused the level of PT (prices and transactions). He rejected explanation of the autonomy of price as the result.[38]

Money as a medium of exchange in orthodox monetary theory

Thus monetarists argue that for money to serve its second functional role in the orthodox commoditized theory of money (and its "quantity theory" of money variant), it must be limited in quantity.[39] The gold standard limited the quantity of money as only so much monetary gold could be added to existing stocks in a given year. Orthodox monetary theory – whether monetarist or not – now worries with Friedman that since the link with a metallic commodity has been severed, "the world is now engaged in a great experiment to see whether it can fashion a different anchor, one that depends on government restraint rather than on the cost of acquiring a physical commodity."[40] The assertion that

---

[36] Irving Fischer (assisted by Harry G. Brown), *The Purchasing Power of Money: Its Determination in Relation to Credit Interest and Crises* (New York: Macmillan, 1911).

[37] Friedman, *Money Mischief*, p. 39. [38] Ingham, *Nature of Money*, p. 21.

[39] Friedman, *Money Mischief*, p. 42. [40] *Ibid.*

the success of this "experiment" depends upon "government restraint" is a belief shared by orthodox economists and contemporary actors in the financial markets, and it is a belief whose consequences for monetary and financial governance this book explores.

In the orthodox view of money as a medium of exchange money serves a functional role indicated by theories of the rational utility of money simply as a tradable commodity whose exchange functions reduce transaction costs in trade. Attempts by neoclassical economists to establish micro-foundations of money – by demonstrating that transaction costs are reduced for the individual by the use of money as a medium of exchange – "express the logical circularity" of the methodological individualist approach to rational utility theory. Money can only provide this utility for the individual "provided that all other agents do likewise . . . to state the sociologically obvious: the advantages of money for the individual presuppose the existence of money as an *institution* in which 'moneyness' is established."[41]

Endogenous money creation through credit

There are two central assertions from orthodox monetary theory that we can identify now that lead us to a problem with which we must deal to understand why so much current effort within monetary economics and central banking is directed toward restraining governments. One is the clear assertion that as a medium of exchange, the function of money in the economy is that of a "medium for the gaining of utility through the exchange of commodities" whose quantity must be limited to serve as a "store of value." Governments must be restrained from monetizing debt with fiat money, thereby devaluing money as a store of value, depleting its utility as a medium of exchange to reduce transaction costs, and distorting its utility as a unit of account. This amounts to an assertion that money is introduced exogenously into the economy by the agency of the state. This exogenous view of money supply neglects the endogenous sources of money creation (and destruction) that characterize modern financial systems, and which have been present since the development of private, commercial banking systems.

As Geoffrey Ingham suggests, modern capitalist finance "is distinguished by entrepreneurial use of credit-money produced by banks to

---

[41] Ingham, *Nature of Money*, p. 23. Emphasis in the original.

take speculative positions regarding the production of commodities for future sale."[42] New money is created by private commercial banks which turn the credit that they extend to borrowers into money by expanding their loan portfolios beyond the cash they have on reserve as deposits to back the loans. Central banks create the cash to back the loans, in this case, after the loans have been extended by creating deposits whose reserves have yet to have been created "by the simple entry in a ledger."[43] Schumpeter had understood the social fact of credit-money when he observed that when credit is extended – beyond the cash on hand of the bank extending it – then "depositors and borrowers have simultaneous use of the 'same' money . . . and . . . new lending creates new money."[44]

In order to illustrate this concept let us consider an example in which a borrower goes to a commercial US bank to borrow $100,000 to buy a house. The bank evaluates the borrower's creditworthiness and assesses the risk that the loan will not be repaid. It asks for "security" in terms of collateral, and/or a significant deposit of the borrower's own money which will be at risk if the borrower defaults on the mortgage. At the end of the day of the creation of that debt, the commercial bank – which is required to keep a fixed percentage of its cash on reserve with the Federal Reserve system at no interest – is frequently required to demonstrate that it can meet those reserve requirements. If it cannot do so (if it has loaned more money to acquire the debts that are its "assets" than it has on deposit as its "liabilities" to cover the loans it has made) it must do one of two things. (1) It must borrow the money needed to top up its reserve funds to meet the Fed's requirements from another bank at a rate of interest determined by the supply of money provided to the banking system by the Fed (known as the "Federal Funds" rate), or (2) it must "go to the discount window" and borrow the money directly from the Federal Reserve system at a penalty rate of interest. The Fed creates the money by creating a deposit in the commercial bank's account at its local Federal Reserve branch. When it has done so it has

created money with a key stroke of the computer terminal (computer accounting having replaced "the stroke of a pen") . . . Once it was created, it

---

[42] *Ibid.*, p. 26.   [43] Greider, *Secrets of the Temple*, p. 59.
[44] Cited in Ingham, *Nature of Money*, p. 27.

[this deposit] increased the overall money supply and was free to float from one account to another through the entire banking system.[45]

From the earliest days of nascent central banking, the banking system, both private and public, has been concerned with the creation of credit-money, and central banks have been rewarded with a monopoly of the creation of "legal tender," as a medium of exchange. The innovation of the public bank may be seen as a seventeenth-century Italian novelty. Banks were formed as early as the late sixteenth century in Venice; they accepted deposits and effected transfers between accounts, accepted bills of exchange payable to clients (proto-checks) and securitized and effectively monetized the short-term debt of the Venetian state by converting it into discountable, resalable bonds. The Bank of England, originally chartered as a private institution, was given the function of managing, and securitizing the government debt, and was in return granted a monopoly of note issue. The Banque de France, said Napoleon, "does not solely belong to the shareholders but also belongs to the state which granted it the privilege of creating money."[46]

That privilege had already likely been claimed *de facto* by private commercial houses in seventeenth-century Venice and Genoa. But the rise of the public bank strongly enabled, and finally formalized, the credit-money creation process of securitizing and monetizing public as well as private debt. This is most evident with the creation of the Bank of England to finance Britain's Nine Years' War with France in the late seventeenth century, and is wholly evident when it was incorporated in 1661 as a joint stock company upon extending a £1.2 million loan to the crown at 8 percent interest. The Bank of England in turn was granted the privileges of a monopoly of joint stock banking, of handling the government's account, of the right to deal in bullion, and to discount approved bills of exchange, which amounted to credit vehicles for settling international payments. Credit-money was consequently quite easily created by the Bank of England because "with the government's promise to pay it, the Bank could issue notes to match the sum lent to the government" which in turn were lent out "so that interest was earned twice over, both from the government and from the private sector."[47]

[45] Greider, *Secrets of the Temple*, p. 32.   [46] Feguson, *The Cash Nexus*, p. 110.
[47] *Ibid.*, p. 39.

Private commercial banks have even been similarly involved in the creation of money. How have they done it?

They did it by new lending, by expanding the outstanding loans on their books. Routinely, a bank borrowed money from one group, the depositors, and lent it to someone else, the borrowers, a straightforward function as intermediary. But if that was all that occurred, then credit would be frozen in size, unable to expand with new economic growth. On the margins, therefore, bankers expanded their lending on their own and the overall pool of credit grew – and the bank turned credit into money... money has been created by the simple entry in a ledger... the businessman [debtor] would go out and spend the money, writing checks on his new account, and everyone would honor their value. The creation of new money, thus, was really based on bank-created debt.[48]

This is precisely the sort of mechanism that Keynes had in mind in his 1930 *Treatise on Money* when he wrote that "the marginal efficiency of capital is determined by forces partly appropriate to itself."[49] For our purposes, Keynes realized that "money in the form of deposits is being socially constructed by discretionary bank lending, according to norms and conventions which render them relatively autonomous from savers' deposits."[50]

But to the extent that orthodox monetary theory accounts for the endogenous creation of the money supply through private sector financial innovation, it theorizes it in orthodox, commoditized, rational-instrumental, and functional terms. The supply of money, if it is not controlled by the government, should be left to the market, which should also determine its value, according to some economists. The "free bankers" among them, as well as the monetarists, see monetary history as the history of the "misuse of political power to further monopoly and rent-seeking interests... [while]... democratic states print money in order to finance spending to appease mass electorates."[51] A highly conservative, yet somewhat socialized, view of money emerges from their discourse. However, it is still a view dominated by a commoditized vision of money as a store of value and a medium of exchange. In this view, stable money is a public good. This view touts the mistaken notion of money as exogenously given to the

[48] Greider, *Secrets of the Temple*, p. 59.
[49] John Maynard Keynes, *A Treatise on Money* (London, Macmillan, 1930).
[50] Ingham, *The Nature of Money*, p. 51.   [51] *Ibid.*, p. 35.

economy and society by central bankers, who enjoy a monopoly of its creation.

There emerges from the commoditized theory of money a highly conservative social purpose of commoditized money "as part of our inheritance – like language . . . it is collective property, a good that once destroyed takes generations to rebuild, an asset not to be abused under the pretext of helping some social group."[52] Recognizing the deflationary impact of tighter money on employment, and on social groupings whose access to credit is limited when credit is dear, the conservative, still commoditized and exogenously produced view of the social purpose of money asserts in quite normative terms that it is "immoral . . . to defraud a person of his or her money through inflation."[53] As we shall see in later chapters, these normative claims exert a powerful influence on the current theory and practice of central banking, and the role that these practices play in the present constitution of the international monetary system.

Money destruction

Money, once created, through the banking system or by the central bank, may subsequently be destroyed. We have seen how central banks create money in response to direct loans to commercial banks, or by purchasing government debt securities on the open market. But just as money is created by central banks, it can be destroyed or retired by central banks. In Greider's description of the operations of the Fed, "when the Fed's Open Market Desk sold bonds or a commercial bank repaid its discount loan, money was extinguished by the Fed. By a simple entry in a ledger, the money was automatically withdrawn from circulation."[54]

However, just as money creation has private as well as public sources, so does money destruction. This was brought to the attention of the monetary policymakers in the Fed with alarming clarity when the Fed had, at Paul Volcker's instigation, changed its "operating system" from a discretionary system to a system that targeted the money supply in order to tackle the "Great Inflation" with which the industrialized world had been struggling from the late 1960s into

---

[52] Deane and Pringle, *The Central Banks*, p. 346.
[53] *Ibid.*, p. 343.   [54] *Ibid.*

the early 1980s. As rate tightening actions by the Fed began to take hold and to seriously change expectations of agents regarding the future rate of inflation and cost of money, the Fed suddenly found that its actions had done more than simply generate a decline in the growth of the money supply. As Greider reports:

Now money was disappearing... Week by week, as each commercial bank reported its currency and demand deposits, Fed economists calculated the total for the entire system... Instead of growing, M-1 was abruptly getting smaller... Money was vanishing – and at a very rapid rate... This did not require any shredding of $100 bills or melting down of coins; most of the money supply, after all, did not exist as cash in people's pockets. Most of the nation's money existed merely as numbers in the account books at banks – the total balances of checking accounts. The Federal Reserve had not intended anything like this.[55]

The Fed had not acted directly to extinguish, in the case Greider reports, over $17 billion in money, but it was extinguished nonetheless, by actions set in motion when people in the real economy finally came to believe that the Fed would continue its bout of interest rate tightening until double-digit annual inflation rates were crushed. This was not a direct act of the US central bank, but in fact:

The money that ceased to exist was, in fact, destroyed by everyone – humble consumers, small businesses, banks and major corporations... People paid off their debts – that was one fundamental cause... millions of consumers not only stopped their new borrowing, but they also rushed to pay off old bank loans or charge accounts. This process extinguished money because it reversed the magical way in which the bank lending created money in the first place. When a customer paid off his bank loan, the bank erased the numbers of both sides of its ledger – the loan disappeared and so did the demand deposit from which the customer had drawn the money.[56]

Since the advent of double entry bookkeeping, the accounting structure of banking systems has been in terms of "assets" and "liabilities." The manner in which banks account assets and liabilities is somewhat counter-intuitive to us humble souls who see banks as intimidating institutions that permit us to park our money with them for a short time until we spend it, paying us a bit of interest as a sop for the fees the bank will charge for its various "financial services." Commercial

---

[55] Greider, *Secrets of the Temple*, p. 194.   [56] *Ibid.*, p. 195.

banks are in the business of "intermediating" between creditors and
debtors. They accept the deposit of the creditor, pay interest on that
deposit, and loan that deposit to a debtor at a higher rate of interest,
pocketing the difference as a profit. Since the bank has loaned out
money lent to it by depositors, it has ostensibly exchanged cash for a
promise of repayment with interest. Though in fact, as we have seen,
the bank often exchanges a deposit it creates without the cash on hand
immediately to back it. The bank has ostensibly performed its fiduciary responsibility of correctly assessing the creditworthiness of the
borrower, and perhaps acquired a legal guarantee of collateral – some
tangible asset belonging to the borrower – to indemnify itself against
the risk of loss through non-repayment that it incurs in the process.

Now, at the end of the transaction, the borrower has a demand-
deposit that can be spent as agreed, and the bank has whatever collateral and security it has obtained from the borrower, and the *promise*
of a cash-stream of a specified amount per unit time for a specified
period of time. Aside from foreclosures against collateral, and the fees
it charges for the various financial services it provides, the majority of
the bank's income and profits derive directly from these cash-streams
resulting from borrowers delivering on their *promises* of the payments
to which they have contracted. Thus the bank regards its portfolio of
such *promises* as its "assets." Its "liabilities" are its own *obligations*,
largely the deposits of cash it receives from its customers – and the
interest it pays them to retain these deposits – which it claims the
right to loan out by virtue of paying interest on the deposits, thus
temporarily acquiring the use of the monies they constitute.

The reader will here note that I have, in this description of a bank
loan transaction, highlighted the terms "promise," "obligation," and
"right." I have done so to stress the fact that in entering into the
loan contract, the banker, the depositor, and the borrower have all
three generated social institutions, and in consequence their economic
relationship is an institutional relationship that is a subset of their
broader social relations. I will elaborate on the importance of this
observation later in this chapter.

Central banks render a similar accounting of assets and liabilities on
their balance sheets. Assets for central banks are "gold and foreign
currency reserves, investments in government and other securities;
and loans to commercial banks" while they list among their liabilities "notes and coin; balances of commercial banks placed with the

central bank, and usually a small amount representing the central bank's capital and reserves."[57] Those items which the central bank regards to be liabilities are bound up with its role as an issuer of legal tender and guarantor of liquidity in the banking system for a given country. These central bank "liabilities" consequently "form the base for all the money in the economy . . . 'central bank money' or 'high powered money.'"[58]

Money as a unit of account in orthodox monetary theory

A key problem arises in the treatment of orthodox monetary theory simultaneously as a medium of exchange, unit of account, and a store of value. Orthodox monetary theorists will report, for example, the use of "cigarette money." Milton Friedman related in his lectures to students of economics a tale in which he exchanged a carton of cigarettes he purchased at the PX for $1.00 for fuel for his vehicle in Germany valued at $4.00, asking them what happened to the missing $3.00, while intimating that "an amazing variety of items have been used as money at one time or another."[59] And he provides us with a list of commodities that have, in his view, been used at various times as "money" including "cattle . . . salt, silk, furs, dried fish, tobacco . . . feathers . . . stones . . . beads and cowrie and other shells, such as the American Indians' wampum."[60] In discussing "cigarette money" Friedman goes on to observe that a carton of cigarettes was deemed to constitute too high a value for most transactions, so cigarettes were exchanged by the pack, or by the single cigarette,[61] indicating that those who employed them and accepted them as payment for goods and services in kind attributed different units of account to cigarettes, packs of cigarettes, and cartons of cigarettes.

But this treatment of commodities like cigarettes as "money," employed as a unit of account, seems to derive entirely from the fact

---

[57] Deane and Pringle, *The Central Banks*, p. 116. It is worth noting that when reserves grow to highly inflated levels, it indicates a highly defensive posture for a central bank with respect to the stability of the currency. See e.g. Hans Genberg, Robert N. McCauley, Yung Chul Park, and Avinash Persaud, *Official Reserves and Currency Management in Asia: Myth, Reality and the Future*, Geneva Reports on the World Economy 7 (Geneva: International Center for Monetary and Banking Studies, 2005).
[58] *Ibid.*   [59] Friedman, *Money Mischief*, pp. 12–13.
[60] *Ibid.*, p. 13.   [61] *Ibid.*

that the cigarettes were clearly employed as a medium of exchange. It is unclear that because commodities are bartered in exchange they consequently take on the clear unit of account functions required for a coherent orthodox monetarist account of the requirements of money. Cigarettes were exchanged during World War II in prisoner-of-war camps for a variety of goods; however, "the fact that non-smokers were willing to offer their goods for cigarettes does not make them, in Keynes's terms, anything more than a 'convenient medium of exchange on the spot.'"[62] Items may be, in Adam Smith's terms "trucked and bartered" without taking on the orthodox "functions" of money. Nor does such a barter economy constitute a market.

A genuine market which produces a single price for cigarettes requires a money of account – that is, a stable yardstick for measuring value... The very *idea* of money, which is to say, of abstract accounting for value, is *logically anterior and historically prior to market exchange.*[63]

Efficient markets clear at the equilibrium price negotiated between buyers and sellers, according to the equilibrium hypothesis of neoclassical economics. A buyer has determined the value the product holds for him and the seller has determined the value s/he must obtain in order to part with the product. In the functional logic of economics, money as a unit of account serves a very specific and important function in bringing the transaction about. "As a unit of account, money simplifies comparison of values. It is a *numéraire*, or standard of measurement" of value.[64] Keynes pointed out that money's function as a unit of value was indispensable to the functioning of a free market economy based upon free exchange among individuals when he observed that the

individualistic capitalism of today, precisely because it entrusts saving to the individual investor and production to the individual employer, presumes a stable measuring rod of value, and cannot be efficient – perhaps cannot survive, without one.[65]

---

[62] Ingham, *Nature of Money*, p. 24.   [63] *Ibid.*, p. 25. Emphasis in the original.

[64] Charles P. Kindleberger, *A Financial History of Western Europe* (2nd edn) (Oxford and New York: Oxford University Press, 1993), p. 19.

[65] John Maynard Keynes quoted in S. Herbert Frankel, *Money: Two Philosophies: The Conflict of Trust and Authority* (Oxford: Basil Blackwell, 1977), p. 40.

In sociological terms, money then serves as an "intersubjective scale of value"[66] which constitutes a shared meaning and understanding, between subjects, of a unit of purchasing power. But this intersubjectively shared understanding only retains social or economic utility if it is relatively stable. It can be renegotiated and retain utility, but if the renegotiation proceeds at too rapid a pace, all utility is lost. Not only contractual, but social, relationships then fail. This leads us to the discussion of the role of trust in establishing money's utility, acceptability, and its intrinsic essence in a system of economic relationships.

Trust: money as a promise

Some theorists of money came to understand that credit, such as is allocated by the banking system, can function as money. Theorists such as Henry Dunning Macleod developed a credit theory of money in which money became the highest and most general form of credit. In this view a piece of money in your hands is:

witness and the proof, that you have at some time done some work, which instead of profiting by, you have allowed society to enjoy . . . this crown piece witnesses that you have rendered a service to society, and moreover it states the value of it. It witnesses besides that you have not received back from society a real equivalent service, as was your right.[67]

In this view money is a claim on society. It represents a debt owed by society to its possessor that is not yet paid. Never mind that a lot of people with money made their money the old fashioned way – they inherited it. In that case money still represents a claim by a forebear for services rendered to society but not yet redeemed. That this claim has passed to another – who continues to press it on behalf of the forebear by the mere possession of money's promise to redeem that claim – has no bearing on the validity of the claim, nor any bearing on the trust that the money's possessor places in the promise.

We may begin to find the social content of money in its acceptability and usage. These are the metrics of the trust and faith that people place

---

[66] Ingham, *Nature of Money*, p. 25.
[67] Macleod quoted in Frankel, *Two Philosophies*, p. 35. Frankel cites H. D. Macleod, *The Principles of Economical Philosophy*, vol. I (2nd edn) (London: 1872).

in it, as "money is worthless unless everyone believes in it."[68] In purely economic terms trust is:

the binding cement of all contractual relationships. Whether unforeseen circumstances are likely to arise which could prevent the fulfillment of promises or obligations; through no fault of the parties concerned; is not a question of trust but of probability. This is the essential difference between a debt and an investment. The first involves a promise, the second only the expectation of a return. When we trust . . . we are going beyond the mere assessment of probabilities.[69]

Thus, following Frankel's notion of the relationship of trust, when we trust in money, we are not actuaries calculating the probability that the promise that money represents will be redeemed. We are engaging in an act of faith.

This may trouble those of us who may think of ourselves as such modern people that we relegate acts of faith to another age. Yet Anthony Giddens has argued that trust is an essential act of modernity. Giddens's work on capitalist modernity sees modernity as characterized by "disembedding mechanisms" that entail the "'lifting out' of social relations from local contexts of interaction" and which depend upon trust, which Giddens characterizes as "a form of faith."[70] Two classes of disembedding mechanisms that are involved in the advent of modern social institutions, and discussed at length by Giddens, are "symbolic tokens," like money, and trust in "expert systems" defined in terms of "systems of technical accomplishment or professional expertise."[71] Every time we get on an airplane, or step into an elevator, we place our trust in an abstract system that we are certain someone understands; thus the expert systems constituting air travel and elevators will (magically, for all we know) deliver us safely at our destination in another city, or on the thirty-fourth floor of the high rise building in which we work.

For the layperson, the "symbolic tokens" in which we similarly place our trust to advance our claims include not only money, but shares of equity, deeds, mortgages, bonds, and other debt securities, and for the

---

[68] Greider, *Secrets of the Temple*, p. 226.
[69] Frankel, *Two Philosophies*, p. 36.
[70] Anthony Giddens, *The Consequences of Modernity* (Stanford, CA: Stanford University Press, 1990), p. 26.
[71] *Ibid.*, p. 27.

more sophisticated (or foolhardy) among us, financial derivatives such as puts, calls, options, and futures contracts. It is by no means clear that even a bare majority of the people who trade derivatives really understand them. This is a problem that is on the rise with the advent of active derivatives trading strategies within the banking system. It appears probable that many investment professionals who lost a great deal of their firm's money in purchasing CDOs that were built upon the structure of disintermediated subprime mortgages did not understand the complex financial products in which they were investing.[72]

Under conditions of modernity, even the most flint-faced of secular people among us are required to commit daily acts of faith, and the functioning of modern society is predicated on "generalized trust in the ability of systems to maintain circumstances and performance within certain limits; that trust depends on a reflexive willingness to accept fictions because they function."[73]

S. Herbert Frankel pointed out rather effectively that

a monetary economy implies the maintenance of a monetary order: one in which trade is conducted, in which debts and obligations are freely entered upon and discharged and services remunerated by money, the maintenance of the value of which is accepted by society, in its customs and laws, as its responsibility.[74]

A monetary economy is not possible without trust that money as a unit of account will retain its capacity as a store of value to continue to function as a reliable medium of exchange, in orthodox terms.

We have generated marvelous institutions for support of the modern faith that lies at the core of our trust in our modern "symbolic tokens." This faith is

based on an ancient cultural reality about money that was still valid in the age of enlightenment and computers. Above all, money was a function of faith. It required an implicit and universal social consent that was indeed mysterious. To create money and use it, each one must believe and everyone must believe. Only then did worthless pieces of paper take on value. When a society lost faith in money, it was implicitly losing faith in itself.[75]

---

[72] Jennifer Hughes, "Investors 'Did Not Understand What They Were Buying,'" *Financial Times*, 5 December 2007.
[73] Frankel, *Two Philosophies*, p. 39.   [74] *Ibid.*
[75] Greider, *Secrets of the Temple*, p. 53.

When people lose faith in money, the monetary economy begins to deteriorate. Writing in the time of the "Great Inflation" in the late 1970s, Frankel observed that

when private individuals or institutions have, as now, to buy gold, commodities or foreign currency, to ensure greater security for themselves in the face of monetary and currency uncertainties, this is a sign of retrogression of and deterioration in the domestic monetary system.[76]

It is this post-Bretton Woods tendency toward monetary "retrogression and deterioration" that has continuously prompted the search for a new "nominal anchor" to stabilize the myriad monies of the international monetary system, ever since gold parity through a convertible dollar ended in 1971. As we shall see later in this book, the device in which governments, finance ministers and other monetary authorities worldwide appear to be putting their faith, is the device of granting extraordinary authority to central bankers – who are the nominal source of "exogenously" supplied money. Precisely because money is a social construct, whose value depends upon our modern faith in it as an extension of faith in our own societies,

the social content, the fantastic implications attached to money – all were sustained by concealment, an austere distance from popular examination. The Fed provided that, with its secrecy and obscure language, with its tradition of mystery and unknowable processes. Ignorance was comforting, perhaps even necessary for belief, and the Federal Reserve's mystique allowed people not to look directly upon these questions. Beyond politics and economics, the Federal Reserve's odd social powers were derived from the collective irrationality surrounding money.[77]

As the nominal source of the United States's ostensibly exogenously given money, the Fed has earned the nickname which provides the title of Greider's famous 1987 book, of "the temple" – not only because its columned Greco-Roman façade powerfully reminds those visiting Washington of the temples to the gods whose remains still lie in the ruins of the Roman Forum – but because "like the [ancient] temple, the Fed did not answer to the people, it spoke for them. Its decrees

[76] Frankel, *Two Philosophies*, p. 41.
[77] Greider, *Secrets of the Temple*, p. 226.

were cast in a mysterious language people could not understand, but its voice, they knew, was powerful and important."[78] A sacral aura attends the pronouncements of central banks, and especially of the central bank that generates the global currency of the US dollar.

Social institutions often speak in quasi-sacral languages. Former Fed Chairman Alan Greenspan raised the impenetrable, quasi-sacral language of "Fedspeak" to an art form with a mode of speech in public fora, and in testimony before Congress, that has been described as "'evasive', 'nebulous', 'opaque', or even 'oracular' and 'Delphic.'"[79] Central bankers, and particularly Fed chairmen, have seemed to feel it part of their job to shroud their actions (and particularly their likely future actions) in secrecy, and their explanations of their views in mystery. Greenspan once quipped to a US Congressman, during congressional testimony during his first term in office: "If I seem unduly clear to you, you must have misunderstood what I said."[80] Greenspan's predecessor, Paul Volcker, could joke about the power of the Fed to rein in the money supply to the effect that "'We have a haunting fear that someone, someplace may be happy,'" and while upholding the Fed's mystique with opacity in testimony before Congress by "confronting a contentious senator in a committee hearing... he would lead a hostile questioner deeper and deeper into the esoterica of monetary policy until the embarrassed senator was lost in confusion."[81]

What we cannot understand, but has power over us, we have to trust. But when we lend, as we are incapable of ensuring repayment, we must also trust. A lot of money is created by precisely this highly social relationship between creditors and lenders. So "the fact that a debt represents a *promise* from the debtor to the creditor, or his successors in title, is crucial."[82] In this context, Friedrich Kratochwil has explored the obligatory character of promises. Kratochwil has dismissed the suggestion that the reliance of the promisee's expectations that the promise will be fulfilled establishes this obligatory character from some first principle. Drawing upon Hume, he notes that the act of promising indeed generates expectations, and Hume resolved the question of

---

[78] *Ibid.*, p. 240.
[79] Catherine Resche, "Investigating 'Greenspanese': From Hedging to 'Fuzzy Transparency'" *Discourse and Society* 15(6) (2004): 723.
[80] *Ibid.*   [81] Greider, *Secrets of the Temple*, p. 70.
[82] Frankel, *Two Philosophies*, p. 46. Emphasis added.

why expectations resulting from promises are so strong relative to expectations resulting from declarations of intent, or resolutions.[83] Hume argues that in the case of promises:

The hearer's expectations, which expectations are supposedly the ground of the obligation, must be based on the belief that *ceteris paribus*, the act will be performed even if the promiser does change his mind (i.e., his "inclinations" etc.). It is because this expectation is so strong, that people rightly come to rely on promises in a way that they don't on statements of intent.[84]

Reliance upon promises is not based upon any enforcement mechanism. As Frankel suggests, there are no formal rules of a "game" of promising. When we promise, "we are engaged in a moral transaction."[85] Some promisers are more reliable than others, but both Kratochwil and Frankel point out that the promiser risks much if s/he is unable to perform what has been promised. The illocutionary force of the promise is an assertion of moral rectitude on the part of the promiser. This moral rectitude comes into question if the subject of the promise is not discharged. As Kratochwil explicates the matter:

Promises are not simply invalid if the promisee does not give too much credence to the promise... we cannot simply ignore and belittle the illocutionary effect of the promise. Doing so would mean we do not take the person seriously, that we deny him/her the status of a *moral agent* by discounting his/her utterances or that we imply he/she is like a child or an imbecile who does not know what he/she is doing.[86]

Frankel puts it similarly:

For not only do I signify my intention or resolution, my conviction that I can and shall perform the described action, I also present myself as a *moral agent* whose moral reputation and continuing moral relations with the person to whom I promise are at stake in the performance of the action. This I am able to do because I connect the performance of the action promised with my status as a *morally responsible agent* – to promise is to signify...that

---

[83] Friedrich V. Kratochwil, *Rules, Norms and Decisions: On the Conditions of Practical and Legal Reasoning in International Relations and Domestic Affairs* (Cambridge: Cambridge University Press, 1989), pp. 146–7.

[84] Hume is quoted in *ibid.*, p. 147.   [85] Frankel, *Two Philosophies*, p. 46.

[86] Kratochwil, *Rules, Norms and Decisions*, p. 147. Emphasis added.

one has tied his status as a *moral agent* to the performance of the action in question.[87]

These observations strongly and effectively emphasize not only that debt is a social, not just an economic relationship, but also that it is a social relationship with an ethical basis by which the debtor must successfully represent herself to a creditor not only as an economically viable agent, but as a moral agent.

Here, clearly, quite tangible benefits may result from the capacity to successfully represent oneself as a moral agent. The fact that the debtor may be an institution, such as a firm, rather than an individual, does not alter the social relations involved. Nor does the fact that the debt may be formalized by a contract that binds the debtor legally to discharge the terms of the debt contract alter the social relations involved. The development of the limited liability corporation may limit the exposure of its directors to the consequences of unfulfilled promises, but the rectitude of the fictitious personality of the firm as a moral agent capable of, and intent upon, fulfilling its obligations is advanced when the firm issues a debt instrument. The evaluation of the value of these promises by bond-rating agencies is a multi-billion dollar industry.[88]

As legal enforcement of contractual obligations is costly, lenders avoid borrowers whose moral agency (the illocutionary force of their promises to repay) is sufficiently weak for legal enforcement of the lending contract to seem needful. A successful assertion of moral agency lies at the heart of any social relationship between debtor and creditor, when the relationship is entered into freely by both parties. Thus, as we have seen in the manner in which credit functions as money, we have to consider the manner in which not only social agency, but moral agency, is implicated in the process of money creation.

When money is instead created through the agency of the state, through the mechanism of its central bank, have the social characteristics of money-as-a-promise been lost? Contrary to nominalist critiques

---

[87] Frankel, *Two Philosophies*, p. 47. Emphasis added and original emphasis omitted.

[88] Timothy J. Sinclair, *The New Masters of Capital: American Bond Rating Agencies and the Politics of Creditworthiness* (Ithaca, NY and London: Cornell University Press, 2005).

of the commodity theory of money, I will argue that moral agency is still advanced when money is created through the agency of the state. The state still "promises" when generating money. The state promises – for the neoclassically minded – that money will retain its functions as a "store of value" and remain a viable "medium of exchange" whose standard "unit of account" will not vary. As Frankel argues:

Notwithstanding Keynes's frequent appeals to morality, his claim that all "civilized money"...is..."a creation of the State" is in effect a claim to place discussion of the nature, meaning and significance of money outside moral discourse and beyond the moral structure of a free community.[89]

Frankel does not allow that Keynes accomplished his aim with this move. Nor should we. The opprobrium that greets those who default on their debts, or who breach their contracts, or who cheat on their taxes, indicates that this treatment of money is *de facto* rejected by social and economic agents alike in practice. And the opprobrium that greets states which do any of the above, or who perpetrate a *de facto* default on their debts by devaluation – either through outright repudiation, moratorium, or currency inflation – similarly signals a practical rejection in the empirical world of the ethical content of statist and nominalist theories of money.

In the statist view, which arises as another critique of the orthodox commodity and quantity theories of money, money does constitute a medium emerging from exchange. The unit of account function takes precedence, and money emerges largely as a state-generated unit of account for the settlement of debts – particularly tax debts to the state, which creates money by decreeing what it will and will not accept for payment of tax debts.[90] This doctrine is most highly developed in the work of German economist Georg Friedrich Knapp, who argued that while money is also privately created through the credit mechanism, the state's "acceptation" decisively defined money.[91] Contrary to the more orthodox interpretations of his contemporaries, who insisted that the value of money could only be established in exchange, Knapp insisted that the creation of money, and the assignment of value, was

---

[89] Frankel, *Two Philosophies*, pp. 47–8.
[90] Ingham, *Nature of Money*, p. 47.   [91] *Ibid.*, p. 48.

the function of the state, and thus that the value of the units thus established was purely nominal.[92] In other words, he argued that "money is the measure and not the thing measured... money is abstract value."[93]

This statist, nominalist critique of the commodity view of money has some utility as well as some disadvantages for the theorist seeking to gain insight from a more socialized conception of money. Its advantages include a reminder that authority relations are implicated in the creation of money. Knapp argued that authority relations were a logical, necessary condition for the existence of money.[94] The state also serves as the legal guarantor of the value of money, in the nominalist view. Certainly there can be no doubt that where the state has a monopoly of the issue of bank notes, and where the state is the guarantor of the value of its debt obligations, its actions are crucial to executing the "promises" to pay entailed by its issue of both bank notes and sovereign debt instruments. And as we shall see, the statist, nominalist view captures a notion that we will shortly develop of money as an "institutional fact" – as a social institution imbued with deontic power to purchase.

However, the nominalist view, and Knapp's statist view of money in particular, contains within it some critical difficulties. Not the least of these is that in arguing that the state and only the state creates money, the nominalist view of money conflates the broader social (and economic) concept of money with the more circumscribed vehicle of "legal tender." This concept of legal tender rather precisely characterizes a subset of financial assets (normally bank notes issued by the central bank) that a government will accept for payment of – as is stated clearly on every US Federal Reserve note – "all debts public or private." But because credit is money, and because credit is a promise backed by moral agency, "in real life nothing can be created out of nothing. Credit is not something which can be created at will. It always rests finally on trust: on the *belief* that the borrower will... keep his promise to re-pay what has been borrowed."[95] This belief is a product of the creditor's assessment of the moral agency of the borrower. If the borrower lacks this social asset, this belief will be wanting, and the

---

[92] Frankel, *Two Philosophies*, p. 48.   [93] Ingham, *Nature of Money*, p. 48.
[94] *Ibid.*, p. 49.   [95] Frankel, *Two Philosophies*, p. 49.

social asset of credit will not be available to generate tangible benefits through the mechanism of credit's social and economic acceptance as money. This is as true for a state as for an individual or for a firm – as many states have learned, and continue to learn, to the great economic distress of their citizens.

3 | Instituting facts and constituting rules

Economists typically believe in models. This methodological approach can be useful for lots of purposes, but . . . I am not trying to construct a model; I am trying to advance a theory that states an important set of facts about how society actually works.

John R. Searle

"Now, what I want is, Facts. Teach these boys and girls nothing but Facts. Facts alone are wanted in life. Plant nothing else, and root out everything else. You can only form the minds of reasoning animals upon Facts: nothing else will ever be of any service to them . . . Stick to Facts, sir!"

Mr. Thomas Gradgrind, in Charles Dickens's *Hard Times*

The scientific study of social phenomena must, as we would expect with all scientific endeavors, concern itself with the explication, stipulation, and explanation of facts. To apprehend social reality, just as with physical reality, we want to concern ourselves with facts. Economists concern themselves with a plethora of facts and they have devised numerous metrics to render these facts in a measurable form. Economic concepts such as gross domestic product, the capital account deficit, the exchange rate between currencies, and the non-accelerating inflation rate of unemployment (NAIRU) are all considered by economists to be measurable facts that can be assigned a quantitative value. But these facts all have something in common. They are a special form of fact that we may call an "institutional fact." The economic realm is, as is the social realm, not predominantly concerned with material facts, but with institutional facts. Institutional facts describe observer-dependent phenomena, while brute or "objective" facts describe observer-independent phenomena. Most metrics, while they are designed to measure phenomena thought to be objective, often "in fact" measure observer-dependent phenomena. A capital

45

account deficit relies upon the observer-dependent concept of deficit vs. surplus, accomplished across myriad transactions, for example.

Institutional facts and deontology

In general, Searle argues that

> observer-relative features are always created by intrinsic mental phenomena of the users, observers, etc., of the objects in question. Those mental phenomena are ... ontologically subjective; and the observer-relative features inherit that ontological subjectivity. But this ontological subjectivity does not prevent claims about observer-relative features from being epistemically objective.[1]

The test of whether features of phenomena are observer-independent or observer-dependent concerns the answer to the question "could the phenomena have existed if there had never been any conscious human beings with any intentional states?"[2] Irrespective of the attempts of economics to become, or the pretensions of economics to be, a "science" of objective "facts," it is in fact a human "science" of observer-dependent, institutional facts. Investigation of institutional reality entails the investigation of observer-dependent phenomena.[3] The application of mathematics (which is itself a human creation and human tool) to observer-dependent phenomena does not lend them "objective" characteristics, or render them knowable in accordance with an entirely objective ontology. Mathematics renders phenomena "knowable" in accordance with an observer-dependent ontology, and does so only when these phenomena are coded into concepts that are intelligible to this observer-dependent ontology. Phenomena that are knowable in accordance with an objective ontology do not require apprehension or experience by a conscious subject in order to exist, while those knowable in accordance with a subjective ontology must be experienced by a human, or at least by an animal, subject in order to exist.[4] Thus in accordance with our criterion of objective and subjective ontological reality, the answer to the ancient Zen question of whether a tree falling in the woods alone makes any sound if no one (or nothing) is there to hear it, the answer, according to the subjective ontology, is "no." The tree is objectively there and objectively falls.

---

[1] John R. Searle, *The Construction of Social Reality* (New York: The Free Press, 1995), pp. 12–13.
[2] Searle, "What is an Institution?", p. 3.   [3] *Ibid.*   [4] *Ibid.*, p. 4.

It objectively disturbs the air when it falls, and that "sound" will be registered (heard) by any conscious creature in the vicinity. But if no conscious creature whose auditory organs register the vibrations of the air caused by the falling tree is present, it made no "sound" as "sound" is a phenomenon that is dependent on the consciousness of a human or animal subject.

Yet we can make objectively true statements out of a social universe of subjective attitudes, beliefs, and intentions, and "can have an objective science of a domain that is ontologically subjective"[5] if we correctly apprehend the nature of "facts" in the social realm as "institutional facts." Our economic reality is a subset of this social reality, and the institutional nature of economic reality and economic "facts" is upon examination, if anything, even more obvious than the institutional nature of other social facts and social phenomena. We will, then, wish to discover the logical structure of institutional facts and understand how it differs from that of brute or "objective" facts. Searle's work suggests to us the logical structure of institutional facts. The discussion above, of the nature of observer-dependent vs. observer-independent facts, suggests the first crucial structural element of institutional facts – they are constituted first through collective intentionality.

As Alexander Wendt has suggested, intentionality implies that agents engage in purposive action "on the basis of their desires and beliefs about the world. Desires and beliefs are mental phenomena, which differ from physical phenomena in at least one crucial way: in some sense they contain within them the objects to which they refer."[6] This intentionality places the exploration of social and institutional facts outside of the realm of exploration of brute or observational facts, as Kratochwil has explained:

There is a crucial difference between causal explanations of the world of observational facts and that of intentions. In the case of natural phenomena...cause and effect have to be determined *independently* from each other through neutral measurements. But the same is *not* true in the case of motivational accounts where "causal" motives can only be imputed by the observer *after* a goal is assumed to be controlling.[7]

[5] *Ibid.*
[6] Alexander Wendt, *Social Theory of International Politics* (Cambridge: Cambridge University Press, 1999), p. 172.
[7] Kratochwil, *Rules, Norms and Decisions*, p. 25.

Moreover, social facts must be constituted by the "collective intentionality" of two or more actors. Collective beliefs and desires constitute
social facts, and the institutional facts which are a subset of social
facts. For example, the collective belief and desire that we are a nation
requires that we collectively conceive of ourselves as a nation, and
these beliefs and desires, in Wendt's lexicon, contain within them the
idea of the nation which becomes the object to which we have referred
when we act upon these beliefs and desires.

A second component of the logical structure of institutional facts is
"assignment of function" to an object, person, or group which does
not intrinsically have that function but acquires it "only by virtue of the
assignment of function."[8] This can be accomplished by an individual,
but for the purpose of generating institutional facts, functions must be
collectively assigned. This entails "a collective assignment of a certain
status, and the object or person performs its function only in virtue
of collective acceptance by the community that the object or person
has the requisite status."[9] The collective assignment of status functions
is essential for generating the constitutive rules of institutions, which
typically take the logical form X counts as Y in context C, where "X
identifies certain features of an object or person or state of affairs, and
the term Y assigns a special status to that person, object, or state of
affairs."[10]

What interests us most about constitutive rules is their role in the
"constitution of meaning."[11] Constitutive rules arise from, and help
to create, intersubjectively shared social meanings and understandings
between agents, and the assignment of status functions is crucial in
generating shared social meanings between subjects. That pieces of
paper and small metallic disks printed or stamped with the portraits
and cameos of deceased politicians (in the United States) or living
monarchs (in the United Kingdom) are intersubjectively understood to
constitute money – and that they give the bearer power to purchase
real goods or services – is an obvious result of the assignment of a

---

[8] Searle, *Construction of Social Reality*, pp. 43–8 and Searle, "What is an
Institution?", p. 7.

[9] *Ibid.*

[10] *Ibid.* See also David Dessler, "What is at Stake in the Agent–Structure
Debate?" *International Organization* 43(3) (1989): 441–74.

[11] Anthony Giddens, *The Constitution of Society* (Berkeley, CA and Los Angeles:
University of California Press, 1984), p. 20.

status function. The assignment of the function as a "store of value," "medium of exchange," "unit of account," or a "promise" of society to the bearer generates a number of constitutive rules of money and its use. These can be written in the logical form X counts as Y in context C. As we shall see, the constitutive rules of a monetary system also rely upon status function assignments.

Constitutive rules constitute – e.g. define in a manner to which collective assent is given – the intersubjectively shared social meanings of objects, persons, and states of affairs within institutional structures. Once social meanings constitute an institution, interaction between persons, objects, and states of affairs within the institution is then regulated by prescriptive or proscriptive "regulative rules" of the logical form "do X in context C" or "do not do Y in context C." These constitutive rules generate institutional facts through collective intentionality, collective acceptance of intersubjectively shared (or created) social meanings, and the collective assignment of status functions. These institutional facts create common understandings which consequently characterize objects, persons, or states of affairs that subsequently circulate in social discourse as "objective facts," though they remain, in social reality, institutional facts.

The function assigned that will interest us is the third component of the logical structure of institutional facts. This is the specific function collectively assigned to the person, object, or state of affairs – the "status function." Searle argues that status functions "are the glue that holds human societies together."[12] The collective assignment of status functions renders a particular social order because they create a deontology. The *Oxford English Dictionary* (*OED*) defines "deontology" as "the science of duty; that branch of knowledge which deals with moral obligations; ethics."[13] Searle's particular use appears to derive from the *OED* definition attributed to Gladstone's 1868 usage of the term which refers to "a system which may be called one of deontology, or that which ought to be, and to be done."[14] Assignment of status functions generates deontic powers. Deontic powers, in the social realm, create social relations of power, such as rights, duties, and obligations. Searle argues:

[12] Searle, "What is an Institution?", p. 8.
[13] *Oxford English Dictionary* online version accessed November 2005.
[14] *Ibid.*

Human institutions are above all enabling, because they create power...a special kind of power...marked by such terms as rights, duties, obligations, authorizations, permissions, empowerments, requirements and certifications. I call all of these deontic powers.[15]

Deontic powers, deriving from the collective assignment of status functions, thereby constitute social structures of power relations by generating institutional facts that function as structures that generate "desire-independent" reasons for action.[16] As Kratochwil argues, "what acquires here the status of an 'objective' fact is not the thing described but rather the intersubjective validity of a characterization upon which reasonable persons can agree."[17]

Thus we must recognize the importance of language in the social realm as what Searle argues is "the fundamental social institution"[18] because language is not simply a tool to describe social and economic reality, but partly constitutes social and economic reality. We can employ language without generating social institutions but we can not generate social institutions without language because we must collectively assign status functions to generate institutions and institutional facts. Status functions "must be represented in order to exist at all, and language or symbolism of some kind provides the medium of representation."[19] Just as high medieval scholars and churchmen had argued "No bishop, no King!" to describe the contemporarily universally accepted claim of the Church to mediate secular rulership between God and man,[20] Searle argues "no representation, no status function...no language, no status functions. No status functions, no institutional deontology."[21] Thus human social and economic power relations are constituted through the creation of institutional deontologies (assignment of rights, duties, obligations, etc.) by representing status functions through the medium of language, and symbolic mechanisms constructed through the possession of language.

---

[15] Searle, "What is an Institution?", p. 10.   [16] *Ibid.*, p. 11.
[17] Kratochwil, *Rules, Norms and Decisions*, p. 229.
[18] Searle, "What is an Institution?", p. 11.   [19] *Ibid.*, p. 12.
[20] See Rodney Bruce Hall, "Moral Authority as a Power Resource" *International Organization* 51(4) (1997): 591–622.
[21] Searle, "What is an Institution?", pp. 12–13.

Deontic powers and institutions

In order to be recognized, status functions require status indicators. Deontic powers are collectively assigned to persons, objects, and states of affairs by the ascription to them of special social functions that impart rights, duties, and obligations on the bearer (or subject) of the deontology. But Searle points out that

> the deontic powers stop at the point where the larger society requires some official proof of the status function ... collective recognition is not enough. There has to be official recognition by some agency, itself supported by collective recognition, and there have to be status indicators issued by the official agency.[22]

Searle gives us the examples of uniforms, wedding rings, marriage certificates, driver's licenses, and passports as such status indicators. In monetary relations, charters of central banks, articles of agreement of international monetary institutions such as the IMF, confer deontic power on these institutions. For money proper, watermarks, portraits of national icons, serial numbers, signatures of finance ministers, and numerals indicating specific values confer deontic power as a "store of value" or "unit of account" on bank notes, and confer on the bearer of the bank notes the deontic power to purchase. Other monetary examples of deontic powers applied to money include par values of currencies per ounce of fine gold under the gold standard, convertibility arrangements under Bretton Woods, whereby US dollars were convertible into gold at a fixed price of US$35 per ounce, and other official convertibility arrangements, such as currency board arrangements, whereby, for example, the government of the Hong Kong Special Administrative Region (SAR) of China at this writing pledges to exchange every 7.79 Hong Kong dollars presented to it for one US dollar. Bond ratings issued by Moody's or Standard and Poor's Corporation are status indicators *par excellence* for the assignment of the deontic power of "creditworthiness" to sovereign and other debtors. The deontic power to assess the creditworthiness of sovereign nations or major transnational corporations is still collectively assigned – even while executed through private firms through creditworthiness grading, if indirectly – by the fact that so many government-run investments

[22] *Ibid.*, p. 15.

such as pension schemes require debt instruments held by such funds to maintain at least an "investment grade" rating to be classed as "assets" at "face value" of the investment.[23]

States of affairs dependent upon deontic powers that might interest us, in addition to bond ratings, include the IMF's capacity to bestow or withhold a form of "seal of approval" of the "viability" of a government's economic policies. In this context, Jacqueline Best claims that the IMF is explicitly engaged in a norm-building exercise through the promulgation of various financial standards whose functions are both regulative and constitutive.[24] This analysis is broadly consistent with Michael Barnett's and Martha Finnemore's recent work describing how international organizations both constitute the social world, and then regulate that world once constituted.[25] In this way the diffusion of new norms (conventions that function as institutions that are constituted by institutional facts) transforms actor identities and interests, thus constituting new rule-governed social and economic orders.

The deontic powers associated with "authorizing" and "certifying" states of affairs are assigned by status functions associated with what Searle refers to as "free standing Y terms," with reference to the Y as which X counts, in the logical structure of a constitutive rule. Such status functions lack a physical object on which the status is conferred – unlike those conferred upon coins and banknotes. Examples of "free standing Y terms" include limited liability corporations – whereby a legal personality that constitutes a legal fiction incurs rights, duties, and obligations, etc. Electronic money is an example provided by Searle. A particular example to which I would draw the attention of the reader is the example of credit (as a "promise" – and thus as an institution – or as a form of money generated endogenously by society, rather than exogenously supplied by government through the central bank). Any number of constitutive rules of monetary relations that may be constructed from these examples may be found to function in the "real economy." I shall write them in the logical form of constitutive rules,

---

[23] Sinclair, *New Masters of Capital*.

[24] Jacqueline Best, "Bringing Power Back In: The IMF's New Constructivist Strategy in Critical Perspective" (manuscript presented at workshop on Economic Constructivism, Radcliffe Institute for Advanced Study, Harvard University, February 2005).

[25] Michael Barnett and Martha Finnemore, *Rules for the World: International Organizations in Global Politics* (Ithaca, NY: Cornell University Press, 2004).

X counts as Y in context C, and represent X, Y, and C for each example in quotation marks. For example, a constitutive rule of a limited liability corporation is:

1. "The legal personality of the General Electric Company" counts as "the shareholders of the capital stock comprising the assets of the corporation" in the context of "incurring and discharging debt obligations to finance the operations of the firm"

A constitutive rule of electronic money is:

2. "The positive digital balance of the demand deposit confirmed by electronically querying computers of the XYZ Bank plc with the data encoded on a magnetic strip on a plastic card, coupled with the correct entry of a personal identification number" counts as "purchasing power for the bearer of the card and PIN number in the amount of £25" in the context of "the bearer's purchase of a bread toaster at the local appliance store."

The constitutive rules of credit differ for the creditor and the debtor. For the debtor, a constitutive rule of a mortgage credit vehicle is:

3a. "This mortgage document bearing the signature of our bank officer" counts as "our promise to create a demand deposit in the amount of $200,000 in partial payment of the purchase price of a home" in the context of "your promise to pay our bank an amortized income stream on the following terms for 30 years;"

while for the creditor:

3b. "This mortgage document bearing your signature" counts as "your promise to pay our bank an amortized income stream on the following terms for 30 years" in the context of "our promise to create a demand deposit in the amount of $200,000 in partial payment of the purchase price of a home."

The free standing Y terms in the examples above, then, are a legal personality in the first case, electronic purchasing power in the second case, and credit *qua* promises in the variation of the third case. The crucial role of language in ascribing deontic powers to these institutional facts is evident in their creation in each case by performative declaration.

We can see here that currency is not required for the existence of money as the deontic power to purchase, or for the deontic purchasing power attached to credit. What will interest us is that which used to be true of many commercial banks (such as in the "free banking" era of the nineteenth-century United States) remains true of central banks – namely that they have the deontic power to create both money and credit through what amounts to a performative speech act. This is why advocates of a commodity-based standard for money derisively refer to modern currencies as "fiat money." And this is why President Nixon, in the press conference nominating Arthur Burns to succeed the long-serving William McChesney Martin, Jr. as chairman of the Federal Reserve in 1969 "would turn sheep's eyes on him and say, 'Please, Dr. Burns, give us some money....'"[26] Fiat money. Let there be money! Burns obliged, and in so doing is widely thought to have contributed significantly to the inflationary spiral of the late 1960s to early 1980s which has become known among economists as the "Great Inflation."

So money is an institution created by the deontic powers of other institutions (here, endogenously by the extension of personal or commercial credit, or exogenously by central banks acting with the collective assent provided by their role as an agent of the state). This is Searle's test for the existence of an institution. If there is a collective deontology associated with a thing, person, or event, then it is an institution. Searle identifies four tests for identifying whether an item (W) is an institution.

1. Is W defined by a set of constitutive rules?
2. Do those rules determine status functions, which are in fact collectively recognized and accepted?
3. Are those status functions only performable by virtue of the collective recognition and acceptance and not by virtue of observer-independent features of the situation alone?
4. Do the status functions carry recognized and accepted deontic powers?[27]

If all four tests are met by an object, person, event, or state of affairs, then it is an institution.[28] Institutions are truly ubiquitous – far too ubiquitous to be left out of any coherent account of social life.

---

[26] Martin Mayer, *The Fed: The Inside Story of How the World's Most Powerful Financial Institution Drives the Markets* (New York: The Free Press, 2001), p. 93.

[27] *Ibid.*, p. 19.   [28] Searle, "What is an Institution?", p. 18.

Money as an institution

Money is an institution that clearly meets these requirements. Any number of constitutive rules of money, in the form of simple specie or bank notes, can be derived that constitute variations on the theme – "this bank note" counts as "an indicated amount of purchasing power" in the context "of a transaction requiring settlement in cash." Cash is collectively accepted and recognized as "legal tender for the settlement of all debts public and private" in the case of coin and bank notes, which have been assigned the status function of "legal tender." No observer-independent features lend intrinsic value to currency as a "store of value," a "medium of exchange," a "unit of account" or a "promise." The bank note is an intrinsically, materially worthless piece of paper, until it acquires these deontic powers by virtue of collective assignment of status indicators through the medium of agencies of a government. The status functions assigned clearly carry the deontic powers assigned to them by the commodity theory of money that we examined in chapter 2, and further assign to the bank note the "deontic power to purchase."[29] What should not escape our attention at this juncture is that the "functions" ascribed to money as intrinsic to it in the commodity theory of money in orthodox monetary economics emerge here as deontic powers resulting from the creation of the social institution of money. I shall say more about this observation below.

Matters are not so different in the investigations of economic sociology. For example, the sociologist Richard Swedberg has recently pointed out that while Max Weber demonstrated no particular interest in developing a theory of money in his famous work on *Economy and Society*, he was interested in:

the most general sociological consequences of the use of money. These consequences include, for example, the fact that with money one can suddenly exchange goods for an enormous range of other goods (indirect exchange) ... [and obtain] an improved capacity to store values for future use, to calculate profit, and to calculate marginal utility.[30]

For Weber, the functions of money intrinsic to it in monetary economics were simply the consequences of its use. The concept of

[29] *Ibid.*, p. 16.
[30] Richard Swedberg, *Max Weber and the Idea of Economic Sociology* (Princeton, NJ: Princeton University Press, 1998), p. 44.

calculable marginal utility, so central to economic thought, all but presupposes the development and use of money. But while Swedberg argues that Weber had relatively little to say about the nature of money, and spilled little ink in attacking the orthodox monetary theory of his day, his view of it was in any event rather socialized. He clearly asserts that "money is not a mere 'voucher for unspecified utilities' which can be altered at will...[but]...a weapon...[in]...the struggle of man against man."[31] A spear – a pole with a sharp pike on the end – is an objective fact. A weapon is an institutional fact. A struggle is an institution. At this point it would be useful to quote at length Searle's most recent, applicable definition of an institution by way of summarizing these concepts:

An institution is any collectively accepted system of rules (procedures, practices) that enable us to create institutional facts. These rules typically have the form X counts as Y in context C, where an object or state of affairs X is assigned a special status, the Y status, such that the new status enables the person as object to perform functions that it could not perform solely in virtue of its physical structure, but requires as a necessary condition the assignment of the status. The creation of an institutional fact is, thus, the collective assignment of a status function. The typical point of the creation of institutional facts by assigning status functions is to create deontic powers...we have created a situation in which we accept that a person S who stands in the appropriate relation to X is such that (S has power (S does A)). The whole analysis then give us a symmetric set of relationships between collective intentionality, the assignment of function, the assignment of status functions, constitutive rules, institutional facts and deontic powers.[32]

What will interest us most in application of this summary to an institutional account of money, as briefly suggested above, is that the "functions" ascribed to money in the commoditized theory of orthodox monetary economics all derive from deontic powers assigned to money in the institutional account. Money is a "store of value" as it has been collectively assigned this function, collectively assented to as an institutional fact. When you hand me a £10 bank note to repay me for the £10 I loaned you last month, I accept this in payment of your debt because I agree with you that the note represents the same £10 of

---

[31] Swedberg quotes Max Weber, *Economy and Society: An Outline of Interpretive Sociology* (Berkeley, CA: University of California Press, 1978), p. 108, in *ibid.*
[32] Searle, "What is an Institution?", pp. 21–2.

purchasing power when repaid to me that it represented when it was loaned. The note is a "medium of exchange" because the collectively derived laws of society have assigned the note the deontic power as "legal tender" to settle debts in the UK. The note is a "unit of account" because it has been ascribed the status function of 10 units of purchasing power rather than 5 units by the collectively recognized "status indicators" of the numeral 10 instead of 5, on a larger note, with a portrait of Darwin and a hummingbird, rather than a smaller sized note, bearing a portrait of Elizabeth Fry on the back. The note is also a promise by the government and the Bank of England that the £10 worth of goods it will purchase today is equivalent to the £10 worth of goods it will purchase next year. Maintaining "credibility" of this promise (price stability), and the promises of the government that the debt obligations they undertake will be redeemed (price and exchange rate stability), is, as we shall see, no small part of the real business of central banks.

Deontic powers of central banks

The powers of central banks, in the same fashion, are uniformly deontic powers in the form of rights, duties, obligations, authorizations, permissions, empowerments, requirements, and certifications that endow the central bank with social and economic power as a result of the collective assignment to it of status functions. Economist Stanley Fischer – who served as First Deputy Managing Director of the IMF, and later as the Governor of the Bank of Israel – has effectively developed the "status functions" of a central bank from an economist's perspective as "functions" and "mandates" in his seminal essay on "Modern Central Banking."[33] Fischer argues that one of the major functions (deontic powers, for our purposes) of a central bank devolves from its "status" as a "bank of issue" which lends it "responsibility for managing the supply of credit and money and correspondingly determining market interest rates."[34] Some central banks have responsibilities for maintenance of the exchange rate and for managing the nation's foreign reserves, which are essential both for ensuring the flow of

[33] Stanley Fischer, "Modern Central Banking" in Stanley Fischer, *IMF Essays from a Time of Crisis: The International Financial System, Stabilization, and Development* (Cambridge, MA: MIT Press, 2005), pp. 169–222.
[34] *Ibid.*, p. 170.

international payments, and for upholding and defending the value of the national currency. Central banks play a major role in promoting financial stability in the economy "by supervising the [commercial] banks and other financial institutions, by serving as a lender of last resort, and in some countries by administering deposit insurance."[35] Central banks also serve as bankers for the government and "manage all or part of the national debt"[36] and administer exchange controls where they are applied.

Political scientist Sylvia Maxfield develops a similar list of "functions" of central banks in a recent book on the international political economy of central banking in developing countries.[37] Maxfield reports that central banks "control the supply and price (interest rate) of money...protect financial stability, guarantee the domestic and international payments system, and provide some range of financial services to the government."[38] To "guard against financial instability" central banks "regulate commercial bank licensing, set standards for minimum bank capital [capital adequacy requirements], and supervise at least a portion of the financial system through the use of in-house examiners or auditors hired from an outside firm."[39] Should these efforts fail to stem financial instability in specific or multiple domestic financial institutions, the central bank "can serve as a lender of last resort" or even "refuse to lend and thus oversee liquidation of the bank."[40] Maxfield ratifies Fischer's assertions regarding the responsibilities of central banks to manage foreign exchange reserves and that "guaranteeing an effective payments system" is part of the financial stability mandate, adding that an effective payments system is "one in which individuals willingly accept money and money substitutes in exchange for goods and services."[41] Let us explore the deontic powers of central banks that engender these "functions" of money, as stipulated by neoclassical orthodox monetary theory. Below I will explain how the best-known "functions" of central banks result from deontic powers ascribed to them by collective assignment of status functions.

---

[35] *Ibid.*   [36] *Ibid.*
[37] Sylvia Maxfield, *Gatekeepers of Growth: The International Political Economy of Central Banking in Developing Countries* (Princeton, NJ: Princeton University Press, 1997).
[38] *Ibid.*, p. 5.   [39] *Ibid.*   [40] *Ibid.*, p. 6.   [41] *Ibid.*

Rate determination: money creation and destruction powers

Significantly a central bank "can finance the government in several ways: it can buy government securities, it can make unsecured loans from its reserves, and it can print money. Theoretically, the central bank can impose fiscal discipline on the government"[42] by refusing to finance its operations by buying government debt securities (thereby "monetizing" the debt) when demand for these sovereign debt instruments is slack on the global bond markets.

This deontic power of a central bank to effectively monetize government debt by buying government debt instruments for its own portfolio has far-reaching effects that can be illustrated as follows. When the open market desk (OMD) of the Federal Open Market Committee (FOMC) of the US Federal Reserve, for example, buys US Treasury securities, it increases the reserves of the banking system and consequently increases the money supply, driving down the interest rates that banks pay for funds when they borrow from one another (the Federal Funds rate) or from the "discount window" of one of the twelve regional district Reserve Banks of the Federal Reserve system.[43] Similarly when the OMD sells government securities it reduces the reserves available to the banking system, diminishing the money supply. Commercial banks will have to bid up the Federal Funds rate, or in an exigency, go to the "discount window" for a direct loan from its district Reserve Bank, in order to obtain funds to make new loans or meet its periodic reserve requirements. In Germany matters worked very similarly for years, but the two rates controlled by the famously inflation-hawkish Bundesbank were called the "discount rate" and the "Lombard rate."[44] In the UK they are called the "discount rate" and Libor (London interbank overnight rate). As a rule, commercial banks will borrow from one another rather than a central bank to obtain funds. This is particularly true of fundamentally solvent banks in the United States which may need to borrow funds to meet their reserve requirements. "Nobody borrows from the district banks: it's considered a mark of weakness to do so."[45] It invites unwanted auditory scrutiny and can also generate capital flight.

---

[42] *Ibid.*   [43] Mayer, *The Fed*, p. 144.
[44] Deane and Pringle, *The Central Banks*, p. 128.   [45] Mayer, *The Fed*, p. 78.

Federal Funds are "the excess reserves of banks that were not fully loaned to customers."[46] Commercial banks in the United States may loan these reserves overnight, or for longer terms, to other banks that need to obtain funds to meet their periodic reserve requirements. Currently commercial banks that are members of the Federal Reserve system must keep a percentage of all deposits on reserve at their regional Federal Reserve Bank as a liquidity requirement, and as insurance against an unexpectedly high demand for cash by their customers (more commonly known as a bank run). As they are paid no interest for these reserve funds, they amount to an interest-free loan to the Federal Reserve system. This requirement violates every instinct of a profit-maximizing commercial banker who must count reserves as "liabilities" and does not wish to keep a dollar more than required on reserve.

The deontic power to buy securities, make unsecured loans from reserves, and print money in many ways all amount to the same power – the deontic power to create money to back up government debt and bank credit, by fiat. We explored this deontic power, in different terms, in chapter 2, and noted that the central bank has the power to create a deposit in the reserve account of the commercial bank that comes to it directly for a loan (comes to the "discount window" in the United States or the UK) with key strokes on a computer, and by fiat. By loaning the commercial bank the amount of money it might have been short on a given day, subsequent to completing its daily loan activity transactions, the central bank has essentially created *ex post facto* (or ratified the creation by the commercial bank) the money that had already been created by the commercial bank when it loaned money to a commercial borrower that it did not yet have. The money was created endogenously by the commercial bank's credit creation activity, and then it was supplied to the banking system exogenously by the central bank which is uniquely "authorized" to take the decision to create in the Reserve system money initially created by the extension of commercial credit. Or the Reserve Bank might, during a credit tightening cycle, decline to do so. This *ex post facto* lending is the mechanism by which the endogenous creation of credit-as-money in the private sector is exogenously authorized by the deontic power of the central bank acting as agent for the government. As Benjamin

---

[46] *Ibid.*, p. 170.

Strong, an early governor of the New York Fed, told an audience he addressed at Harvard in 1922:

Practically all borrowing by member banks from the Reserve Banks is *ex post facto* borrowing. The condition that gives rise to the need for borrowing had already come into existence before the application to borrow from the Reserve Bank was ever made.[47]

The central bank also has acquired, through its collectively assigned "status function" as a "bank of issue," the deontic power to destroy money by contracting the reserves in the banking system. This is normally accomplished by the selling of government securities. This will raise the costs of borrowing for commercial banks and restrict their lending by restricting their access to funds, or at a minimum by raising the costs of credit and money for individuals and businesses – dampening their appetite for credit over time, or quite suddenly with a large single rise in rates. In the United States the contraction of reserves raises the cost of money for commercial banks by raising two key interest rates. Such action by the FOMC raises the "discount rate" – the rate of interest that the Fed charges commercial banks who "go to the discount window" at a district Reserve Bank. It also raises the more effective Federal Funds rate – the rate commercial banks charge one another for short-term funds to meet reserve requirements, to avoid "going to the window" at nearly all costs.

Financial system stabilizer and lender of last resort: liquidity creation and risk socialization powers

The function of a central bank as domestic lenders of last resort also arises from its collectively assigned "status function" as a "bank of issue," and from its collectively assigned status function as an agent of the government "authorized" to socialize societal economic risk at its discretion. The assignment of these status functions endows the central bank not only with the deontic power to destroy money, but with the deontic power to dilute, at its discretion, the value of existing money in a crisis through a massive injection of liquidity into the system. It may create this liquidity (money) by fiat, on the spot, without prior consultation with any elected official of the government, or its

---

[47] Strong is quoted in Mayer, *The Fed*, p. 96.

appointed representative. A very early illustration of these deontic powers was the bail-out of the South Sea Company in 1720. So great were the financial stakes when the famous South Sea financial bubble burst that, the result was a classic, and very early, example of a firm "too big to fail." When the bubble did burst its debts were partly taken over by Parliament (which effectively socialized that risk by taking it on as a public debt) and the Bank of England took over £4.2 million of its nominal capital, converting this to bonds paying 5 percent.[48] Of course this example does express, in that case, some shared responsibility between Parliament and the Bank of England.

A more recent, and quite excellent, empirical demonstration of these deontic powers involves the actions taken by the Greenspan Fed in the wake of the stock market crash of October 1987, shortly after Alan Greenspan's appointment as Chairman of the Federal Reserve system by the Reagan administration. The "Black Monday" crash of 29 October 1987 saw a 508-point, single-day plunge in the Dow Jones Industrials index of blue chip stocks that wiped out more than $1 trillion of wealth, and 22.6 percent of the value (market capitalization) of 30 premier US firms, with comparable losses in the Standard and Poors 500 and NASDAQ indices. As a point of historical perspective, the single-day "Black Tuesday" market crash of 1929 that had ushered in so many bank failures, and the Great Depression, had constituted an 11.7 percent single-day loss.

The impact of systemic shocks on the financial system is unpredictable. What might have been predicted is that news of the crash threatened to bring the payments system to a grinding halt as financial institutions that had suffered great losses lacked the liquidity to make payment on the losses. Those with liquid assets were anxious to hold on to them. After "Black Monday," Gerald Corrigan, then Governor of the New York Fed, watched with horror as the payments system seized up and telephoned Fed Chairman Alan Greenspan to let him know that it was time for the Fed to exercise its lender of last resort powers to inject massive liquidity into the financial system to halt the seizure of the payments system and the unknowable financial wreckage that would follow. According to one account, the discussion went as follows:

---

[48] Ferguson, *Cash Nexus*, p. 114.

"Alan, you're it," Corrigan said. "Goddamit, it's up to you. This whole thing is on your shoulders." Corrigan . . . believed there was no time for procrastination and little for analysis. The availability of money in the system would be critical. In one form or another, Wall Street securities and brokerage firms, and their clients, would need bank credit, their lifeline, to cover their losses.

"Thank you, Dr. Corrigan," Greenspan said.[49]

At 8:41 a.m. on Tuesday, Greenspan issued a one-sentence statement to the press highly effectively designed to reassure the markets that risk would be pooled and money created in the quantities necessary to ensure the continued functioning of the payments system:

The Federal Reserve, consistent with its responsibilities as the nation's central bank, affirmed today its readiness to serve as a source of liquidity to support the economic and financial system.[50]

While this statement was credited with enormous deontic power in calming the markets (White House Chief of Staff, Howard Baker, reportedly suggested to Greenspan of his statement that "Those are the best lines I've read since Shakespeare") the statement's full impact had clearly not been absorbed when the markets opened at 9:00 a.m. on Tuesday. The Fed had already been active in pumping liquidity into the reserve system by purchasing Treasury bills overnight, but matters were not so sanguine among the "specialists" on the trading floor of the New York Stock Exchange when the markets opened Tuesday, as banks had been unwilling to extend credit to them in the face of their own liquidity concerns. Mayer reports that "the specialists needed credit from banks to keep functioning – and they didn't get it."[51]

One observer argues of Greenspan's quintessential and timely "lender of last resort" statement that:

The message to Wall Street professionals was unmistakable. The Fed would reverse its tight money policy of the past few months and supply liquidity – that is, it would pump as much money into the system as was needed to

[49] Bob Woodward, *Maestro: Greenspan's Fed and the American Boom* (New York: Touchstone, 2001), p. 39.

[50] Greenspan's statement is quoted in Steven Solomon, *The Confidence Game: How Unelected Central Bankers are Governing the Changed Global Economy* (New York: Simon & Schuster, 1995), p. 60. The statement is also quoted in Tuccille, *Alan Shrugged*, p. 180, and Woodward, *Maestro*, p. 40.

[51] Mayer, *The Fed*, p. 136.

keep it afloat. Specifically, the Federal Reserve entered the marketplace and bought $2.2 billion worth of US Treasury securities, supplying the markets with an immediate infusion of cash. It also lowered the rates at which banks borrow money from one another [the Federal Funds rate] and from the Federal Reserve [the discount rate]. Both short- and long-term rates headed downward instantly . . . the Fed fund rate dropped nearly two full percentage points, and the thirty-year Treasury bond yield declined a point and a half . . . Banks stepped up their lending to brokerage firms, ensuring that none would be threatened with insolvency by further sell orders from their clients.[52]

Gerald Corrigan meanwhile tirelessly worked the phones to the larger banks in a massive exercise in moral suasion, backed up by the deontic powers of the Federal Reserve system to create and deploy theoretically unlimited liquidity. He pressured the banks to make their payments to their creditors to cover their own trading losses, to extend credits to brokers (who were themselves calling in margin call loans) and floor specialists in individual equities, and to remind them of the unintended consequences of individually rational action – namely that no bank could insulate itself from a collapse of credit and a seizure in the payment system.[53] This hands-on moral suasion and pressure by the powerful Governor of the New York Fed, whose district Reserve Bank contained the trading desks that constituted the technical apparatus for the execution of the Fed's open market operations, was a crucial element in ensuring that the Fed's deontic power to socialize risks by pumping liquidity into the banking system was credible and effective. Martin Mayer suggests that Corrigan's heroics "changed the definition and function in the economy of the lender of last resort."[54]

However, it is worth pointing out that the deontic powers that endow this lender of last resort capability on central banks is not equally available to all countries that have created central banking institutions. Some countries have opted for currency boards, and can only issue as much local currency as the supply of foreign reserves on hand to which that currency is pegged will permit at the pegged exchange rate. Other countries, including Ecuador and Panama, have entirely dollarized their economies, and circulate the US dollar as legal tender in substitution for a former national currency that the dollar

---

[52] Tuccilli, *Alan Shrugged*, pp. 180–1.
[53] Woodward, *Maestro*, pp. 41–2.   [54] Mayer, *The Fed*, p. 137.

has replaced. Motivations for "currency substitution," according to Benjamin Cohen, include:

[a] high or accelerating inflation rate, which reduces a currency's purchasing power both at home and, through exchange depreciation for transactions abroad. Residents accordingly, have an incentive to turn to some more stable foreign money as a preferred store of value – an inflation hedge for their savings... Foreign money, in effect, becomes the public's financial refuge, a convenient defense against abuse of the seigniorage privilege by government.[55]

Economies can, of course, become "dollarized" *de facto* by entirely endogenous mechanisms which amount to capital flight, or exogenously, and "officially," by an act of government. Dollarized economies scarcely require central banks. Dollarized economies and economies with "hard pegs" to foreign currencies can not generate liquidity at will. They have essentially surrendered monetary sovereignty and their monetary policy to that of the US Federal Reserve, or another foreign central bank. China, for example, replaced its hard peg to the US dollar in 2005 with a new hard peg to a "basket of currencies," which now includes the euro as well as the dollar. Thus Chinese monetary policy is now in the hands of the ECB as well as the Fed, among other foreign central banks. China maintains a vast array of capital controls on both inflows and outflows, however. Thus while China remains subject to overvaluation of the renminbi, which will rise with the dollar and the euro, the Chinese central bank retains administrative control of the nature and to a significant extent, the level of capital inflows and outflows, as well as administrative controls to manage the exchange rate.

Yet other countries have fixed but adjustable regimes (FBAR), or "adjustable pegs" that feature "crawling pegs" or "flexible pegs" to permit occasional adjustment of the exchange rate within either small or large exchange bands. Some domestic monetary flexibility is possible for countries employing these adjustable pegs in an environment of low capital mobility where the risk of speculative attack against the exchange rate is low, but there is extremely limited to no monetary discretion available to the central bank in an environment of high global capital mobility, where the risks of speculative attack against

[55] Cohen, *The Geography of Money*, p. 96.

the exchange rate are proportionately (or perhaps disproportionately) high.[56]

The choice of exchange-rate regime is no doubt an important determiner in the level of discretion available to the central bank for the conduct of monetary policy in general, and of liquidity lending or last resort lending to a domestic economy in crisis. But even for many countries that embrace entirely floating exchange rates and which permit the value of their currencies to float freely on the FOREX markets, backed only by the "confidence" that traders exhibit in their economies, liquidity lending must be rather circumscribed, and is likely to be extremely circumscribed. Indeed, liquidity lending to domestic financial institutions is likely to be abandoned entirely in a crisis, for fear that precious reserves of foreign exchange will not be available for international debt settlements, or to defend the exchange rate in the face of a concerted speculative attack upon it in the global financial markets. Most central banks must exercise these deontic powers of liquidity creation and risk socialization quite carefully.

Exchange-rate and foreign reserves management: international product valuation power

The function of many central banks as managers of the exchange rate and of their country's foreign reserves arises from their collectively assigned "status function" again as agents of the government "authorized" to socialize societal economic risk at their discretion, in this instance by the deontic power to revalue (or attempt to revalue) the international purchasing power of their nation's money. The assignment of these status functions endows the central bank, in many countries, with the power to "manage" the exchange rate of the national currency by buying and selling the currency in the global foreign exchange markets to increase or decrease demand for it, and thus its price. This authorization entails deontic powers to determine how much of the nation's tradable wealth will be held in reserve by the central bank in the form of foreign exchange. It endows the deontic power to determine how much of this will be spent to uphold a "value" of the domestic currency to be determined by the central bank or finance ministry when the exchange rate comes under pressure from "market

[56] Corden, *Too Sensational*, pp. 42–52.

forces." More often, it endows the deontic power to determine how much of the nation's wealth should be squandered in an often (even normally) futile battle to uphold the exchange rate when it falls under speculative attack.[57]

The international valuation of every commodity, good, and service – extant or produced in the country that is subject to an international transaction – is directly impacted by the exchange rate of the national currency. In some countries, such as the United States, the Treasury (or finance ministry) has primary responsibility for managing the exchange rate. In the United States exchange rate policy belongs to the Treasury and the Fed implements that policy through open market operations and the mechanism of the foreign exchange trading desk located at the New York Fed. But the deontic power of the central bank to determine the supply and cost of money generates a *de facto* power of the central bank to strongly impact the direction of exchange-rate policy. For example, in November 2005 the US Federal Reserve was in a tightening cycle and consistently raised the discount rate by 25 basis points (one quarter of a percentage point) in subsequent meetings of the FOMC, which was expected to continue tightening well into 2006. Meanwhile the Bank of England was making "dovish" sounds having recently lowered rates by 25 basis points at the last meeting of the monetary policy committee (MPC) in that timeframe, and weakness on the High Street (weakness in retail sales) and other signs of weakness in the UK economy induced speculation in the currency markets that the MPC would continue to cut rates, or at least hold them steady. In consequence the price of sterling against the dollar consistently fell in that period.

So while the deontic power of exchange rate policy lies with the US Treasury in Washington, and with the Chancellor of the Exchequer in London, *de facto* power lies with the central bank in each country as a result of deontic power resulting from assignment of a very different status function. The central banks were assigned the status function of setting the cost of money, and its supply, and thus the deontic power of money creation and destruction. Central banks have acquired, from the international currency markets, the *de facto* status function of helping

[57] For a primer in the manner in which movements on the international currency markets are typically disconnected from movements that would be justified by economic fundamentals, see George Soros, *The Alchemy of Finance: Reading the Mind of the Market* (New York: Wiley & Sons, 1987).

to establish the exchange rate, thus the deontic power of revaluing domestic goods and services internationally.

But this *de facto* status function is not collectively assigned to the central bank by the citizens of the nation, as their agent or the agent of their government. This *de facto* status function of helping to indirectly determine the exchange rate through monetary policy is collectively assigned to the central bank by the international currency markets. If the currency markets believe that the central bank's expressed determination to restrict the supply of money (the central bank's exercise of the deontic power to destroy money from the collective assignment by the central bank's national citizens of the status function of determiner of the cost and supply of money) is "credible" they will allocate the status function of determiner of exchange-rate policy as well as monetary policy to the central bank, even if the expressed exchange-rate policy of the finance ministry or treasury is directly at odds with the direction induced by the central bank's monetary policy. The *de facto* power of the central bank to determine the exchange rate through the credibility of its "promise" to destroy money and credit becomes, from the perspective of the currency markets, deontic power to revalue national goods and services internationally as the agent of the markets.

I will refer to this effect as a second order deontology. It is a structural effect of a hierarchy among institutional facts. The deontic powers engendered by the currency market's assignment of status functions can trump the deontic power engendered by the nation's assignment of status functions to its fiscal and monetary institutions. This is best illustrated in situations where the central bank makes a clear commitment to defend its currency in the face of speculative attack by the currency markets. The central bank can commit enormous foreign reserves to the defense of its currency, as did the Thai central bank in the days leading up to 2 July 1997, when it was forced to abandon the defense and let the currency float because it had exhausted its reserves. The volume of private transactions selling the baht overwhelmed the volume of transactions that the Thai central bank could generate to buy the baht.

"'We have no reserves left' . . . has always been seen as an admission of defeat,"[58] and the very last words a central banker would wish to utter. Such an utterance announces the defeat of the central bank's

---

[58] Deane and Pringle, *The Central Banks*, p. 172.

mandate to defend the currency, and often an admission of a global vote of no confidence in the economic policies of the government for which the central bank acted as an agent. It also spells the end of monetary policy autonomy for a central bank that had enjoyed it, at least temporarily, and of fiscal and macroeconomic policy autonomy for the government whose currency actors in the FOREX markets have devalued. Foreign reserves serve as a cushion from exogenous shocks to the national economy, and a source of macroeconomic policy autonomy for the countries that enjoy them.[59]

Foreign reserves must be more readily available (liquid) for small, developing countries whose currencies are less frequently traded, and which are generally not accepted as a means of payment for international settlements. They require ready availability of liquid foreign reserves for occasional (or sometimes frequent and panicked) intervention in the foreign exchange markets, and to smooth out less than steady capital flows, import payments, and export receipts. These funds will be held in the form of highly liquid investments, such as cash, certificates of deposit, and treasury securities, denominated in the currencies in which they expect to make payment, often in the central banks that serve as the "bank of issue" for those currencies, such as the Federal Reserve Bank of New York, or leading commercial banks in leading global financial centers of common reserve currencies, such as New York, London, and Tokyo. Others employ the good offices of the BIS, in Basle, Switzerland. The operational management of the reserves on a day-to-day basis may then be "contracted out" to major foreign central banks or to large commercial and investment banks.[60]

Reserve monies may be defined in the form:[61]

$$RM = (a + b) - (c + d + e)$$

where a is the domestic credit outstanding of the central bank (or claims on commercial banks or the government), b represents net foreign assets. The term $(a + b)$ is the net assets of the central bank. These are balanced against net liabilities which include the sum of c, the currency in circulation, d non-government deposits with the central bank, and e any other net accounts. For most countries, especially

---

[59] *Ibid.*   [60] *Ibid.*, p. 179.
[61] Wilbert O. Bascom, *The Economics of Financial Reform in Developing Countries* (New York: St. Martin's, 1994), p. 40.

developing countries, the term *a* (the central bank's claims on domestic commercial banks or the government) can not contribute to increasing *b* (net foreign assets) in time to help meet a balance of payments crisis or a currency crisis. For this reason the reserves held by the world's central banks have risen dramatically, particularly as countries have moved increasingly to flexible exchange-rate regimes.[62] The United States is a notable exception, and before the collapse of Bretton Woods it alone in the world enjoyed the privilege of making international settlements in its own currency, while all other countries had to make settlement in dollars as well, or the gold bullion into which only the dollar was then directly convertible.

For many countries, when foreign reserves are expended, national austerity immediately results. Thus central banks in developing countries will – and increasingly have, if they have the capacity to do so – develop large foreign reserves in spite of the opportunity costs to the domestic economy of keeping large, liquid, non-interest bearing or minimal interest bearing reserves on hand to avoid the austerity and economic contraction that inevitably follow a currency crisis.

In Thailand in 1997, as elsewhere, the problem was not simply that the supply of baht exceeded demand, in accordance with orthodox monetary theory's view of money. The problem was that the "promise" of the central bank that the baht's exchange value that had been upheld in the past through the "credible" economic policy of the Thai government was no longer upheld. A larger problem was that the "promise" that the value of the baht's future exchange value would and could be upheld – through (1) government policies that could credibly redress the growing current account balance, and through (2) the "promise" that sufficient intervention in the foreign exchange markets by the Thai central bank that could be sustained long enough to counter the huge wave of private transactions dumping the baht in favor of more "stable" currencies – was not credible. In other words, the Thai central bank was unable to credibly present itself, or the government which it served, as a moral agent capable of upholding the promises that the valuation of the currency prior to July 1997 represented. The deontology resulting from the status function assigned to the central bank

---

[62] Deane and Pringle, *The Central Banks*, p. 183. For an account of the dramatic rise in foreign reserves held by Asian central banks due to the impact of the Asian financial crisis see Genberg *et al.*, *Reserves and Currency Management*.

by the Thai people was dismissed by actors in the FOREX markets. One institutional fact established itself as more credible than another. The institutional fact of the value of the baht against other currencies on, say, 15 June, was no longer an institutional fact by 3 July. Collective acceptance for the former fact had, by 3 July, dissipated, and a quite different institutional fact had been established, with enormous real implications for the international exchange value of every good or service produced in Thailand prior to and from that date. The cost of every good or service imported into Thailand from that date rose dramatically, and the real standard of living of every man, woman, and child within the borders of Thailand declined accordingly.

Government debt management: deontic power to monetize debt

The function of central banks as managers of the government's debt arises, in part, from their collectively assigned status function as "banks of issue," and their collectively assigned status function as agents of the government "authorized" to underwrite government debt. The assignment of these status functions endows the central bank with the deontic power to convert government debt into newly created money, diluting the government debt burden by fiat. Economists refer to this practice as "monetizing" government debt. As an example, Greider describes how this practice works in the United States as follows:

the central bank bailed out the Treasury by inflating the currency. The circle went like this: The executive branch borrowed money from the private sector by selling new Treasury notes and bonds. The Fed then diluted the value of this debt by buying up old Treasury notes and bonds from the private sector and paying for them with newly created money. The Federal Reserve, in effect, wound up holding more and more of the government's debt paper in its own cloistered portfolio – and the private economy wound up with a bloated money supply.[63]

This works to reduce the real value of national foreign debt as well. All that was once required, before the real costs of inflation were better understood, was to "pump the money creation process into high gear, all in the politically appealing name of growth. Foreigners would be

---

[63] Greider, *Secrets of the Temple*, p. 560.

repaid with worthless, inflated dollars"[64] or yen or rupiah, or baht, or what have you.

The earliest central banks were developed in no small measure to underwrite government debt, particularly for the purposes of war finance. Some of the stabilization functions of central banks fell out as a natural outgrowth of these functions. For example, while the primary purpose of the Bank of England was underwriting and management of the debts of the British government, the privilege of the "regional monopoly of note issue and its extensive commercial business gave it a natural interest in, and hence in time responsibility for, currency stability, which meant the convertibility of paper notes into specie."[65] Loans to the city-state in the early modern period were effectively monetized when early modern bankers created the mechanisms by which those who supplied goods and services to the city-state governments acquired the capacity to draw upon accounts created for them by the nascent banking system prior to receipt of payment from the debtor government.[66] The state's financing needs in the sixteenth and seventeenth centuries were essential to the founding of nascent central banks and the creation of state credit-money, and Ingham explicates this innovation as a result of a political struggle between supporters of credit and coin as two distinct forms of money.[67] While the Bank of England was created at the behest of the British state for the purposes of war finance and monetization of the attendant debts, this monetization of national debt also mitigated the risks of default, and generated a form of monetary stability and a form of "Dutch finance" that found support among the mercantilist class as well.[68]

But the monetization of debt through inflation is an ancient art, and amounts, as it did in ancient times, to "seigniorage" and even outright debasement of the currency. Benjamin Cohen defines seigniorage as "the excess nominal value of a currency over its cost of production."[69] Niall Ferguson refers to it in more polemic terminology as "the inflation tax" which "permits the government to swap intrinsically worthless pieces of paper (or their electronic equivalent) for actual goods and services,"[70] reducing by inflation the government debt so long as it is denominated in the local currency. Such debt monetization imposes a

---

[64] Solomon, *The Confidence Game*, p. 186.
[65] Feguson, *Cash Nexus*, p. 109.   [66] Ingham, *Nature of Money*, p. 116.
[67] *Ibid.*, p. 125.   [68] *Ibid.*   [69] Cohen, *The Geography of Money*, p. 39.
[70] Ferguson, *Cash Nexus*, p. 144.

number of social costs on the domestic populace. As Cohen suggests, "public spending financed by money creation in effect appropriates real resources at the expense of the private sector, whose purchasing power is subsequently reduced by subsequent inflation."[71]

While inflation likely has many sources, monetarists who insist that excess money creation is its only cause would draw our attention to the social costs of inflation induced by monetizing debt. Stanley Fischer, in a famous essay on modern central banking, attempts to draw our attention to the social costs of inflation in a table that runs on throughout three full pages of the essay, stipulating no fewer than twenty-five "direct effects" of inflation that may be counted as social costs. To stipulate just the top few of these is sobering: they include "increase in government revenue (inflation tax), economizing on currency, reduction in private net wealth, resource costs of price change, increased real income tax bill [income tax bracket creep] and reduction of net tax return on lending relative to pre-tax real rate."[72]

Most contemporary economists argue that the economic policy environment leading to the Great Inflation of the late twentieth century, dominated as it was by Keynesian thought, consistently underestimated the costs of inflation. The monetary policy errors were compounded by exogenous supply shocks such as oil and other commodity shortages in the face of global excess demand, and false expectations of continued low inflation as had been enjoyed as a result of an extended period of rather conservative post-war economic policies.[73] Not the least problematic was a clear over-accommodation in the realm of monetary policy, particularly by the US central bank in the hands of Arthur Burns.

Inflation can be employed by the state as a covert form of taxation as it "permits the government to swap intrinsically worthless pieces of paper (or their electronic equivalents) for actual goods and services" reducing the real value of the government debt so long as this is denominated in the local currency.[74] This became much easier for the state

---

[71] Cohen, *The Geography of Money*, p. 39.
[72] Fischer, "Modern Central Banking", table 7.2, pp. 178ff.
[73] Charles Freedman, "Central Bank Independence" in Paul Mizen (ed.) *Central Banking, Monetary Theory and Practice: Essays in Honour of Charles Goodhart*, vol. I (Cheltenham, UK and Northampton, MA: Edward Elgar, 2003), pp. 97–8.
[74] Ferguson, *Cash Nexus*, p. 144.

with the advent of paper money, which had been introduced in China as early as the eleventh century, but made no appearance in the West until *circa* 1690.[75] Neither physical debasement of precious metals nor "clipping" or "sweating" of coins was any longer required to generate the benefits of seigniorage. Government debt reduction through inflation and debt monetization became all but impossible in the nineteenth century with the advent and spread of the gold standard, but the collapse of the latter returned debt monetization through inflationary finance to the toolbox of state financial statecraft. This possibility was at best a mixed blessing, to which the horrendous consequences of German inter-war hyperinflation and the corrosive consequences of the post-war Great Inflation and stagflation in the last century have testified.

The issue of paper money by newly created central banks in the years immediately following decolonization in the mid-twentieth century also proved to be at best a mixed blessing for developing countries. Here we see that central banks had promised to serve a social as well as an economic purpose for newly independent countries. They proved to be more effective at the former purpose than the latter. A central bank and a national currency were status indicators *par excellence* of national independence, so "the first thing every colony did on achieving independence was to abolish the [colonial] currency board"[76] that had pegged the local currency to that of the former colonial metropole. Many developing countries employed their new central banks as "efficient engines of inflationary finance" that were systematically abused to monetize debt acquired for purposes of economic development projects, but also for the finance of political patronage.[77] Deane and Pringle argue "without the restraints imposed by the fixed exchange rate system, or by the currency board system, there was a systematic tendency toward monetary expansion resulting in either inflation, or chronic payments crises – or more commonly both"[78] with the result that "average inflation in developing countries remained at or above 20% in every year from 1973–1993."[79]

In addition to the normal means of government debt monetization described above, the relatively closed developing economies of the post-colonial world devised a number of novel mechanisms to raise

---

[75] *Ibid.*, p. 46.   [76] Deane and Pringle, *The Central Banks*, p. 87.
[77] *Ibid.*, p. 88.   [78] *Ibid.*, p. 92.   [79] *Ibid.*, p. 93.

the fiscal abuse of central banks to a new level. They were employed to rig the financial market in favor of the government's debt instruments by capping the interest that might be offered on commercial bond issues which might locally compete with government paper. They were employed to increase the reserve requirements on commercial banks well beyond what might have been necessary for prudential lending reserves or for the purposes of monetary control. They were employed to force domestic exporters to sell all of their foreign exchange receipts to the central bank at prices lower than those at which the central bank would make foreign exchange available to exporters to finance their export operations.[80] Thus we see that a number of deontic powers were acquired by central banks in the developing world that enhanced the already considerable deontic power to convert public debt into newly created money.

The view of money advanced here emphasizes that central bank money or high-powered money arises from social relations of debt, that debt remains a promise, and that the newly formed central banks of the developing world in the 1960s and 1970s failed to redeem that promise. The role of central banks in the monetization of state debt should not bear too much opprobrium, however, because this has historically been an essential mechanism of credit expansion and thus of money creation. In the case of the creation of money through monetization of government debt, Ingham is anxious to point out that "even under a gold standard, it is not the *commodity* but the government's *obligation* that produces the money."[81] The government's promise to pay is at the bottom of this creation of high-powered money in the monetization of the government's debt. This is of great consequence, because as Kratochwil reminds us, "promising is constitutive of 'agency' and our ability to bind or commit ourselves by an act of will."[82] Promising is thus at the heart of a government's capacity to create money through the monetization of debt as an act of will. This is so whether money creation begins with public or with private debt creation.

The capacity to monetize private debt effectively began when instruments of debt, such as the "bill of exchange," replete with deontic

---

[80] *Ibid.*, p. 108.
[81] Ingham, *Nature of Money*, p. 75. Emphasis in the original.
[82] Kratochwil, *Rules, Norms and Decisions*, p. 149.

power of a promise of repayment, began to be transferable to third parties, by sale or by discounting. Such instruments began, from the sixteenth century, to circulate alongside sovereign specie as "fiduciary money" and as discounted and rediscounted bills of exchange, though they constituted private promises of payment that were transformed into a form of public money.[83] Victorian English literature is replete with evidence of a nineteenth-century market in "queer bills" whereby a party could buy the already discounted and unpaid debt of another party through a rediscounted purchase of that bill (or proto-check) and press for its full or partial payment as a precondition to cancelling the note.[84] While today significant amounts of government debt are monetized through the disintermediated bond markets (about which I will have much to say in later chapters), huge amounts of private credit-money are also created, as we noted in the first chapter, by bank lending. But the capacity for banks to create money is ultimately limited by the decision of the central bank to ratify that money creation by lending to increase the pool of reserves. And the central bank's power derives from its production and control of the "most sought after promise to pay"[85] which belongs to the government. This promise to pay is only most sought after if the government's past promises to pay have been reliably redeemed and the government has established itself as a credible moral agent.

Promises remain obligatory even for those whose reputations as moral agents have been sullied by past non-performance. Thus central bank credibility as a guarantor of the government's promises is highly prized in an era of capital mobility. And it will be more highly prized by states that maintain open economies dependent on capital flows. In this context we should not be surprised to see the recent moves to granting independence from the government to central banks in that portion of the developing world that is integrating into the global economy, as well as in the developed world. The value of central bank independence "rises as a signal to investors"[86] that the government's promises are trustworthy, and the government is creditworthy. The

---

[83] *Ibid.*, p. 116.

[84] See, for example, the narrative beginning with the chapter "Lodgers on Queer Street" in Charles Dickens, *Our Mutual Friend* (Ware, Hertfordshire: Wordsworth Classics, 1997).

[85] Ingham, *Nature of Money*, p. 142.

[86] Maxfield, *Gatekeepers of Growth*, p. 45.

obligation to ensure the value of money that will uphold the government's promise to pay results from the deontic power of the central bank to create money. It further results from the central bank's capacity to monetize government debt. Independence enhances the central bank's credibility as a moral agent with the capacity to exercise discretion and ostensibly to impose restraint on behalf of the government to ensure that government debt creation will not obviate its promises. These promises are assertions of creditworthiness, and as Kratochwil reminds us it is "precisely because the uptake of an obligation is so fundamental to our basic moral conceptions, promising is most probably paradigmatic for a wide variety of rule-bound actions, including the institution of asserting something (telling the truth)."[87] This will be demonstrated to be quite significant later; as Pufendorf demonstrated centuries ago in his investigations into the hypothetical laws of nature, when we make assertions, we are engaged in an activity governed by institutional rules.[88]

Directed lending and "window guidance": deontic power to allocate credit

To this list of "functions" or "mandates" of central banks, from which they derive deontic powers, we might add, for central banks in some Asian countries and developing countries around the world, the allocation of credit. This was a function that was *de facto* allocated to nearly all central banks in the post-war period, when central banks in the industrialized world were marshalled to the task of reconstruction of war-ravaged national economies:

After the war, the Bank of England and the *Banque de France* were nationalized, and everywhere central bankers were given the task of allocating credit, persuading, influencing, and ordering the banks in their countries to finance only those activities that promoted the national "plan".[89]

Credit allocation methods were developed and deployed masterfully by Hitler's finance minister, Hjalmar Schacht, who employed credit allocation methods in the 1920s to structurally transform the German economy by sectoral and regional credit allocation directives to

---

[87] Kratochwil, *Rules, Norms and Decisions*, p. 149.
[88] *Ibid.*   [89] Mayer, *The Fed*, p. 82.

German banks. These methods placed enormous power in Schacht's hands as successive Weimar German governments fell from 1924 until his pre-Hitlerian resignation in 1930.[90] Wartime Japan had sent Bank of Japan officials to Berlin to learn from the Reichsbank's techniques, among them Hisato Ichimada, who became a key figure in post-war Japan's central banking structure. It is worth noting that the wartime Japanese government formally subordinated the Bank of Japan to the government's finance ministry in 1942 by simply translating Hitler's Reichsbank Law of 1939 from German into Japanese and introducing it as the new Bank of Japan Law.[91]

Japan spearheaded its meteoric post-war economic recovery and rise with a highly government-directed credit allocation process by which the Bank of Japan, then wholly subordinate to the Ministry of Finance, allocated credit when regional commercial banks "came to the window" for their reserves. The Governor of the Bank of Japan would decide by what amount total loans should grow for a given period of time, and the head of the Banking Department would then allocate the increased reserve credit to individual banks in the form of loan quotas. The commercial banks would be asked to share their lending plans with the Bank of Japan on a monthly basis, and the latter would then revise the lending plan to fit the predetermined credit allocation plans and hand it back to the commercial banks. As Richard Werner explains, "since the banks came to the Bank of Japan to be told virtually over the counter (the teller window) of the Banking Department how large their loans quota was going to be, the procedure became known as 'window guidance' (*madoguchi shidō*)."[92]

There are, of course, enormous developmental advantages to applying such government-directed lending through the central bank, not the least of which are the advantages of directing credit to the most productive sectors of the economy and avoiding diversion to less productive sectors. This "window guidance," which is more generally known as "government directed lending," is one of several tools of the "developmental state"[93] pioneered by Japan, whose model was followed

---

[90] Richard A. Werner, *Princes of the Yen: Japan's Central Bankers and the Transformation of the Economy* (Armonk, NY and London: M. E. Sharpe, 2003), p. 53.

[91] *Ibid.*, p. 54.   [92] *Ibid.*, p. 62.

[93] See, for example, Meredith Woo-Cumings, *The Developmental State* (Ithaca, NY: Cornell University Press, 1999) and Alice H. Amsden, *The Rise of "The*

with enormous success by South Korea, Taiwan, Hong Kong, and Singapore, and more recently by Malaysia, Thailand, and other East Asian nations. As has been succinctly argued, "high household savings plus high corporate debt/equity ratios plus bank-firm-state collaboration, plus national industrial strategy, plus investment incentives conditional on international competitiveness equals the 'developmental state'."[94]

This particular form of government-directed lending was criticized when it would occasionally reach the public eye, and formal window guidance was abolished more than once, first in 1958. But it was replaced by a more covert move by the Bank of Japan to maintain the reserve positions of banks in such a way that the expansion of credit throughout the Japanese financial system would result as desired, so window guidance, while formally abolished, continued in practice. Window guidance also continued in practice after it was again formally abolished in 1965. However, the criticism of the financial system that led to these reforms required the Bank of Japan to begin buying and selling government bonds as a more expensive means of financing economic stimulus than the simple credit expansion through reserves in which it had earlier engaged in with impunity.[95]

In fact, Werner provides evidence in his interviews with Japanese commercial bankers that window guidance was alive and well as a government-directed credit allocation practice through the Bank of Japan well into the 1980s, where it played an unfortunate roll in helping to inflate the disastrous bubble economy. According to one Japanese banker interviewed by Werner and his collaborators:

In the bubble period, we wanted a certain amount [of loan increases], but the BoJ wanted us to use more than that. After 1985, the BoJ said, "Use more!" Normally, we would not get as much as we wanted to use... Especially in 1986 and 1987, for around one year, the Bank of Japan said: "Use more because we have a recession." Window guidance can be used not just to make borrowing smaller, but also to make it bigger. We actually thought, "This is a little bit much." But we couldn't leave anything unused of the

Rest": *Challenges to the West from Late-Industrializing Economies* (Oxford: Oxford University Press, 2001).

[94] Robert Wade and Frank Veneroso, "The Asian Crisis: The High Debt Model Versus the Wall Street-Treasury-IMF Complex" *New Left Review* no. 228 (March/April 1998): 3–24.

[95] Werner, *Princes of the Yen*, p. 68.

quota given to us. If we did, other city banks that received a similar quota might beat us. Thus in order to keep our ranking [among banks] we had to use it all up... Also, if we got a reputation for being weak, we would get less in the future. (Bank officer 4).[96]

Deane and Pringle argue that "window guidance" in the form of direct control lending by the Bank of Japan has ended.[97] Has it? Cargill, Hutchinson, and Ito[98] argue otherwise. They suggest that window guidance is still around after the 1998 law granting independence to the Bank of Japan. Deane and Pringle, writing in 1994, saw a "modified window guidance" arguing that the Bank of Japan "still... knows exactly what each commercial bank plans to lend and makes clear its preferred policy."[99] Since the Bank of Japan previously still took its marching orders from the Ministry of Finance at the time of their writing, the latter received the blame for the excessive credit expansion of the bubble economy, and the subsequent decade of economic stagnation and deflation. This was the stimulus for the New Bank of Japan Law of 1998 granting operational independence to the Bank of Japan, with a primary objective of price stability.

Article 43 of the new law removes the Ministry of Finance's former power to direct the Bank of Japan's business, and a wide range of other business. But Article 38 rather vaguely states that

the Ministry of Finance may request the Bank of Japan to conduct the business necessary to maintain an orderly financial system, including the provision of loans, when it is believed to be especially necessary for the maintenance of the orderly financial system.[100]

This could as easily refer to a lender of last resort function, and systemic risk of the failure of a particular financial concern or sector, but is adequately vaguely worded to suggest that the Ministry of Finance can lean on the Bank of Japan to engage in some government-directed lending. The wording also clearly indicates, however, that the Bank of Japan may decline to do so. Enormous pressure was placed upon East Asian states in the wake of the Asian financial crisis to

---

[96] Japanese bank officer quoted in *ibid.*, p. 134.
[97] Deane and Pringle, *The Central Banks*, p. 250.
[98] Thomas F. Cargill, Michael M. Hutchison, and Takatoshi Ito, *Financial Policy and Central Banking in Japan* (Cambridge, MA and London: MIT Press, 2000).
[99] *Ibid.*, p. 251.　　[100] *Ibid.*, p. 104.

terminate government-directed lending, and other key economic practices associated with the Asian model of development,[101] with varying success.

Thus it is clear that central banks, in some states, have acquired the deontic power to allocate credit, which amounts to the deontic power to structure the national economy, expanding some sectors and contracting others through the provision or denial of credit to specific sectors or firms – though this power is shared with national planning authorities. This is denounced by many economists as the benighted practice of "picking winners and losers," which neoclassical economics argues paradigmatically is a process best left to market forces. However, irrespective of the developmental advantages of "window guidance" it is equally clear that these central banks have also acquired the deontic power to extend a surfeit of credit, and generate destructive asset bubbles, with enormous negative consequences for longer-term economic national well-being.

Economics as institutional facts and deontic powers: why does it matter?

So having generated an institutional account of money, and the "functions" of central banks as deontic powers constituted by institutional facts and constitutive rules, the reader might ask why this matters. First, this observation is extremely important for establishing the parameters for fruitful investigation of social (and consequently of economic) life, because social life is mediated by institutional facts generated by constitutive rules, and regulative rules that are subsequently indicated from these. Much social and economic behavior is rule-following behavior, regulated at a minimum by norms of behavior established by the construction of institutions. As Kratochwil has observed:

Since rule-following does not involve blind habit (except in limiting cases) but argumentation, it is through analyzing the reasons which are specific to different rule-types that the intersubjective validity of norms and thus their "deontic status" can be established.[102]

---

[101] Rodney Bruce Hall, "The Discursive Demolition of the Asian Development Model" *International Studies Quarterly* 47(1) (2003): 71–99.
[102] Kratochwil, *Rules, Norms and Decisions*, p. 97.

The short answer is that it matters if the monetary realm is an institutional realm, because if we adhere to the commodity-based theory of money we cannot understand money as an institutional fact constituted by social relations of debt *qua* promising. We cannot understand the deontic powers of money or the social institutions of credit and debt that constitute these, or the central banks that were created by governments to redeem the promise that money constitutes. We do not have an adequate account of the social relations that lend central banks their social and economic power to create and destroy money, to determine its price both domestically and internationally, to create liquidity and socialize risk in a crisis, to convert government and private debt into money, or to allocate credit to structure a national economy – or to over-allocate it to over-monetize a national economy, generating destructive inflation and/or asset bubbles.

In addition to these problems, understanding money, credit, and central banks as social institutions permits us to begin to discover the monetary and economic realms as rule-governed spheres of social action. It helps us make an analytic cut into the rule-based architecture of international monetary affairs which, as we shall shortly see, has always been governed by an institutional logic of institutional practices in response to institutional facts and the constitutive rules that arrange these into social reality – rather than as the wholly uncoordinated actions of means–ends instrumentally rational actors. We need a "logic of appropriateness" and not simply a "logic of instrumentalism" to explain central bank behavior,[103] and market behavior as well, in both national and international monetary affairs.

An institutional account permits us to read the rules of exchange-rate regimes and the never-ending search for a stable "nominal anchor" for the system, as a nearly entirely rule-governed order. It lets us see the current move to central bank independence as an attempt to sustain that order by assigning the independent central bank the status function of that nominal anchor. This nominal anchor in turn serves as a constitutive rule of the international monetary system in the form, "a nominal anchor" counts as "international monetary stability" in the context of an international monetary system characterized by fiat money, capital mobility, and floating exchange

---

[103] Stephen Bell, "The Limits of Rational Choice: New Institutionalism in the Test Bed of Central Banking Politics in Australia" *Political Studies* 50 (2002): 488.

rates, as well as an important emerging mechanism of global financial governance.

Before turning to develop the international monetary system as a social institution, and the emerging mechanisms of global financial governance arising from these social relations, the next chapter pauses briefly to situate the notion of the deontic powers of the central bank that I have developed from Searle's institutional philosophy with respect to some other accounts of constitutive and monetary power relations to be found in the contemporary literature on international relations theory. While these accounts are useful for explicating power relations among actors in monetary systems, they differ sufficiently from the notion of deontic power for me to simply pause in the next chapter to take note of these analytic relationships. I will then move on in chapter 5 and its successors to further apply the notion of deontic power to additional actors whose use of it plays important roles in the emerging system of global financial governance.

4 | *Constitutive power relations*

Neorealism "fetishizes" material capabilities in the sense that it embues them with meanings and powers that can only correctly be attributable to human beings.

Alexander Wendt

Constitutive relations cannot be reduced to the attributes, actions, or interactions of pregiven actors. Power, accordingly, is irreducibly social. In other words, constitutive arguments examine how particular social relations are responsible for producing particular kinds of actors.

Michael Barnett and Raymond Duvall

The study of power relations lies at the heart of the modern academic discipline of political science. Yet power relations have been oddly understudied in the literature on international political economy and particularly in the literature arising in the North American academy. In large measure this has been because of the manner in which international political economy has developed in attempting to extricate itself from the state-centric North American "canonical" texts in international relations as they have emerged from structural realism and neoliberal institutionalism. In the North American debates scholars were required to struggle to develop the power of market actors and the forces they bring to bear on outcomes in the international economic realm as autonomous actors in international politics.[1]

A large measure of the reasons why the study of power relations in international political economy has not heretofore come to develop a sustained discussion of the forms of power relations with which the present work is concerned stems from the focus of the literature

---

[1] See e.g. Benjamin J. Cohen, "The Transatlantic Divide: Why are American and British IPE so Different?" *Review of International Political Economy* 14(4) (2007): 197–219.

in international relations on the direct power effects resulting from the interaction of autonomous actors in an "anarchic" international system.[2] Neoliberal institutionalist scholars, for the sake of engaging structural realist scholars in debate, adopted this interactive methodological individualist framework and developed a literature predicated on the "puzzle" of how liberal international economic regimes and institutions persist in the absence of a "hegemon" to maintain them through coercive interaction or the provision of their benefits as a public good.[3] Literature from these schools of thought dedicated specifically to investigation of the political economy of monetary institutions has retained a focus on the power relations and outcomes resulting from interaction effects, while broadening the study of these effects to include coalitions of domestic actors within the state and interaction between sub-state and state-level actors.[4] In all of this work, such studies of power relations as have been generated have been focused squarely on power exercised through interaction.

Deontic, constitutive and interactive power relations

In response to the long-standing criticism that constructivist work in international relations lacks a theory of power relations, Michael Barnett and Raymond Duvall have generated such a theory. In doing so they have generated a four-element taxonomy of power relations in international politics that encompasses the power relations exercised through the interaction of actors who are either autonomous of one another or stand in relations of super- and subordination to one another, directly or indirectly through institutional relations. But they have also been careful to address the power relations arising from social relations of agential constitution and mutual co-constitution exercised both directly and diffusely.[5]

Barnett and Duvall's work develops two forms of power relations – derived from their explorations of the social relations of constitution,

---

[2] Kenneth Waltz, *Theory of International Politics* (Boston, MA: Addison-Wesley, 1979).

[3] Robert Keohane, *After Hegemony* (Princeton, NJ: Princeton University Press, 1984).

[4] See e.g. Bernhard *et al.*, "The Political Economy of Monetary Institutions."

[5] Michael Barnett and Raymond Duvall, "Power in International Politics" *International Organization* 59(1) (2005): 39–75.

rather than interaction – that provide additional utility to exploring the consequences of the forms of deontic power that I have developed from Searle's institutional philosophy. In this chapter I will explore the relationship of these forms of power deriving from social relations of constitution to the concept of deontic power, as developed in Searle's institutional philosophy, and demonstrate how these constructivist concepts can be employed to elaborate on the articulated forms of the deontic powers of central banks that I have derived from Stanley Fischer's neoclassical economic description of the "functions" of central banks in global financial governance.

Barnett and Duvall develop four major forms of social power by deducing the social power relations resulting from variation in the "relational specificity" of the actors implicated in power relations (these are direct or diffuse) and by the extent to which social agency or social structure governs the resulting power relations. Where the exercise of social agency is strongly implicated in generating power relationships, the forms of power relationships resulting are (1) "compulsory" when interaction between actors is direct, and the resulting power relations are designated as (2) "institutional" when the relational specificity is more indirect. Compulsory and institutional power relations then result from the interaction of actors either directly or more indirectly. When social structures more strongly govern relations between actors, however, power relations are those resulting from social relations of constitution rather than from the interaction of specific actors. The direct mutual constitution (or co-constitution) of social actors generates power relations among these actors that Barnett and Duvall designate as "structural" power relations, and they designate the more "diffuse" constitutive relations to produce the situated social capacities of actors as "productive" power relations. Of particular interest in this context is Barnett and Duvall's development of those forms of social power arising from social relations of constitution and mutual constitution (or co-constitution) – namely their "structural" and "productive" forms of power.

Deontic power is also a form of power arising from social relations of constitution. But deontic power arises from a specific form of constitution – from that form resulting from collective assignment of status functions. This collective designation of status functions generates human institutions. In this view institutions are not a result of interaction effects. They are constructions built of institutional facts that, per Searle, "are generated by constitutive rules which rely upon collective acceptance and intentionality and the collective assignment of status functions."[6] Thus constitutive rules, which result from collective intentionality and more particularly from collective assignment of status functions, are generated as institutional facts. Human institutions are aggregations of these constitutive rules. And deontic powers result from the formation of these human institutions. Human institutions "are above all enabling, because they create power...a special kind of power...marked by such terms as rights, duties, obligations, permissions, empowerments, requirements and certifications."[7]

As Barnett and Duvall explain, social relations of constitution, such as the deontic powers Searle develops, do not result from the interaction by which actors exercise "power over" one another, but are social arrangements by which actors acquire "power to" perform various acts or functions. In the case where social actors acquire "power over" one another through interaction effects, social relations and the attendant power relations are treated as "comprised of pre-constituted social actors toward one another" and power is treated as "an attribute that an actor possesses and may knowingly use as a resource to shape the actions or conditions of action for others."[8] Power resulting from social relations of constitution, however, derives from:

social relations that analytically precede the social or subject positions of actors and that constitute them as social beings with their respective capacities and interests. Constitutive relations cannot be reduced to the attributes, actions, or interactions of pre-given actors. Power, accordingly, is irreducibly social...constitutive arguments examine how particular social relations are responsible for producing particular kinds of actors.[9]

Human institutions produce particular kinds of actors. Institutions, Searle reminds us, "are structures of power relationships."[10] Institutional structures "create desire independent reasons for action" which like norms cannot be conflated with "causes" of actions. They presuppose that there is "a [collective] recognition of the deontic [power] relationships."[11]

Thus structural and productive power as developed by Barnett and Duvall are particular forms or articulations of deontic power. Human

---

[6] Searle, "What is an Institution?", p. 19.   [7] *Ibid.*, p. 10.
[8] Barnett and Duvall, "Power in International Politics," p. 45.   [9] *Ibid.*, p. 46.
[10] Searle, "What is an Institution?", p. 10.   [11] *Ibid.*, p. 11.

institutional subjectivity is generated and specified by both structural and productive power, though wielders of structural and productive power take differing approaches to the generation of subjectivity in their exercise. Barnett and Duvall argue that structural power involves the "co-constitution of subjects" with the result of "hierarchical and binary relations of domination."[12] The structural binaries of master/slave and capitalist/laborer are employed by Barnett and Duvall as examples.

Structural power results from "mutual constitution of the capacities of action" whereby "structural positions" are "co-constituted."[13] It would appear that collective intentionality is necessarily involved in the generation of structural power, even though some actors are significantly disadvantaged as autonomous agents in the process. One can be an object rather than an agent in the construction of a social institution resulting from the collective intentionality of others. Slavery and capitalism are both social institutions, and both require the collective intentionality of numerous autonomous actors to generate and to maintain them as human institutions. Both require the collective assignment of status functions to come into being and to generate constitutive and regulative rules in order to maintain them as institutions. The status functions enjoyed by master and capitalist necessarily entailed the assignment of less enviable status functions and social subjectivities to slave and laborer, but assigned they were, through the collective intentionality of actors benefiting from these institutions. The consent (intentionality) of slave and laborer clearly need not be involved in either the generation or maintenance of the social institution within which they have been assigned subordinate status functions. These subordinate subjectivities will discover in direct interaction with the social institutions of slavery and capitalism that their behavior is structurally constrained to performing those functions assigned to them by those whose collective intentionality generates the superordinate status functions of master and capitalist. They will experience the effects of the "compulsory" power of those at the top of the status hierarchy in such direct interactions. Those at the top of the binary status hierarchy enjoy rights, authorizations, permissions, empowerments, and privileges. Those allocated subordinate status functions face duties, obligations, and responsibilities. As

---

[12] Barnett and Duvall, "Power in International Politics", p. 56.   [13] *Ibid.*

Barnett and Duvall suggest, "structural positions do not necessarily generate equal social privileges; instead structures allocate differential capacities and typically differential advantages to different positions."[14] Structural power as developed by Barnett and Duvall clearly emerges as a form, or a specific articulation of deontic power that generates structural binary social subjectivities and hierarchical power positions among those binary, co-constituted subject positions.

Barnett and Duvall provide the key to the relationship between their two forms of constitutive power and deontic power in contrasting these constitutive forms of power with power arising from interaction. The latter

point[s] to the exercise of control *over* others... [whereas]... concepts of power tied to social relations of constitution, in contrast, consider how social relations define who the actors are and what capacities and practices they are socially empowered to undertake... [and]... focuse[s] on the social production of actors.[15]

Here the focus is on what the actors have the power to do. The effects of constitutive power, by contrast, include establishing

identities of the occupants of social positions... affecting the behavior of others... setting the terms of their very self-understandings... effects of actors' subjectivities and self understanding... fixing what actors are as social beings... [and defining]... the meaningful practices in which they are disposed to engage as subjects.[16]

Most if not all of these can be recognized as effects of collective allocation of status functions and the associated deontologies. While all of these effects of structural power arise from deontologies, it is not, however necessarily the case that all deontologies generate structural binaries of hierarchical power relations. For example, one deontic power arising from collective assignment of status functions can generate human institutions in which actors constituted as members of the institution enjoy "rights" and "privileges." While one might argue that a deontology generating a "rights holder" necessarily involves generation of a subject who does not enjoy those rights, this cannot be regarded as a "structural binary" in the classical sense as one can always envision subjectivities who do not enjoy these rights and

---

[14] *Ibid.*, p. 53.   [15] *Ibid.*, p. 46. Emphasis added.   [16] *Ibid.*, pp. 46–7.

privileges yet are unaware of and/or unconcerned with the rights and privileges of the institution. Similarly, within the membership of the institution, hieratic structural binaries need not result either. My enjoyment of my rights in law or a society need not have any effect on my fellows' enjoyment of equivalent rights. We all stand in the same relationship to the law, or to the constitutive and regulative rules of society. When our exercise of our positive rights under the law impinges on the rights of others, then the law (constituting itself a social institution through collective assignment of our rights, and often a reciprocal stipulation of duties) must adjudicate the resulting dispute.

Thus we acquire legal subjectivity. In this context, the granter or assigner of rights and obligations (legal authority) stands in a relationship of structural power to the subject of the law. Thus legal subjectivity generates a structural binary only when legal authority has not itself been assigned a legal subjectivity – in those cases where the legal authority promulgates the law (assigns status functions to others) but is not subject to the law. The social institution of "sovereignty-as-dominium,"[17] particularly absolutist forms of monarchy, serves as an example. Totalitarian societies ruled by the law promulgated by a "vanguard" or single, power-monopolizing political party serve as another example of a legal authority lacking legal subjectivity beyond that of "authority." In these cases the social subjectivities of "sovereign/subject" are generated in hieratic, structural binary form.

Productive power is exercised via "knowledge systems and discursive practices... through which meaning is produced, fixed, lived, experienced and transformed."[18] Unlike structural power, productive power is not employed in the co-constitution of subjects, but "concerns the boundaries of all social identity."[19] Productive power is employed in the "discursive production of subjects, the fixing of meanings, and the terms of action" in social life. Generation of "basic categories of classification [what Wendt calls 'social kinds'][20] are representative of productive power as they generate asymmetries of social capabilities."[21]

---

[17] Friedrich Kratochwil, "Sovereignty as *Dominium*: Is there a Right to Humanitarian Intervention?" in G. Lyons and M. Mastanduno (eds.) *Beyond Westphalia* (Baltimore, MD: Johns Hopkins University Press, 1995), pp. 21–42.

[18] Barnett and Duvall, "Power in International Politics," p. 55.   [19] *Ibid.*, p. 56.

[20] Wendt, *Social Theory*, pp. 67–77.   [21] *Ibid.*

But it is important to note that the fixing of social meanings need not always result in the assignment of status function. In this instance productive power differs from structural power as it generates social kinds but not necessarily in hieratic, mutually constitutive binary forms. Deontic power similarly generates social kinds, and fixes certain social meanings of a certain kind. Thus "productive power" seems a more extensive, more diffuse, less specific form of constitutive power than deontic power.

Now let us examine the deontic powers of central banks that I derived from Stanley Fisher's functions of modern central banks and explore what forms of power relations from Barnett and Duvall's taxonomy are operating in consequence of the deontic powers described.

Constitutive power relations in rate determination

Recall that the power to set the interest rates or the price of money is the deontic power to create and destroy money and to make money available or to decline to make money available to the commercial banking system, and thus to the broader national economy. Structural power as developed by Barnett and Duvall is at work in the power relations that emerge from this deontology. The hieratic structural binary relationship "money issuer/money user" is generated. In the absence of a functioning "free banking" system, the commercial bank's capacity to issue credit and back it with money is predicated on the central bank performing its role as a bank of issue. But the hierarchical binary that emerges as socially salient is dependent upon context. The central bank has the deontic power to issue money to back credit and thereby enable the commercial banking system to expand credit, or to decline to do so, and even the deontic power to extinguish money and compel the commercial banking system (through that interaction) to contract credit and lending. Thereby deontic powers derived from constitutive forms of power relations can also generate compulsory interaction effects when employed in interaction.

As we shall see when we discuss the operating systems with which they execute monetary policy, for many central banks this deontic power is operationalized by setting the price of money in the interbank market by specifying a target price of money in the market and then expanding or contracting the supply of money in such a way that transactions in the interbank money markets generate that price. In this context the structural binary subjectivities created between the central bank and the commercial banking system is "price setter/price taker." When the commercial banking system wants more money to back the credit it would like to issue than the central bank is willing to provide (when monetary policy is tight) the relationship constructed between the central bank and the commercial banking system is that of "credit refuser/credit supplicant." Thus deontic power to create and to destroy money is the deontic power to expand or contract reserves in the banking system. It is structural power, in Barnett and Duvall's formulation, to the extent that it generates hieratic power binaries between the central bank and the commercial banking system. Such co-constituted social subjectivities are generated, as I have just illustrated.

Now recall Barnett and Duvall's argument that productive power is exercised via "knowledge systems and discursive practices . . . through which meaning is produced, fixed, lived, experienced and transformed." However, constitutive processes that fix meanings need not always result in the collective assignment of status functions. The deontic powers of the central bank to create and destroy money both fix economic meanings and generate "economic kinds." The deontic money creation and money destruction powers of the central bank provide it with the productive capacity to transform and fix both the supply of money and the price of money.

The institutional power of the central bank through interaction (the exercise of these productive capacities) has the institutional capacity (through diffuse interaction) to transform the demand for money. In more direct interaction, by contracting or expanding the supply of money in the banking system, the central bank has compulsive power over the capacity for the commercial banking system to extend credit or to generate credit-money. When applied in interaction to counter the intentions of the commercial banking system this power is compulsory, as designated by Barnett and Duvall, and when applied in concert with the intentions of the commercial banking system I would designate this power as "enabling" power. Enabling power is the positive analytic equivalent of Barnett and Duvall's notion of compulsory power relations established through direct interaction.

Constitutive power relations in liquidity provision and risk socialization

Recall that the status functions that generate the deontic powers of liquidity provisions and risk socialization (central banking's "lender of last resort" function) include the status of a "bank of issue," and that of an agent of the government authorized to socialize risk by selectively providing liquidity on an emergency basis at the agent's discretion. This also implies the deontic power of diluting the value of the money supply via massive injections of liquidity. The exercise of this deontic power as structural power requires at least one financial institution for which the central bank is authorized to lend on an emergency basis to suffer such significant illiquidity that it is insolvent in the absence of injections of fresh capital.

A financial institution such as a bank is generally considered to be insolvent if its ratio of capital to assets is at, or close to zero, or if its capital assets, including common stock, are of such poor quality that its continued existence is uncertain.[22]

A distressed institution seeking finance that cannot be privately arranged, and a central bank willing to provide this lending at last resort, co-constitute a structural binary of "lender of last resort/bail-out institution."

The power relations are hieratic and co-constituted *in situ*. Operationally there is no lender of last resort without a distressed borrower at last resort. The social subjectivity of the former is predicated on the subjectivity of the latter, even as the latter subjectivity is generated infrequently and not constantly available to enable the lender of last resort to actually act as a lender of last resort in interaction. The lender of last resort as a potential subject was constituted as a potential subject, normally, by national legal statute. But just as with the social institution of slavery, where every man of a certain description with the capacity and legal right to purchase another as chattel is a potential master, a man becomes a master in fact only in acquiring a slave, at his discretion.

The central bank may also have a function to perform as emergency provider of liquidity into the banking system in times of systemic

---

[22] T. P. Finch, *Barrons: Dictionary of Banking Terms* (4th edn) (2000), pp. 236–7.

financial distress, as most recently observed in the August 2007 global liquidity crunch. This ensued (and continues at the time of writing) as a result of spiraling non-performance of structured and CDOs in which high-risk mortgages were securitized along with higher-quality obligations into a single structured bond and sold throughout the financial system to investment banks, pension funds, and insurance companies, among other institutional investors. When borrowers began defaulting on these securities in large numbers, a global crisis of liquidity spread throughout the financial system, in part as a result of the amount of capital involved for many firms with high exposure to these securities, and in part because no liquid market had developed for them, and a liquid market price became nearly impossible to determine, as no market actor believed the "modeled" or computed and imputed value of these securities that had been recorded in the balance sheets of firms as "assets." The ECB, the US Federal Reserve, and finally the Bank of England, decided to accept these securities as collateral against infusions of central bank cash for periods of time as long as ninety days in order to inject emergency liquidity into national and global financial systems.[23] The ECB even opened its window to British banks with significant exposure to these securities, who borrowed at the ECB window through their continental subsidiaries while the Bank of England for a time remained stubbornly averse to such lending for fear of exacerbating moral hazard issues.[24]

Thus central banks act to provide liquidity and socialize risk across financial systems – whose payment systems and willingness to extend credit and liquidity to one another may become frozen for fear of inadequate liquidity, leading financial institutions to hoard liquid assets – in addition to acting as a lender of last resort for individual distressed institutions.[25] However, such direct interaction between central banks and market actors enables (rather than compels) markets to shed "dysfunctional" status and enables distressed borrowers (large failing financial concerns deemed "too big to fail") to shed "uncreditworthy"

---

[23] See e.g. Gillian Tett, Richard Milne, and Krishna Guha, "ECB Injects €95bn to Aid Markets," *Financial Times*, 10 August 2007, and Ralf Atkins and James Politi, "ECB Move to Inject Funds Lifts Markets," *Financial Times*, 23 August 2007.

[24] Martin Wolf, "Central Banks should not Rescue Fools from their Folly," *Financial Times*, 28 August 2007.

[25] Gillian Tett, "Money Markets Squeeze: Sense of Crisis Growing over Interbank Deals," *Financial Times*, 5 September 2007.

status. In interaction this constitutes a positive form of "compulsory" power that I have designated as "enabling power." Direct interaction of specific actors enables other actors to shed unwanted status and to escape threatening structural positions of domination via the application of enabling power resources. These are provided through the agency of the central bank.

Productive power is employed here to change and to fix social and economic meanings. An example given earlier in the book was the brief statement by Alan Greenspan issued during the October 1987 Wall Street plunge assuring unlimited liquidity to the markets, which transformed the meaning of the market crash from an event generating a huge liquidity crisis that could generate other forms of collapse, in the credit markets and in the payments system, into a manageable downturn in the market or at worst a steep market correction. The productive power of the exercise of the central bank's deontic power of emergency liquidity provision transformed the social and economic meanings of the disappearance of trillions of dollars of market capitalization into a painful, but discrete and manageable, event from a harbinger of a major downturn in the availability of credit.

Similarly the social meanings of market conditions and actors are altered by the application of productive power in the central bank's emergency liquidity provision capacity in systemic credit crises like the CDO credit crunch and in lender of last resort stabilization of individual distressed financial institutions. Markets are transformed from "illiquid" to "liquid" status, with enormous causal significance for the manner in which they function (in lieu of dysfunction). "Insolvent" financial institutions are transformed into "recovering" financial institutions. Thus the deontic powers attending liquidity provision and risk socialization have both structural and productive constitutive power effects, as well as institutional and compulsory (and enabling) effects in interaction.

Institutional power over the level and forms of market activity in indirect interaction with the markets (or the central bank's direct interaction with particular distressed financial institutions) are signals to the market as a whole that any truly distressed financial institution is likely to have access to the liquidity it needs to make settlement of existing obligations, and those generated by the deterioration of market conditions. The deontologies described in chapter 3 were, however, required to generate all of these power relations and their effects.

Constitutive power relations in exchange-rate and reserve management

Recall that the status functions that generate the deontic powers of valuation of the international product, in performing exchange-rate and reserve management functions by the central bank, derive from the status functions of the bank as a government agency authorized (1) to socialize risk, (2) to determine the level of national wealth held in reserves in the form of foreign exchange, (3) to determine how many of these reserves to expend to uphold the exchange rate when it comes under pressure. In managing the exchange rate, the central bank thereby revalues national wealth.

From Barnett and Duvall's taxonomy of power, productive power may be more in evidence in operation than structural power in articulating these deontic powers of the central bank. A deontology obviously results in the transformation of the economic meanings of the value, or purchasing power, of the national currency. Consequently a transformation in the meaning of the value of the national wealth denominated in this currency is a productive power effect. A transformation of the prices paid for imports denominated in foreign currencies, and of exports denominated in the local currency, is an institutional effect of interaction between the central bank and the FOREX markets, and interaction of local and foreign producers with the institutional effects of the central banks' productive power exercise – namely adjusted import and export prices.

For both FOREX market participants and participants in the sovereign debt markets such central bank actions generate qualitative changes in the meaning of the credibility of the central bank's determination to defend its currency valuation (or peg, depending on the exchange-rate regime employed) as signaled by the exercise of deontic power to accumulate or expend reserves. It is important to note that market actors' interpretations of the government's fiscal policies have a good deal (perhaps more) of productive power to generate qualitative changes in FOREX and bond market assessments of the meaning of the credibility of the government's promise to generate stable money.

These observations suggest that the reserve management functions of central banks, and the associated deontologies, do generate structured binaries constituted by the exercise of these deontic powers. However, unless a central bank has accumulated enormous reserves that could conceivably be run down to defeat any concerted speculative movement against its national currency's exchange rate – and it is difficult to assess whether any state could achieve this level of reserves given the thunderous volume of daily transactions in the FOREX markets – government fiscal policy is at least equally implicated in the structured binaries that follow. The constitutive rules of FOREX market understandings of the meanings of the terms "credible" and "responsible" are indicative of the effects of the forms of productive power they employ in interpreting the actions of the government and central bank of the currency in which they are trading. For example, historical FOREX market activity might lead us to inductively derive the following constitutive rules of how market actors appear to assess exchange rate futures:

Reserves accumulation + "responsible" fiscal policy *counts as* "credible" peg and stable currency *in the context of* assessing exchange rate futures
and
Reserves depletion + "imprudent" fiscal policy *counts as* "non-credible" peg and speculative attack opportunity *in the context of* assessing exchange rate futures

The productive power of skillful exchange-rate management of the central bank, and skillful management of government fiscal policy to generate specific economic meanings and understanding among market participants, is clearly indicated in these inductively derived "constitutive rules of speculative attack."

The central bank exercises institutional power (which generates interaction effects) by employing its deontic power to intervene in the FOREX markets with accumulated reserves. It may do so either by selling those reserves and buying the domestic currency to defend its peg (or to raise the market value of the currency in the FOREX markets, thus raising the exchange rate). Conversely it may do so by selling the domestic currency in the FOREX markets to buy foreign exchange (or to lower the exchange rate of the domestic currency). The institutional power of the central bank engenders productive power in market actors as they interpret the institutional action of the central bank and the government. This productive power generates social (and economic) kinds – namely "stable" and "unstable" currencies, and "credible" and "non-credible" exchange rates or pegs. It is worth noting in this context that for countries whose economies are strongly export driven, reserve management is an essential tool for managing the trade-competitiveness of national goods sold on their national markets. The employment of the deontic power of exchange-rate management can be employed to fix or transform the meaning of the "competitiveness" of national goods in international markets. It is not difficult to understand why countries like China whose central banks actively manage the currency for this purpose appear to be in no particular hurry to float their exchange rates, or even to let them rise very rapidly, thereby suffering the material consequences of the transformation of their goods from "competitive" to "less competitive" on international markets.

Constitutive power relations in debt monetization

Recall that the status functions that generate the deontic powers of the central bank to monetize government debt derive from the status functions of the bank to create and destroy money (as a bank of issue), and to manage and underwrite government debt. These deontic powers authorize some central banks – nominally exclusive of those central banks that manage a currency board or a similar very hard peg arrangement to a single anchor currency or basket of currencies – to convert government debt into money, just as they convert credit extended by the commercial banking system into money. Central banks with a significant discretion in monetary policy can, however, effectively dilute the government's debt burden through monetization and by fiat. The mechanisms by which this is accomplished were discussed in the previous chapter. The resulting seigniorage reduces the government's debt through inflation, provided that debt is issued and held in the local currency, normally requiring a liquid market in debt issued in that currency. This is always true of US government debt, but equally true of any country that is able to float sovereign debt issues in the local currency. In a world awash with surplus capital that is chasing high returns, a surprising number of countries have found a willing market for their sovereign debt issued in their own national currencies. Yet they remain a privileged minority.[26] And when tighter global credit conditions return their numbers may shrink even further.

This deontic power of debt monetization permits the central bank to transfer the costs of inflationary fiscal policy, for example, to foreign bond-holders and to the domestic public. Debt monetization always results in an erosion of the real value of the currency of issue, and thus of the securities purchased by others prior to or concomitantly with the monetization activities of the central bank. David Andrews and his collaborators would refer to this as an exercise of the "power to deflect" adjustment costs on to others. Andrews defines this as the "capacity of states to pass on transitional costs of adjustment to their economic partners."[27] Central banks, which can issue debt in their own currencies, to domestic investors and especially to foreign investors, can effectively devalue that debt by monetizing a portion of the debt and erode the real value of future repayment costs via inflation. This can be a mixed blessing, however, as the credibility of the future promise to repay may be lost in flagrant monetization, with attendant inflationary effects. In the social relations of credit and debt, money remains a promise. Failure to redeem this promise consistently can result in loss of credibility. This could result in the loss of the capacity of the central bank to issue debt in its own currency, and thus to monetize future debt. Avoidance of this loss is another rationale for granting independence to central banks.

Barnett and Duvall's structural form of power appears in debt monetization when the central bank steps in as a creditor and monetizes government debt by purchasing it for its own account and generating fresh money to pay for it. In theory it creates the co-constituted binary relationship "central bank creditor/government debtor." The government pays the central bank on its obligation from its future revenue streams, but the net national money supply has increased as new money is created to fund the government debt rather than extant money flowing from private hands into the government's hands from existing domestic or foreign money stocks.

---

[26] Andrew Walter, "Domestic Sources of International Monetary Leadership" in David M. Andrews (ed.) *International Monetary Power* (Ithaca, NY: Cornell University Press, 2006), p. 76.

[27] David M. Andrews, "Money, Power and Monetary Statecraft" in Andrews, *International Monetary Power*, p. 13.

In the latter case, if the sovereign bonds are purchased by domestic investors, the government gets a loan of money that is already in circulation from a private source. If the sovereign debt is purchased from a foreign investor then the loan from abroad – also a recirculation of existing monetary stocks – finances current operations in exchange for a promise of the government to pay from future revenue streams. However, the effect of the central bank's issue of new money to purchase the government debt dilutes the value of the currency already in circulation, even as the domestic central bank, as does the foreign central bank or investor, holds a note that constitutes a promise of future repayment from government revenue streams as "collateral" against the loan.

In this fashion deontic power to monetize government debt is deontic power to dilute or reduce government debt in real terms. Thus it constitutes deontic power to abrogate the government's promise to repay both foreign and domestic creditors in money of equivalent value in real purchasing power to that in which the debt was contracted. For independent central banks this deontic power is institutional power in the context of its independent decisions to monetize or to decline to monetize government debt. As an agent of the government so authorized, the central bank can effectively enforce or abrogate the government's promise to pay. When the central bank monetizes government debt it abrogates the government's promise to repay in money of equal value to that which was borrowed, and forces real losses on existing debt holders and existing holders of the currency. Conversely when the central bank declines to monetize government debt it enforces the government's promise to repay in money of equal value, and effectively enforces an implicit contract between the government and its debtors and the holders of its currency. In doing so the central bank may potentially enforce adjustment costs on the government – including potentially the adjustment cost of enhanced fiscal discipline.

This is why central banks also have, in Andrew's terminology, the "power to deflect" adjustment costs on to private foreign and domestic investors as well as upon the foreign central banks, governments, and sovereign wealth funds that hold the central bank's currency as a reserve currency, or hold assets in reserves denominated in that currency. Put differently, an independent central bank has the "structural power" of determining who adjusts: the government or those who hold the government's debt and currency. An independent central bank imposes adjustment costs on governments which must pay higher risk premiums to bond investors if the central bank will not monetize its debt, or imposes costs on bond investors and domestic consumers if it does monetize the debt, thereby diluting the purchasing power of extant monetary issue.

An independent central bank has productive power to change the social meaning of the government's debt – by changing it into money; to change the social meaning of extant currency issue and extant government debt obligations – by diluting its value; and to change the social meaning the credibility of the government's promise to pay – by abrogating or enforcing it through monetization or refusal to monetize government debt.

But while the central bank has these structural and productive powers in consequence of its constitutive capacities to serve as a bank of monetary issue, and to manage government debt, the central bank acts or refrains from acting to monetize this debt. Interactive effects also come into play and institutional power is diffusely employed via interaction with the government and market actors. Interaction effects can even be compulsory in nature if the central bank has adequate credibility through adequate independence from the government. Central banks that lack independence have no compulsory or institutional power over the actions of governments, because they are effectively subordinated to government fiscal policy. They may retain compulsory and institutional power over market actors who hold extant government debt obligations, and may impose costs by diluting the real value of the currency, thus the exchange value of future debt-servicing payments. An independent central bank also has the institutional power to dilute the capacity of bond investors to discipline government fiscal policy by obviating (however temporarily) the putative risk premiums that the latter will charge as a *quid pro quo* for their willingness to issue credit. But compulsory and institutional power will be exercised by market actors when the government next seeks to access domestic and international sources of private credit. They will raise the cost of long-term lending for the government by demanding higher risk premiums in anticipation that the government's promise to repay in money of equal value to that it borrowed is no longer credible.

Constitutive power relations in credit allocation

Recall that the status functions that generate the deontic powers of
some central banks to allocate credit on a sectoral basis throughout
the national economy, and thus play a significant role in helping to
structure the national economy, derive from the status functions of
the bank to control the supply of money to the commercial banking
system. These deontic powers authorize some central banks – which
are normally not independent of the government – to selectively control the dissemination of money to back commercial credit to commercial banks and to direct their lending to specific industrial sectors
in the national economy. This sectoral allocation schema is normally
developed by working in conjunction with national industrial planning
authorities, or by simply executing the policy of such authorities as an
agent of government credit allocation decisions. Unfortunately, when
misapplied, the central bank in such systems also has deontic power
to over-allocate credit and consequently to generate destructive asset
bubbles.

In accordance with Barnett and Duvall's taxonomy, several structural power relations binaries are created within the domestic economy as a result of the practice of credit allocation by the central
bank. Industrial sectors emerge as supplicants for money they wish
to obtain to expand their business operations. The commercial banking system, however, can only allocate them as much credit as the
"window guidance" provided by the central bank permits unless
the commercial bank in question wishes to risk lower quotas from
the central bank in future. Thus we might express the structural
power relationship between the central bank (often acting as an
agent for the government) and industrial sectors in the economy as
co-constituted as "credit provider/credit supplicant" with the same
relationship obtaining between commercial banks and individual businesses within a given industrial sector. Government-established performance criteria for assessment of the efficiency with which these
funds are applied by businesses impose discipline on businesses to
generate a target return on capital with the funds made available.
Thus we might express the structural power relationship between
the central bank (again, often acting as an agent for the government) and businesses representing industrial sectors in the economy as

co-constituted as "performance adjudicator-discipliner/performance adjudicated-disciplined."

The consumer sector was often an unsuccessful sectoral supplicant in East Asia during the heyday of the developmental state in East Asia. But the central bank often stands in a structurally subordinate relationship to the industrial planning authorities of the government, which ultimately plan and determine which sectors of the domestic economy will have privileged access to finance for developmental growth, and which sectors (often consumer-oriented industries in the past) will suffer a relative dearth of investment finance. Thus the co-constituted structural power relation between the government and the central bank in these economies with respect to national industrial planning and sectoral allocation of finance is "generator/executor."

The status-structural hierarchy among institutions is:

> government planning authority
> ↓
> central bank
> ↓
> commercial banks
> ↓
> sectoral industries

The commercial banks normally have some discretion regarding which specific firms may obtain a specified level of funds. But clearly Werner's account of the Japanese commercial bank official who spoke of Bank of Japan pressure to commit more money to commercial loans during the "bubble period" of the late 1980s suggests that reputational concerns among Japanese banks – which serve as a basis for credit allocation to specific lending institutions – served as adequate inducement to abandon prudential lending practices and to loan without due diligence.

Such a "ranking system" among Japanese banks constitutes another deontology. Collective assignment of status function is clearly at work in this example as "status" is the very object of participating or taking notice of a ranking system. Fear of loss of status had clear motivational and behavioral effects on the Japanese bank in question, inducing it to generate unwise loans for fear of loss of ranking status, and presumably for fear of loss of access to as much credit "as we want to use." Reputation is a pure deontology, with enormous behavioral effects, badly understudied in the social sciences.[28]

In the case of the power relations described above the central bank appears to enjoy institutional power over commercial banks and industry, while structural power relations are co-constituted between government planning authorities and commercial banks and industrial sectors. The central bank is in possession of the applicable power resources – in this case credit/money. But as the resources are allocated at the behest of national industrial planning authorities, the central bank's power is exercised by virtue of the fact that it "stands in a particular relation to the relevant institutional arrangements."[29] Here the particular relation is allocation of credit to commercial banks in accordance with government coordinated allocation planning. The central bank holds the power resources that are applied (the money it creates) and thus compulsory power, in addition to institutional power, in deciding how much credit each commercial bank gets to pass on to specific industrial sectors. However, the compulsory power to allocate discrete levels of credit to specified industrial sectors is shared with, if not entirely in the hands of, government industrial planning authorities.

In accordance with Barnett and Duvall's taxonomy, productive power relations are naturally exercised in the process of adjudication of the deontologies created by the various status hierarchies described in the credit allocation process. This is obviously in evidence in the prioritization of industrial sectors for allocation of credit. The social kinds created here are, for example, "essential industries/non-essential industries." While I have expressed these social kinds in binary format, there are no structural power relations between them and they do not co-constitute one another. Both are subjectivities generated by the exercise of productive power by others. Similarly status ranking of commercial banks by the central bank as "efficient allocators/non-efficient allocators" of credit to particular businesses within industrial sectors, or any other less binary ranking schemas created and applied,

---

[28] For an important exception see Jonathan L. Mercer, *Reputation and International Politics* (Ithaca, NY: Cornell University Press, 1996).
[29] Barnett and Duvall, "Power in International Politics," p. 51.

are clear examples of the generation of social kinds with the productive power of the central bank. As the Japanese bubble economy demonstrated, commercial banks will occasionally lend well beyond the levels that an objective observer might regard as consistent with the financial institution's material interests in order to maintain or raise their ranking within this productively generated social kind.

International monetary power relations

This chapter should not conclude without directly addressing another important and quite recent contribution to the literature on power relations as they pertain to international monetary systems, namely the work of David Andrews and his collaborators. Eschewing a purely material approach to power that treats power as an object or resource, Andrews argues that he and his collaborators

adopt a social theory approach to power... treating power as a relational property. Social power exists when one actor's behavior changes as a result of its relationship with another actor... international monetary power exists when one state's behavior changes as a result of its monetary relationship with another state.[30]

Andrews and his collaborators enrich the literature and our understanding of their topic by proceeding with an understanding of "international monetary power as a relational property."[31] They point out that they are "adopting a particular view of causality... A's relationship with B is causing B to behave in a certain way with respect to policy C... [while]... B's relationship with A is causing B to behave differently than would otherwise be the case."[32]

The focus on power as a social relationship rather than a commodity to be employed as a bludgeon is highly welcome to the social analyst of money and monetary relations. The purposes of these scholars' monetary power analysis are very different from mine, however; thus the critique of the utility of their conceptual apparatus for my purposes that follows is somewhat unfair to them, as their analytic framework was developed for their own analytic tasks, and it appears to serve admirably to illuminate monetary power relations between states. However, for our purposes the "self-consciously state centric"[33]

[30] Andrews, "Money, Power and Monetary Statecraft," p. 2.
[31] *Ibid.*, p. 8.   [32] *Ibid.*   [33] *Ibid.*, p. 1.

approach they employ does limit the application of their power analysis to many of the actors and processes that are of particular interest to the current study. When we self-consciously examine power relations among states we necessarily limit analysis of the sub-state actors, market actors, and transnational private authorities that are demonstrated in the current offering to exercise so much authority over global financial governance structures.

A purely causal analysis of power relations cannot develop the constitutive power relations from which causal interactive effects ensue. This problem is not resolved by referring to power as a "relational property." The definition employed by Andrews and his collaborators appears to leave open the question of whether power is a relationship between A and B or a property (an attribute of A). There are usages throughout the work that appear to have it both ways. And while Andrews is careful to point out that his analysis of monetary power entails a necessary "counterfactual corollary" requiring us to understand that A's power over B implies that B would have behaved differently in the absence of that power, this corollary requires us to rely upon the theory-dependence of counterfactual claims in order to credit the assertion. To claim to know how B "would otherwise" behave in the absence of the posited monetary relationship with A is to "predict" B's counterfactual behavior on the basis of some theory of how B would have "otherwise" behaved. Thus in formulating this counterfactual corollary less is said in explanatory terms than might be imagined, given our inability to "test" the counterfactual proposition empirically.

The focus of analysis of "monetary power" in the work of Andrew and his collaborators is squarely on power relations between states, and centered on the political questions of "who adjusts?" and "who benefits?" The role of the central bank in financial governance is often obscured in this form of analysis as the central bank is generally depicted as a willing tool of the finance minister. The actions of specific central banks in specific instances (the Australian and European central banks, and the central banks of the United Kingdom, Russia, Japan, the United States) arise in these essays, but no sustained discussion of the power relations between central banks and states or market actors is engaged in.

Four different major forms of "monetary power" are developed and discussed by Andrews and his collaborators, but significantly the two forms of monetary power relationships that are best developed in this collaborative study – the "power to delay" and the "power to deflect" adjustment costs – are studied exclusively at the level of macro-political economy, and clearly arise through interaction. The monetary power relations most consistent with what we have come to recognize as constitutive forms of power relations – the "power to rearticulate" actor interests and the power to "reconstruct actor identities" – are studied exclusively at the level of micro-political economy, and appear to arise through social relations of constitution.[34] This formulation appears to self-consciously replicate the constructivist notion of the co-constitution of identities and interests and the importance of analyzing the attendant changing structure of actor identities and interests.[35] Somewhat incongruously, constitutive power relations between actors, and particularly between transnational actors at the macro-level of political economy, do not appear to be considered. This tendency to discount constitutive power relations between sub-state actors, like central banks, and transnational market actors and global credit ratings agencies is a major difference in approach between the work of Andrews and his collaborators and the present study.

Yet while these concepts of power relations are developed by Andrews and his collaborators specifically to study international monetary power relations between state actors, they lend some utility to our purposes. As we have already seen earlier in this chapter, deontic powers of some central banks lend their governments "power to deflect" adjustment costs to domestic and foreign investors. Andrews's definition of this power as the "capacity of states to pass on transnational costs of adjustment to their economic partners"[36] is an artifact of the purposes for which he and his colleagues developed the concept. This does not rob it of analytic utility for our purposes.

Similarly, Andrews's notion of the "power to delay" the costs of adjustment as a capacity that "can be enhanced by improving the state's liquidity position"[37] is not without utility for the analysis of credible, independent central banks whose reputations permit their finance ministers to access international capital markets for finance at

---

[34] *Ibid.*, p. 11, and Eric Helleiner, "Below the State: Micro-Level Monetary Power" in Andrews, *International Monetary Power*, pp. 72–90.

[35] Alexander Wendt, "Anarchy is What States Make of It" *International Organization* 46(2) (1992): 391–425.

[36] Andrews, "Money, Power and Monetary Statecraft," p. 13.   [37] *Ibid.*

low cost, or that can monetize government debt without surrendering credibility. It is worth noting in this context that in the summer and autumn of 2007, French President Nicolas Sarkozy clearly hoped to induce the ECB to loosen monetary policy in order that a French state suffering a continuing fiscal crisis might delay the costs of adjustment that would necessarily be visited upon the French public if Sarkozy were to resolve the fiscal crisis and redeem his reformist campaign promises to his people.[38] Lacking both fiscal discipline and the capacity to monetize French government debt with a French central bank, Sarkozy's France lacks the power to delay adjustment and at this writing (late 2007) appears to be in the process of adjustment, starting with reform of public sector pensions.

In further developing the macro-political economy or "macro-foundations of monetary power" Benjamin Cohen provides us with a description of the "power to delay" that is comprised largely of macroeconomic variables, rather than social relations. This power is said to stem from "a country's international liquidity position... both foreign reserves and access to external credit. The more liquidity there is at a country's disposal, relative to other states, the more it can postpone adjustment to its balance of payments."[39] This assertion is somewhat problematic from our perspective as it suggests that the power to delay adjustment results entirely from the state's liquidity position, its ability to meet its short-term obligations. However, Cohen of course recognizes the importance of what he calls "creditworthiness" or what we call credibility, in a state's capacity to arrange finance for its deficits. More importantly for our purposes he recognizes that limitations on this capacity to finance deficits through external credit "are not set by borrowers at all. Rather they are set by creditors, both public and private. It is they who gain the power that overextended debtors lose."[40] Thus Cohen is explicitly recognizing the deontic power of actors in the sovereign debt markets to adjudicate the credibility of the promise to pay that is implicit in the issue of a sovereign debt obligation, and the deontic power of domestic bond market actors to do the same.

---

[38] See e.g. Bertrand Benoit and Ben Hall, "Sarkozy and Merkel at Odds over ECB," *Financial Times*, 22–23 September 2007.

[39] Benjamin J. Cohen, "The Macrofoundations of Monetary Power" in Andrews, *International Monetary Power*, p. 42.

[40] *Ibid.*, p. 44.

What is somewhat quixotic about Cohen's formulation, as with all of the work in this study edited by Andrews, is the certainty of "adjustment" as a privileged variable. States ever conduct their monetary and fiscal policies in the shadow of some certain, dread day-of-reckoning in this macroeconomic formulation of monetary power relations. Even as Andrews and Cohen and their collaborators labor to develop a more socialized account of monetary power relations than is normally prevalent in the literature, a macroeconomic tautology lies lurking in the background to anchor the work developed in a "certainty" of neoclassical economics that is actually merely a theoretical construct from which macroeconomics proceeds – namely, the certainty of "adjustment." The certainty of macroeconomic systems returning to "equilibrium" is another such *ad hoc*, non-falsifiable assumption commonly deployed in the literature on macroeconomics or the literature that is styled upon it.

As "adjustment" is thought to be certain – there arises a point at which it is no longer avoidable – and Cohen informs us that

it is the markets that are enforcing a limit on its power to delay. The more states rely on borrowing capacity rather than on owned reserves for their international liquidity, the greater is the role of creditors, public and private, in determining who ultimately will be forced to undergo real adjustment.[41]

This is both true and important but the employment of the certainty of "adjustment" as an explanatory panacea may mask as much as it explains. Adjustment can encompass a bewildering array of social, macroeconomic, and microeconomic outcomes for a given state. What does emerge as agreement between Cohen's analytic formulation of monetary power relations and our formulation is that the power of market actors to adjudicate the credibility of government fiscal policy and central bank monetary policy is formidable. As Cohen suggests, "the perpetual opinion poll often changes its mind – and when it does, the ability to postpone adjustment through borrowing is changed as well...what creditors giveth by way of a power to delay they may also taketh away."[42]

Cohen's treatment of the "power to deflect" is similarly predicated on macroeconomic variables that characterize a national economy, such as its degree of openness to trade and capital flows, national

---

[41] *Ibid.*   [42] *Ibid.*, p. 45.

factor endowments, and the diversity of industrial production. Cohen notes that smaller economies are disadvantaged and more likely to experience macroeconomic shocks that require adjustment. He intones that "the power to deflect is limited by the economy's underlying attributes and endowments."[43] While it is certainly the case that smaller economies are more vulnerable to economic shocks and less likely to easily deflect the costs of adjusting to those shocks on to others, Cohen's formulation neglects the fact that smaller states may, in an exigency, deflect them nonetheless. The Argentine government and its central bank did precisely this when Argentina defaulted on at least $132 billion of sovereign debt obligations and severely limited withdrawal of domestic savings in 2001, not only "deflecting adjustment costs" but inflicting enormous financial pain alike on foreign creditors and domestic citizens.[44]

Andrew Walter addresses many of the power relations that stem from strong credible currencies in his discussions of the domestic sources of international monetary leadership. His work resonates somewhat with the current study in arguing that currency or monetary leadership "requires conservative monetary policy ... credibility embedded in its domestic political and economic institutions ... [whose arrangements can] ... facilitate the emergence of highly developed financial markets."[45] Walter's argument relates strongly to Niall Ferguson's argument regarding the institutional preconditions for the emergence of British financial and monetary leadership in the eighteenth and nineteenth centuries.[46] Importantly, Walter clearly allocates authority in establishing and maintaining these power relations to market actors as in his view monetary leadership "can only be sustained through the ongoing persuasion of market agents."[47] Social relations of credit and debt are emphasized in Walter's description of monetary

---

[43] *Ibid.*, p. 49.
[44] See e.g. Paul Blustein, *And the Money Kept Rolling In (and Out): Wall Street, the IMF, and the Bankrupting of Argentina* (New York: Public Affairs, 2005); Padma Desai, *Financial Crisis, Contagion, and Containment: From Asia to Argentina* (Princeton, NJ: Princeton University Press, 2003); Michael Mussa, *Argentina and the Fund: From Triumph to Tragedy* (Washington, DC: Institute for International Economics, 2002).
[45] Walter, "Domestic Sources of International Monetary Leadership," p. 51.
[46] Ferguson, *The Cash Nexus*.
[47] Walter, "Domestic Sources of International Monetary Leadership," p. 52.

power relations among state and non-state actors who are currency "followers." Walter argues that it is the

> *legitimacy* enjoyed by the leader that explains why followership can be largely *voluntary* in nature. *Persuasion* is more typical of monetary leadership than is explicit... coercion. Market agents... are difficult to coerce and must generally be *persuaded*.[48]

Social relations of persuasion, trust, credibility are also emphasized; Walter's stipulation of the incentives for "monetary followers" to employ the currency of "monetary leaders" reads like a stipulation of the preconditions for generating and maintaining a credible reserve currency. Those who employ the currency of a "currency leader must be *socialized* into accepting the leader's preferences as their own"[49] through "the monetary policy *credibility* and the high financial development that flow from the leader's domestic institutional arrangements"[50] as well as *"normative convergence* through *socialization"*[51] because "money is, after all, a *social convention."*[52] Credible currency leaders feature domestic institutional arrangements that foster "deep, stable, efficient and open financial markets"[53] and institutions of "limited, constitutional government"[54] are thought to reduce arbitrary outright default "but also the potential for partial default via inflation"[55] as well as various "institutional mechanisms that ensure policy consistency."[56]

Most importantly, Walter ascribes authority to people who make the market in currencies – namely foreign central bankers and above all, private actors in the FOREX markets. For example, regarding the deontology that renders a given currency a "reserve currency" he argues "in the long run, it is private market agents who are most important in terms of a lead currency's status."[57] It is they who collectively assign a given currency (currently the US dollar) this status function, thus creating a social institution of its status as a reserve currency. Since their collective intentionality is responsible for this deontology it is their collective intentionality that can revoke it. However, the managing director for global central bank services at UBS wrote in the

---

[48] *Ibid.*, p. 53. Emphasis added. [49] *Ibid.*, p. 55. Emphasis added.
[50] *Ibid.*, p. 61. Emphasis added. [51] *Ibid.* Emphasis added.
[52] *Ibid.*, p. 62. Emphasis added. [53] *Ibid.*, p. 56. [54] *Ibid.*, p. 57.
[55] *Ibid.* [56] *Ibid.*, p. 58. [57] *Ibid.*, p. 67.

summer of 2007 that it is a continuing "myth," in spite of the discomfort that its fluctuations on the FOREX markets generate for central banks around the world that hold dollars and dollar-denominated assets as reserves, that the US dollar is in decline as a reserve currency. As he points out:

> The US dollar is extraordinarily stable in relative terms as a reserve currency and growing massively in absolute terms; fluctuating between 62 per cent and 72 per cent for most of the past three decades, it has now stabilized around 67 per cent of total reserves. No other currency provides access to such a wide pool of liquid, high quality assets, the chief preoccupation of reserve managers.[58]

Nor did the difficulties experienced in late 2007 by the Hong Kong Monetary Authority (HKMA), which administers the SAR's currency board, ever lead it to reconsider its dollar peg. In the fall of 2007, when China permitted mainland investors to begin investing on the Hong Kong Stock Exchange in addition to the Shanghai Exchange, speculation ensued that investor demand for the Hong Kong dollar (the currency which must be purchased in order to trade shares on the Hong Kong Exchange), coupled with falling US interest rates and the perils of importing inflation from mainland China as the renminbi appreciated against the US dollar to which the Hong Kong currency was pegged, would lead the HKMA to abandon the long-standing dollar peg. The unprecedented liquidity and depth of the markets in dollar-denominated assets removed any such temptation and on 1 November 2007, Joseph Yam, the HKMA chief executive reported "We again reaffirm that the [Hong Kong] government has been clear in its financial policy and is committed to maintaining the peg."[59]

There is surely a limit to the size and duration of current account deficits a "monetary leader" can run, and limited depths to which it can permit its currency to fall on the FOREX markets (at this writing the euro is trading near $1.50 and the pound sterling near $2.10 while the dollar will only buy 110 yen) and the global purchasing power of Chinese reserves exceeding $1.3 trillion has fallen precipitously. Yet it is far from clear that central banks globally are likely to start

---

[58] Terrence Keeley, "Myths About the Sovereign Menace to Treasuries," *Financial Times*, 29 June 2007.
[59] Tom Mitchell, "Hong Kong Committed to Sticking with the US Dollar," *Financial Times*, 2 November 2007.

dumping US Treasury securities to reduce their dollar-denominated reserves. Fear of China dumping US Treasory-bills arises with some frequency in the press. However, the Chinese central bank knows at least two important things about the consequences of such an action that the pundits appear to neglect. First, China could not but cripple the global purchasing power of its reserves by dumping dollar-denominated assets precipitously, inducing a further decline in their price (even though a collapse is unlikely, even under this scenario). More importantly, China at this writing is thought to have an unemployed and underemployed workforce as large as the entire workforce of the United States. The size of this army of reserve labor already mounts a potential challenge to domestic and social stability in China, and is thus an enormous source of concern for the Chinese authorities. As China largely employs a peg to the dollar to anchor its currency, China's capacity to manage the value of the renminbi, holding it down to promote Chinese exports to increase domestic employment, would be significantly impaired by the contraction of the Chinese money supply that would result from significant dumping of assets in a major anchor currency. The supply of euro-denominated assets, as a viable alternative for reserves, is comparatively limited. Domestic stability in China would not be well served by a precipitous decline in employment, and the capacity to manage the value of the domestic currency, to maximize exports and export-related employment, is predicated on holding large reserves in viable anchor currencies. These are limited in variety and supply. Market actors will likely continue to adjudicate the credibility of the US Federal Reserve to be superior to the credibility of other central banks in the absence of an alternative to the depth and breadth of liquidity of dollar-denominated markets for reserve accumulation. The "monetary power" that interests us most in this context remains in the hands of these private market actors.

5 | Rules and international monetary systems

Monetary economics is a field where an understanding and appreciation of history is arguably more important than a lot of high powered mathematical and statistical analysis.

Michael Mussa

The first casualty of war may not be truth but money.

J. K. Galbraith

The international monetary order is a rule-based order. Its history is the history of the construction and demolition of rules: constitutive and regulative, explicit and tacit, substantive and procedural, national and transnational. Thus neoclassical economist Michael Mussa does well to suggest that an examination of the history of monetary economics may offer more insight into the nature of the topic than the more formal, also rule-based, constructed artifice of mathematics. It is rather odd that relatively little attention has been devoted to explication of the history of the international monetary order as rule-based order. This is so particularly as international monetary history is often organized according to a changing periodization of constitutive and regulative rules.

Economic historian Gianni Toniolo, for example, periodizes international monetary history in the late nineteenth to twentieth centuries as characterized by (1) a classical gold standard ending 1914; (2) a system of pegged exchange rates from 1914 to 1924 and again from the mid-1930s to late 1940s, interspersed with (3) a gold exchange standard (attempts to reconstruct gold parities) from 1924 to 1931 to 1936, depending upon accounts of when these attempts were abandoned, followed by (4) the Bretton Woods gold–dollar parity from the late 1940s to early 1970s.[1] What we have constructed to replace Bretton Woods,

---

[1] Toniolo, *Central Bank Cooperation*, p. 5.

114

Toniolo, whose history of the BIS ends with the collapse of Bretton Woods, does not say. International legal historian Kenneth Dam periodizes the international monetary system quite similarly, dating the construction of an international gold standard from 1879, when the United States formally went on to gold.[2] Dam dated the gold exchange standard from 1925 to 1931, the Bretton Woods system from 1945 to 1971, the present system as one of floating exchange rates centered on the US dollar as a global reserve currency, and speculated in his writing (in 1982) that a system of multiple reserve currencies might in future emerge.[3]

The future is here, as the euro is now held in various central banks across the globe as a reserve currency with the introduction of various pegs to "baskets of currencies" that include the euro as well as the dollar, and to lesser extents sterling and the yen and other currencies selected according to national trade weighting and patterns. In one recent study of transformations of the reserve currencies held by the central banks of eleven industrialized countries and twelve emerging market countries, Truman and Wong estimate a 6 percent decline in reserve holdings of the US dollar in their sample to an average across these central banks of 50 percent of reserves, a 6 percent decline of holdings of the yen to an average of 7 percent of these reserves, and a 12 percent increase in holdings of the euro to an average of 36 percent of reserves from the years 2000 to 2004.[4]

All of these international monetary systems are systems of social facts that have been constituted, and to a varying extent regulated by rules. To the extent that they have been stable and successful in making good the promise that money constitutes as a social relationship, they have been able to generate a "credible commitment mechanism" as a social fact that has served, in the terminology of neoclassical monetary economics, as a "nominal anchor" for a system of transnational

---

[2] Kenneth W. Dam, *Rules of the Game: Reform and Evolution in the International Monetary System* (Chicago, IL: University of Chicago Press, 1982), p. 19.

[3] *Ibid.*, p. 6.

[4] Edwin M. Truman and Anna Wong, *The Case for an International Reserve Diversification Standard*, Working Paper WP 06–2 (May 2006) (Washington, DC: Institute for International Economics, 2006), p. 26, table B2–1. Note that the authors indicate that the euro's share of increased reserve holdings may be overstated in their study due to the overrepresentation in their sample of Eastern European transitional democracies.

monetary exchange. The emphasis on the "credibility" of a commitment to a particular monetary standard, arising time and again in the literature on monetary economics, is our reminder of the social character of money as a promise. I hope to have established this social character of money in chapters 2 and 3. It is a precondition to establishing the utility in neoclassical economics of abstracting from this social character to discuss money in the parlance of conventional monetary economics, as a medium of exchange, a unit of account, and a store of value.

While floating exchange-rate regimes may rely upon market forces, fixed exchange-rate regimes are rule based, and consequently rely upon policy intervention by governmental actors to function, as any form of exchange-rate regime between rigidly fixed and purely floating regimes relies upon central bank intervention, and ideally upon coordinated central bank intervention.[5] The classical gold standard (pre-1914), the abortive inter-war gold exchange standard (1925–31) and the Bretton Woods, dollar–gold parity standard (1945–71) were all fixed exchange-rate regimes which relied heavily on rule-following behavior by central banks to function and to provide price stability. I will later argue that even many states with a floating exchange-rate regime also rely on rule-following behavior if they have instituted central bank independence. This is particularly true if that central bank has instituted an inflation targeting regime.

In this chapter I will explore two international monetary systems. First I will very briefly develop the rule-based classical gold standard, the myths and realities of its "rules of the game," and the social bases of its credibility and transparency. I will then develop the rules and discretionary practices of our contemporary international monetary system. The contemporary international monetary system is a system of subsystems of international and competing regional currencies dominated by a regime of floating exchange rates, but incorporating a bewildering array of regional subsystems. I will examine the contemporary debates over rule-based vs. discretionary monetary policy frameworks and operating systems before moving on to explore the ways in which central banks work to enhance this social relationship of credibility with their publics and with international financial market actors.

---

[5] Toniolo, *Central Bank Cooperation*, p. 5.

Rules of the game: the classical gold standard

Economic historian Gianni Toniolo argues that the rules of international monetary systems provide public goods, such as transnational price stability and an orderly system of international payments, and that the credibility of the gold standard was based on adherence to the "strict rules of the game" of the gold standard. He asserts that

[a]ll that was needed for a country to be a member of the gold club was for its bank of issue to commit itself to convert bank notes into gold at a fixed rate and to adopt domestic legislation, monetary policy, and financial practices towards the goal of making the conversion pledge *credible*.[6]

Was that "all that was needed"? If we examine "all that was needed" we find that it was rather a lot, in deontic and statutory terms, even as a purely domestic project. The original model by which gold was supposed to automatically flow back to a deficit country is nowhere to be found in this description. Nor does Toniolo mention the deflationary consequences for the "adjusting" country.

The "rules of the game" of the classical gold standard were neither internationally binding in any formalized fashion and nor did their adjustments function with the automatic character touted by gold's champions. Consider, for example, David Hume's original "price-specie flow model." In theory, ignoring for the moment the role played by a central bank in the process, an exporter received payment in gold from which coin was minted. Gold would flow out from a country with a trade deficit, setting off a self-correcting chain of events. Prices then fell in deficit countries with less coin in circulation and prices rose in surplus countries with more coin circulating. Purchases of imports would then fall in the deficit country as their prices rose, etc. The opposite chain of events would transpire in the country experiencing a temporary trade surplus. Thus trade imbalances were thought to be self-equilibrating. This was an early example of a general equilibrium model[7] of the form so central to the later development of neoclassical macroeconomic theory.

In practice matters were really neither so automatic nor mechanistic and a number of deontologies and rules were required for the

---

[6] *Ibid.*, p. 13.
[7] Barry Eichengreen, *Globalizing Capital: A History of the International Monetary System* (Princeton, NJ: Princeton University Press, 1996), pp. 25–6.

"equilibration" of trade flows to occur at all. Nor were they as automatic or mechanistic as the reified portrait of the gold standard generated in the Cunliffe Committee Report of 1918, whereby according to the idealized vision of how the pre-war standard functioned, a balance of payments deficit was supposed to result in an automatic outflow of gold that was stemmed by a rise in the bank rate by the Bank of England.[8] In this version, rather than mints melting transshipped bullion into coin of the realm, the central banks converted currency into gold. Foreign merchants converted sterling into gold at the Bank of England, and then gold into francs at the Bank of France, for example. The money supply would consequently fall in the deficit country and rise in the surplus country as the result of conversion of bullion into bank notes by central banks in the recipient country. As is the case with Hume's price-specie flow model, in the Cunliffe Report version of the "rules of the game" of the classical gold standard, money supplies move in the opposite direction in the two countries.[9]

However, unlike the Hume price-specie model where gold flows in the form of bullion and is then minted by the central bank of the recipient country into coin, "[g]old, rather than moving from circulation in the deficit country to circulation in the surplus country, moves from one central bank to the other."[10] The central bank in the deficit country raises the bank rate to attract gold back, restricting domestic credit and consequently the money supply. In "reducing the money supply, central bank intervention put downward pressure on prices and enhanced the competitiveness of domestic goods, eliminating the external deficit as effectively as a gold outflow."[11]

In the United Kingdom and the United States, as well as with many other central banks around the world, the rate that the central bank sets to loan money to commercial banks is called the "discount rate." This terminology originated from the "discount houses" of the eighteenth and nineteenth centuries in the City of London which would lend money to merchants for a sixty- to ninety-day term to finance, for example, their shipping operations. As Eichengreen relates the matter the

---

[8] Michael D. Bordo and Finn E. Kydland, "The Gold Standard as a Rule" in Barry Eichengreen and Marc Flandreau (eds.) *The Gold Standard in Theory and History* (London and New York: Routledge, 1985), p. 15.
[9] Eichengreen, *Globalizing Capital*, p. 26.   [10] *Ibid.*, p. 27.   [11] *Ibid.*

central bank could advance the bank [or the discount house] the money immediately in return for possession of the bill signed by the merchant and the payment of interest. Advancing the money was known as "discounting the bill"; the interest charged was the discount rate.[12]

According to the "rules of the game" fewer financial intermediaries would be inclined to present bills for discount and to obtain cash from the central bank if the bank raised the rate and made discounting more expensive. By manipulating the discount rate, the central bank could affect the volume of domestic credit. It could increase or reduce the availability of credit to restore balance-of-payments equilibrium without requiring gold flows to take place. When a central bank anticipating losses raised its discount rate, reducing its holding of domestic interest-bearing assets, cash was drained from the market. The money supply declined and external balance was restored without requiring actual gold outflows.[13]

Deontologies of the gold standard

An extensive literature argues that the "rules of the game" were more often observed in the breach, if at all, largely because the central banks of the day were private institutions, mindful of their bottom lines. Domestic deontologies and legal structures, replicated transnationally, were required to institute and execute gold convertibility, lending enormous discretion to the central bank in deciding whether, or to what extent, to "equilibrate" trade flows with gold movements or conversions. Raising rates could result in a loss of business for the central bank to a commercial discount house that might consent to discount bills at a lower rate.

But we can see that rather a lot is going on to make the gold standard function as a mechanism of adjustment, and to ensure the value of money, even after the Bank Charter Act of 1844 subdivided the Bank of England into separate issue (public, note issue) and banking (private banking) departments.[14] For example, we can see that the system rested on entirely domestic legal foundations that were required to be replicated, with some cross-national variation, across the members of the "gold club" for the system to function as an international monetary system. Kenneth Dam has argued that the British gold standard

---

[12] *Ibid.*   [13] *Ibid.*, p. 28.   [14] Dam, *Rules of the Game*, p. 26.

was the legal cornerstone of the system that rested legally (and thus deontically) on the domestic "right of a private party to move freely from gold to currency and back again and to export gold without limitation."[15] Dam notes amendments to this legal foundation, the most important of which were Acts of 1819 and an 1821 amendment, as well as the Bank Charter Act of 1844 (Peel's Act).

Already we can see that a number of deontologies were required for the gold standard to function as a parity mechanism to assure "sound money" and for its "rules of the game" to function as a system of adjustment at all. Recall that deontic powers result from collective assignment of status functions, and that they establish constitutive rules. Even in the days in which Hume's price-specie flow model could be said to have functioned, prior to the widespread issue of bank notes to represent the value of bullion, the melting of bullion into coin relied on the deontic power of a mint, at the behest of the sovereign, to mint "coin of the realm" with a "unit of value" specific to the realm in which the coin was minted. The status function of "issuer of coin" was collectively assigned by a legal charter of some form to the central bank or mint. This authority was delegated by the sovereign, who enjoyed the penultimate deontic powers and collective assignment of status. When bank notes were issued in lieu of bullion, the deontic power of the central bank (in our example, the Bank of England) to issue notes that were "backed" by a quantity of bullion, was collectively assigned by statute – another form of devolution of the authority of the sovereign. The Bank Charter Act of 1944 was specifically designed to not only ensure that the Bank of England had a monopoly of note issue, but that its note issue functions and commercial banking functions were rigidly separated. Thus in theory no discretion in the amount of notes issued (the money supply as determined by reserves of bullion) would be permitted, rendering note issue and money supply a relatively inelastic determinant of reserves.[16]

This commitment to a fixed parity between note issue and gold reserves was the essence of the classical gold standard. The parity was a constitutive rule in the following form: "A note of a certain value" counts as "a set number of ounces of fine gold" in the context of "issue of the note by the Bank of England." It was a public deontology. The status function of sole issuer of fiduciary money was collectively assigned to the Bank of England by Parliament, acting in the name of

---

[15] *Ibid.*, p. 24.   [16] Kindleberger, *A Financial History*, p. 92.

the sovereign. These constitutive relations were replicated, with minor variations, by all countries adhering to the gold standard.

While in institutional terms the parity generated a constitutive rule, in social terms the parity constituted a commitment that "each country would define the price of gold in terms of its currency and keep the price fixed."[17] The mint price of gold was kept constant by purchase and sales. Fiduciary money had to be freely convertible into gold; thus Bordo and Kydland claim that "it is a fixed value of the unit of account that is its [the gold standard's] essence."[18] This was the "commitment mechanism" that was required to "reassure the public that the real value of the [public] debt will not erode in the future as a result of inflationary [monetary] policy."[19] The commitment mechanism proved sufficiently credible for both conservative and radical political economists of the nineteenth century to predict the impending eclipse of the landed aristocracy in Britain by the *rentier* classes who held public debt denominated in sterling.[20] This fixed parity, whose note issue was mandated by statute to never exceed the gold reserves available to back it, constituted the "nominal anchor" for the classical gold monetary standard.

In this context the statutory fixed parity functioned very much like a contemporary currency board, whereby the central bank of note issue pledges to issue domestic notes at a fixed parity to gold or foreign reserves, and to restrain domestic note issue to the level justified by the foreign reserves that anchor the domestic currency. Each form of commitment mechanism essentially eliminates monetary policy. Money supply is in no way discretionary, but entirely constrained by the level of reserves available to anchor note issue as denominated in the local currency. Currency boards are also deontologies, and the result of statutory processes. A currency board system is as close to being an absolutely fixed regime as was the classical gold standard. Currency boards are based upon a commitment

to a firmly fixed exchange rate but also strict regulations that effectively prohibit an independent monetary policy. Neither budget deficits nor rescues of commercial banks can be financed by money creation. The country's money base must be fully backed by foreign exchange reserves.[21]

---

[17] Bordo and Kydland, "The Gold Standard as a Rule," p. 101.   [18] *Ibid.*
[19] *Ibid.*, p. 102.   [20] Ferguson, *Cash Nexus*, pp. 194–5.
[21] Corden, *Too Sensational*, p. 23.

Both the gold standard and currency boards rely entirely on public deontologies to exist. And they exist entirely as institutional facts constituted by rules that have been carefully stipulated by statute. Their "credibility" is largely dependent upon the fidelity of central bankers to their commitment to act in a manner that upholds the integrity of those rules. They are social systems of trust constituted by deontological statute, and upheld by the fidelity of central banks to their constitutive rules.

When trust is absent the credibility of the commitment fails. The monetary authorities charged with upholding the integrity of the currency board will then find the social fact of its pegged value challenged by speculative attacks on the foreign currency markets. Capital flight by foreign and domestic investors alike to more credible "stores of value" normally follows. This is the nature of currency crises. Such loss of credibility can generate currency crises for fixed and floating exchange-rate regimes alike.

In contemporary currency board arrangements, as well as other pegged exchange-rate regimes such as "crawling pegs," the deontologies that collectively assign status functions to economic actors, in our contemporary era of capital mobility, are transnational as well as domestic, and private as well as public. Modern central banks must uphold the credibility of the promise that their money constitutes for private foreign as well as domestic actors. Flight from domestic capital markets by domestic and foreign investors alike – should that promise appear to them to be compromised or suspect – can decimate the levels of capital available for domestic investment. The contemporary international monetary system assigns the status function of converting one currency to another (and one "store of value" to another) at a stable value ultimately to the global FOREX markets rather than to the domestic central bank. At a minimum, our contemporary system assigns to the FOREX markets the status of "adjudicator" of the credibility and integrity of the promise that their hard or crawling peg constitutes. This is a significant form of private authority and private governance in the international monetary system.[22]

---

[22] For theoretical and empirical development of these concepts see, for example the collection of essays in Rodney Bruce Hall and Thomas J. Biersteker (eds.) *The Emergence of Private Authority in Global Governance* (Cambridge, UK: Cambridge University Press, 2002).

The international credibility and efficacy of the gold standard was largely predicated on domestic legal foundations, or by what we now understand to be a domestic, public deontology. The international dimension was that there was to be

> no restriction on the nationality of individuals who presented bullion to the mint to be coined, or who exported coin or bullion to foreign countries...every country following the rule fixed the price of its currency in gold, thus created a system of fixed exchange rates, linking all countries to the same standard.[23]

The system of fixed international exchange rates that resulted was an international benefit, or international public good, that guaranteed highly transparent, and rigidly fixed, exchange-rate stability among all countries adhering to gold. But the commitment mechanism was primarily domestic and the international benefits were in effect a byproduct of a domestic commitment mechanism. As Bordo and Kydland suggest, "[t]o the extent that the commitment was honored in relation to other countries, it served to strengthen the credibility of the domestic commitment."[24] However, "[e]xchange in both goods and capital was facilitated if countries adhered to a standard based on a rule anchored by the *same* commitment mechanism."[25]

Since the demise of the classical gold standard, the architects of successor international monetary systems have, when permitted by national governments, been continuously in search of a similarly sanguine arrangement, whereby domestic adherence across the system to a single universal "commitment mechanism" or "nominal anchor" generates money whose domestic purchasing power enjoys long-term stability, and which generates "equilibrating" flows of capital and trade in response to balance of payments disequilibria. The classical gold standard did provide these benefits. But it did so at the cost of quite serious domestic deflationary events. A government's willingness and capacity to bear these domestic costs of adjustment were a precondition for the monetary standard's credibility. The credibility of contemporary monetary policy is similarly predicated on demonstration of a capacity to bear the domestic economic consequences of adjustment.

---

[23] Bordo and Kydland, "The Gold Standard as a Rule," p. 105.
[24] *Ibid.*, pp. 105–6.   [25] *Ibid.*, p. 106. Emphasis added.

Credibility of the gold standard

This commitment mechanism was predicated on the credibility that
the central bank would move to maintain the parity, which in turn,
de facto, relied upon domestic wage and price flexibility. In practice
this relied upon the credibility that the government would suffer the
central bank to impose the deflationary consequences of adjustment in
the form of rises in the discount rate, and the effects of the attendant
monetary contraction on the domestic populace. In the pre-1914 economy in which this was possible wages and prices were highly flexible,
and in consequence

a shock to the balance of payments that required a reduction in domestic
spending could be accommodated by a fall in prices and costs rather than a
rise in unemployment . . . [thus] . . . the priority that central banks attached
to maintaining currency convertibility was rarely challenged.[26]

Eichengreen notes the political preconditions for perpetrating
domestically painful deflation as an adjustment mechanism that could
be imposed on domestic workforces as a matter of course, and was
enhanced by the limited franchise prevalent during this era.[27] Toniolo
claims that the adjustment mechanisms of the gold standard made
cooperation among central banks possible because commitment to it
required only minor adjustments in the bank or discount rate, because
capital was mobile and labor flexible, and because fiscal and monetary
policy were insulated by worker ignorance and by limitations on the
franchise.[28]

Mobile capital, flexible labor, and politically insulated fiscal and
monetary policy are, it is worth noting, the conditions to which contemporary neoliberal policies have aimed to return us. That neoliberal-
ism seeks to establish capital mobility and labor flexibility is axiomatic.
That insulary of monetary policy is deemed advisable is more than
evident from the current stampede toward granting independence to
central banks. That governments worldwide currently suffer, or at least
are anxious to claim, severe fiscal constraint in light of the requirements of global capital mobility, is scarcely more controversial. This
theme will resurface to interest us later, when we shall recall that the
preconditions for deflationary adjustment under the pre-1914 gold

---

[26] Eichengreen, *Globalizing Capital*, p. 31.   [27] *Ibid.*
[28] Toniolo, *Central Bank* Cooperation, p. 16.

standard largely describe the contemporary conditions of much of the developing world under conditions of capital mobility and the dominance there of neoclassically trained economists in finance ministries. Thus central bank independence as an alternative to gold as a deflationary or disinflationary "nominal anchor" for the system should be relatively easy to carry off for a team of neoclassically trained and neoliberally committed financial officials who have sold the benefits of central bank independence to political elites. In this context it might be argued that anywhere democratic governance is lacking, or hampered by fiscal exigency, we have returned to this pre-1914 environment. For that matter, as international monetary matters are little understood by contemporary publics in advanced, industrialized states, central bank independence as a new nominal anchor for the emerging system of global financial governance should not be terribly difficult to carry off in the developed world. Nor has it been.

So on what basis did the credibility of the gold standard as a nominal anchor and a commitment mechanism rest? While Eichengreen argues that the system was "one of the great monetary accidents of modern times" he points out that the system "presupposed an intellectual climate in which governments attached priority to currency and exchange rate stability" and also "presupposed the flexibility of markets."[29] It is worth noting that no less of a rationalist political economist than Eichengreen emphasizes the importance of shared social understandings and shared priorities between governments and their monetary authorities in the construction, functioning, and maintenance of the gold standard. Unsurprisingly, from a constructivist perspective, the ideas and interests then prevailing in a socially and historically contingent era constrained the range of possible monetary arrangements. As previously noted, each government adhering to the metallic standard fixed its currency's exchange rate at a par value equivalent to an ounce of fine gold. No less a neoclassically trained economist with neoliberal policy leanings than Michael Mussa, who had been chief economist at the IMF during Michel Camdessus's managing directorship, has suggested the importance in the public mind of a cognitive fixing of the national currency to gold as the basis of "sound money." The accident that Eichengreen describes resulted in no small measure from this ideational, cognitive fixing. As Mussa relates the matter:

[29] Eichengreen, *Globalizing Capital*, p. 7.

in terms of the basic conception of the system people did not think of the international exchange value of the dollar against the pound sterling. Rather, because the dollar was fixed in terms of gold, and because sterling was fixed in terms of gold, by convenient accident, the exchange rate between the dollar and sterling was also fixed.[30]

In the earlier era of capital mobility in which the classical gold standard held sway, this was brought off alongside a system of fixed exchange rates, argues Eichengreen, because central banks that were insulated from politics prioritized capital mobility and fixed exchange rates. While numerous scholars have pointed out that sometimes, even frequently, the "rules of the game" were observed in the breach, the credibility of the metallic standard as a nominal anchor and a commitment mechanism did not suffer. "Central banks could deviate from the rules of the game because their commitment to the maintenance of gold convertibility was credible," suggests Eichengreen. One could find repeated short-term violations "over a period as short as a year" but central bank domestic and foreign assets moved together over longer periods. "Central banks possessed the capacity to violate the rules of the game in the short run because there was no question about obeying them in the long run."[31] I will later argue that this is the sort of credibility that central bank independence is intended to restore; Eichengreen has essentially argued that specific rules were epiphenomenal to the credibility of the gold standard, which was iron-clad, except in times of war.

But the gold standard's iron-clad credibility was required for more than simple price stability. It was required to provide a nominal anchor for fiduciary money to lend credibility to the latter in a fashion that imposed state control over note issue. This measure of control had been impossible to achieve in the era of "free banking," in which multiple commercial banks issued notes in England, until Peel's Act of 1844 separated note issue from commercial banking by monopolizing the note issue within the Bank of England. Meanwhile free banking continued throughout the nineteenth century in the United States. Paradoxically, these gold standard "rules of the game" were highly credible despite

---

[30] Michael Mussa, "The Triumph of Paper Credit" in Forrest Capie and Geoffrey E. Wood, *Monetary Economics in the 1990s*, The Henry Thornton Lectures 9–17 (London: Macmillan, 1996), p. 170.

[31] Eichengreen, *Globalizing Capital*, p. 32.

the fact that central bank adherence to them, in a particular instance, was both contingent upon other events and performed at the discretion of the central bank.

Contingent rules

It is important to consider in this context that the gold standard "rules of the game" were both contingent and discretionary, yet they unquestionably upheld a highly functional international monetary system for at least a generation (at the latest 1870–1914). The gold standard was a contingent rule before 1914, as it could be suspended "in the event of a well understood, exogenously produced emergency, such as a war" with the understanding that parity would be restored when the emergency had passed.[32] It was a "rule with escape clauses."[33] Gold reserves were carefully hoarded during wartime. An operational norm that we might say developed into a contingent "war suspension rule" meant that "[o]perationally the rule is to suspend the gold standard for the duration of a war plus a delay period. In all periods with no such emergency, the gold standard is maintained unconditionally."[34] During an extreme emergency, fiat money might be resorted to, and the inflationary consequences tolerated.

Even in Britain, home of the Bank of England, suspension of gold convertibility to enable monetization of government debt during the Napoleonic Wars saw British domestic prices rise by about 80 percent between 1797 and 1818, with much higher price rises on the continent.[35] Another departure from the rule that appeared to be tolerated by the public in the nineteenth century, without adverse consequences to the credibility of the standard when restored, was suspension during banking crises. Such suspensions permitted, for example, the Bank of England (in 1847, 1857 and 1866) to generate the liquidity required for it to serve as a lender of last resort, and to bail out the banking system and stem financial crises.[36] Presumably, however, this had to be done with note issue, which no doubt diluted the parity in a manner opaque to the public. Unfortunately I have been unable to locate studies addressing this issue in order to explore it further.

---

[32] Bordo and Kydland, "The Gold Standard as a Rule," p. 100.
[33] Cited in Ferguson, *Cash Nexus*, pp. 332–3.
[34] Bordo and Kydland, "The Gold Standard as a Rule," p. 104.
[35] Ferguson, *Cash Nexus*, p. 147.   [36] *Ibid.*, p. 333.

A return to gold at the end of the crisis generally enjoyed popular
support, in part because the public had learned to rue the effects of
inflationary finance, and in part because of the psychological benefits of
a metallic standard that publics believed stored value in a manner that
was not wholly dependent upon the state's deontology. Mussa argues
that "when a country temporarily left its metallic standard...there
was usually a popular demand to get back 'sound money' after the
emergency was past. This would normally require painful deflation;
but this was tolerated, even desired, in the interests of sound money."[37]
This popular demand for a return to gold would be expressed in spite
of the painful period of deflation that attended its return. The popular
ignorance of monetary matters alluded to by Eichengreen was no doubt
a contributor to this demand, but Mussa avers that

> there was widespread popular demand for "sound money" in the form that
> people could readily understand...a purely paper money standard, without
> convertibility of paper money into something physically valuable, was not
> easy to understand or accepted...the public wanted a monetary standard
> where they could literally see and feel the metal that they believed gave value
> to money.[38]

Contingency in contemporary monetary arrangements

Contemporary independent central banks also operate according to
"contingent rules." Even formal, statutory central bank independence
is contingent as it relies upon a statute that might be overturned.
Central bank independence is nearly always reversible, thus contingent, particularly in a crisis, even if that statute is constitutionally
enshrined. This is an implicit threat in the charters of central banks,
and in the requirements that central bankers make themselves available for mandatory reporting sessions to domestic legislative bodies.
Even the chairman of the US Federal Reserve system, who enjoys glob-
ally exceptional discretion in formulating monetary policy – by virtue
of the status of the US dollar as the premier global reserve currency,
by virtue of the dual mandate for price stability and economic pros-
perity embodied in the Humphry–Hawkins Act, and by virtue of the
avoidance of a quantitative inflation target, or of the need to target foreign reserves or explicit monetary aggregates – is required to

[37] Mussa, "Triumph of Paper Credit," p. 152.   [38] *Ibid.*

provide testimony before the US Congress biannually. There he is always implicitly and occasionally explicitly reminded that the Fed enjoys its independence at the pleasure and suffrage of Congress.

The contemporary Bank of England was granted operational (but not goal) independence by then Chancellor of the Exchequer, Gordon Brown, in May 1997, and is publicly committed to an inflation target of 2.5 percent as measured by the retail price index. But the Chancellor can change the inflation target at any time. Moreover, until the United Kingdom had been forced to abandon the European exchange rate mechanism (ERM) in 1992 the Exchequer had set rates and the governor of the Bank of England had merely advised the Exchequer and executed its policies. The Bank of England's independence is quite novel. It was established by the Bank of England Act of 1998. Independence can be revised or rescinded at any time by an Act of Parliament.[39] The Bank of Japan has different arrangements. A member of the government from the Ministry of Finance has the right to sit in on policy board meetings. The government representative cannot vote, but his presence is a constant reminder of the contingency of the Bank of Japan's also quite recent independent status. The government representative can request that a vote on a rate change be postponed until the next meeting. The government also has effective control over exchange-rate policy, which is delegated to the Ministry of Finance, and thus over foreign exchange reserve management, which means that decisions to intervene in the FOREX markets are effectively in the hands of the government.[40]

Arrangements in developing countries can render the independence of a central bank even more contingent, or even merely nominal. A recent study of central banking in Africa, for example, indicates that developing countries permit a representative of the government to participate in central bank monetary policy formation meetings, and see the central bank governor participate in meetings of the government cabinet much more frequently than in industrialized countries. The study suggests that meetings between government officials, including finance ministry officials, and central bank officials in industrialized

[39] Alan Blinder, Charles Goodhart, Phillip Hildebrand, David Lipton, and Charles Wyplosz, *How Do Central Banks Talk?* Geneva Reports on the World Economy 3 (Geneva: International Centre for Monetary and Banking Studies, 2001), p. 84.

[40] *Ibid.*, p. 80.

countries are oriented toward keeping each other informed on respective assessments of current and future economic conditions, while these contacts involve much more active cooperation in monetary and fiscal policy formation in developing countries.[41] Central bank officials responding to the survey of the study indicated that

for about half of the participating central banks from emerging market economies the coordination of monetary and fiscal policy is a key purpose of their high-level meetings with the government, while none of the participating central banks of industrialized countries indicate that this is the purpose of any of their meetings with the government.[42]

While the author of the study, participating in a conference at the BIS on central banking in Africa, that was attended, heard and read by African central bankers, was careful to note that "it would be wrong to take this as a sign of a lack of monetary policy autonomy"[43] in Africa, perhaps we need not be so circumspect.

Discretionary rules

The ideational infatuation with the gold standard among the financial community as an "automatic" adjustment mechanism was so highly developed in the immediate inter-war period that it became "universal doctrine" among central bankers in the 1920s. The adjustment mechanism of the pre-war gold standard (rate rises to attract gold in response to balance of payments deficits, and rate cuts to let gold flow to deficit countries in response to balance of payments surpluses) was a discretionary activity. As a private bank with commercial banking concerns, the Bank of England was also concerned about its profitability.[44] While Peel's Act had separated the note issue and commercial banking functions of the Bank of England, in practice the bank found a means by which to harmonize the concerns of the note issue and banking departments in a fashion that respected the bottom line of the latter.

The problem with the "automatic machinery" view of the gold standard, mythologized among the frustrated central bankers of the

---

[41] Paul Moser-Boehm, "The Relationship Between the Central Bank and the Government" in *Central Banks and the Challenge of Development* (Basle: Bank for International Settlements, 2006), p. 49.

[42] *Ibid.*, p. 50.　　　[43] *Ibid.*　　　[44] Dam, *Rules of the Game*, p. 17.

inter-war period, is that the "rules of the game" were actually highly discretionary rules for a private Bank of England, mindful of its commercial concerns. According to the "rules of the game" in the mythical view of gold's "automatic" adjustment mechanism, "if gold flowed out, then a central bank was supposed to act in such a way as to decrease its assets (say, by raising its discount rate, reducing the circulation of notes and thus tightening money market conditions)."[45] In so doing, however, it might lose lending opportunities in its commercial operations. The central bank as a private institution with a public charter had conflicting obligations. It had a "statutory duty to maintain the convertibility of bank notes into gold" and a "commercial duty to pay dividends to its shareholders."[46]

Thus while the "rules" said that the central bank was to raise rates to attract back gold, and thereby restrict domestic credit when the national balance of payments was in deficit, and to lower rates, letting gold flow out of the country, and boosting domestic credit when the country was enjoying a balance of payments surplus, the former operation was much more likely to be executed in response to international gold movements than the latter. Note that an increase in the bank rate was not an act of public policy because the Bank of England was a private institution at this time. A rise in rates led to a contraction of domestic credit and thus reduced employment and reduced the demand for consumable goods, generating a decline in prices in the domestic market. Conversely, in theory an "overexpansion of credit would cause a gold outflow and hence lead to a contraction before inflation had taken hold."[47] However, an expansion of domestic credit generated an increased demand for currency, which was to be supplied in the form of bank notes by the Bank of England. Thus the Bank of England often had to raise the rate of discount to prevent a fall of the currency stock relative to its reserves, as these reserves could only rise with an increase in bullion stock in reserve.[48] The Bank had to attract more gold reserves in order to issue more notes in response to domestic demand, and from 1844 in England to meet its statutory obligations to limit new note issue in accordance with the supply of bullion held in reserves. This generated a temptation for the Bank to raise the discount rate in response to domestic

[45] *Ibid.*, p. 18.   [46] Ferguson, *Cash Nexus*, p. 155.
[47] Dam, *Rules of the Game*, p. 16.   [48] *Ibid.*

demand for bank notes rather than in response to international gold flows.

Peel's Act (the Bank Charter Act of 1844) had required the Bank of England to keep larger reserves than it would otherwise have done to ensure adequate bullion reserves to back all new note issues. Thus the reserve requirement subsequently exhibited a notable influence on the Bank's discount rate movement policies. Rates might now rise as a result of the pressure on reserves from domestic demands for cash rather than as a result of international gold flows. The rate could rise when the demand for cash withdrawals by British depositors depleted reserves,[49] even at times when Britain enjoyed a significant trade surplus, and the "rules" suggested the discount rate should fall to let gold flow abroad to equilibrate the drain on the bullion reserves of foreign trading partners. Perhaps overstating the case, Eichengreen voices his suspicions that central banks were not guided "even implicitly by a rigid code of conduct"[50] during the reign of the classical gold standard. He cites concerns about a loss of profits (by setting the discount rate above the market rate), deflationary impact on the domestic economy, as well as government pressure to avoid the attendant increased costs in debt servicing, as reasons why central banks might have avoided "automatic" rate rises in response to balance of payments deficits. The latter issue was of particular concern at the Bank of France and the German Reichsbank, many of whose officers and employees were appointed by the government in France, and were civil servants in Germany.[51]

The Bank of England's commercial concerns were evident before Peel's 1844 Act as well as after. Before the Act, since the Bank of England had no legal obligation to provide coin of the realm of a recipient country for a private party wishing to export gold, it would charge a premium to provide it.[52] After the Act, the Bank of England manipulated the "rules of the game" with "gold points" and "gold devices" such as subsidies of broker's charges.[53] Legal scholar Kenneth Dam argues in a vein similarly skeptical to Eichengreen's that while the Bank of England came closer to following the "rules of the game" ostensibly relating gold and trade flows during the classical gold standard, it often did not. He suggests that "[i]t is hard to escape the

---

[49] *Ibid.*, p. 27.   [50] Eichengreen, *Globalizing Capital*, pp. 28–9.
[51] *Ibid.*, p. 29.   [52] Dam, *Rules of the Game*, p. 25.   [53] *Ibid.*, pp. 31–6.

conclusion that the gold standard rules of the game were *a post-WWI construct*, not observed and probably not even widely recognized as relevant norms."[54]

However, if there were no rules, how could they have been consciously "manipulated"? Yet Dam and Eichengreen's skepticism, and the evidence they present of violation of the "rules of the game," have two implications of interest to constructivist analysis. First, it is important to note that unlike general propositions of a nomological-deductive character, or Hempelian covering laws, norms and rules are counterfactually valid. We would not suggest that because someone committed murder, for example, in a particular instance, or even if homicide were on the rise in a particular city or country, that there was no valid injunction against killing people in that society. Norms and rules are not invalidated by particular, or even persistent, counterfactual violations of their injunctions. Yet such rule-following behavior as could be historically observed was clearly marred by self-interested behavior. Thus, second, it is reasonable to suggest that post-war reification of a quite imperfect, loosely structured gentlemen's game of coordination into an "automatic mechanism" by frustrated, inter-war financiers and central bankers demonstrates a significant degree of *post facto*, constructed mythology regarding the strictures of this particular rule-based monetary system. Simultaneous play for contingency and discretion in the application of rules by central banks, which construct systems of rules to coordinate their responsibilities, by no means invalidates those rules nor the deontic powers that central banks exercised within that system of rules.

Contemporary monetary arrangements to withdraw contingency and discretion

The "rules" of a presently developing sub-system of floating exchange rates among independent central banks are similarly contingent and discretionary. This contingency and discretion will be described shortly. However, I refer to this as a "sub-system" because, clearly, not all countries with national currencies let the values of their national currencies float on the FOREX markets. For that matter not all countries employ national currencies. Some countries fully (or partially,

---

[54] *Ibid.*, p. 31. Emphasis added.

minting only national coins of small denomination) substitute the currency of another country, and surrender prestige, seigniorage, and capacity to manage their money supply by abolishing the national currency entirely to permit the currency of another country deemed stable and credible in the FOREX markets to circulate as legal tender. This is known as "dollarization" for shorthand, because this is most often done with the US dollar, though the euro, Swiss franc, Australian dollar, and even Turkish lira enjoy full substitution status somewhere around the world.[55] Other countries anchor their national currency rigidly by statute to a stable, credible currency (presently either the US dollar, the euro, or in the case of Brunei, the Singapore dollar).[56] Yet other countries are bimonetary, with two or more currencies circulating as legal tender. Yet others have pooled monetary sovereignty to construct monetary unions.

All fully or partially dollarized economies, and countries with hard pegs to currency boards, have entirely yielded their monetary policy to that of a foreign central bank, which may, but more often will not, take into account their interests and economic conditions when formulating monetary policy. They have entirely abandoned monetary sovereignty for the benefits of price stability and the credibility of the currency they employ to tax, spend, and trade. The major task of the central banks that maintain a fully pegged national currency consists mainly in managing their reserves to ensure that adequate FOREX reserves denominated in the "anchor currency" are on hand to defend the peg, particularly should their currency suffer speculative attack on the FOREX markets. The other significant task is to control new note issue to levels consistent with those reserves, which may only grow with increases in FOREX receipts. Their monetary "rules" are only contingent in the sense that their governments retain the right to reissue a national currency, for dollarized economies, or to dismantle the currency board, for those who have adopted hard pegs. Little that matters in the realm of monetary economics is at their discretion, except for the decision, for countries with hard pegs, regarding how many reserves to accumulate, how many domestically denominated

---

[55] Benjamin J. Cohen, "Monetary Governance in a World of Regional Currencies" in Miles Kahler and David A. Lake (eds.) *Governance in a Global Economy* (Princeton, NJ: Princeton University Press, 2003), tables 6A.1 and 6A.2, p. 165.

[56] *Ibid.*, table 6A.3, p. 166.

notes to issue against these reserves, and in special circumstances, a decision about whether and when to defend the currency, and how much foreign exchange reserve to spend down in the process.

Bimonetary economies and currency union arrangements may be more contingent and discretionary monetary arrangements than these, if the local component of a bimonetary arrangement, or the common currency, is not hard pegged to a more credible, stable anchor currency. Of course bimonetary economies can always ban the use of a foreign currency as legal tender at their discretion, but it is often a decline in the credibility of the national currency that generates the currency competition that induces the government to make the original concession of legal tender status of a competing foreign currency. The foreign currency would in any event continue to circulate as a basis for private transactions without employing the strictest capital controls, and perhaps even with them. Monetary unions that issue currencies that float freely in the FOREX markets enjoy all the contingent and discretionary advantages of national floating currencies within pooled monetary sovereignty arrangements while, like these arrangements, remaining "rule-based" monetary systems.

Rules vs. discretion?

Central banks that are not independent of the government, and whose currencies are not hard pegged to an anchor currency, enjoy all sorts of discretion, or rather the governments that direct their activities do. In particular they can monetize debt, stimulate the domestic economy through credit creation, engage in discretionary lending to specific sectors of the economy through practices such as the Bank of Japan's former "window guidance" (a form of government-directed lending), and help countries compensate for exogenous shocks to the economy and their deflationary consequences, among others. But they may pay a high longer-term price for this discretion through the accumulation of inflationary pressures in the economy, as accumulating quantities of money and credit chase a limited number of goods and services. When this occurs, the social character of money discussed in chapter 2 demonstrates its salience, as market actors come to distrust the "promise" of stable money, leading either to asset bubbles in the markets for property and securities at best, or general inflationary pressures across the domestic economy at worst. They may also suffer capital flight by both foreign and domestic investors, and speculative attack on the rate of exchange on the FOREX markets.

Governments that direct central banks to engage in high levels of public debt monetization and inflationary finance may also pay a price in significantly increased costs of borrowing on the disintermediated bond market. Matters were similar with the gold standard. Ferguson reports that for nineteenth-century sovereign debt issues "[b]eing on gold was worth between 100 and 200 basis points on a country's yields."[57] The credibility of monetary policy formulation by a contemporary central bank that is clearly and credibly independent of the government similarly knocks down risk premiums charged by investors in sovereign debt issues. We will explore the many steps taken by central banks to ensure the credibility of their money in significant detail in chapter 6.

There has been no shortage of contemporary central bankers or monetary economists who have argued that the best way to stem inflationary pressures from excessive monetary growth is the adoption of firm rules for monetary growth. Recall Friedman's assertion that inflation is always and everywhere a monetary phenomenon. He claims that money is "too important to be left to [the discretion of] central bankers."[58] A thoroughly rule-based monetary policy that leaves no discretion to central bankers would have no capacity to play politics with the money supply. Proposals for monetary rules vary from Friedman's monetarism, featuring rigid and predictable annual growth in the money supply, to rigid exchange-rate pegging to an external standard as a nominal anchor for money supply, and to the appointment of "conservative central bankers" who are ideologically predisposed to place price stability before any competing objective of monetary policy.[59]

But all of these proposals have their own problems. Monetary economist Charles Goodhart has argued, adequately persuasively for the assertion to be cited by influential economists such as Stanley Fischer as "Goodhart's law," that "[a]ny universal monetary rule is doomed to failure."[60] I shall discuss these problems in a moment.

[57] Ferguson, *Cash Nexus*, p. 333.
[58] Issing, *Should We Have Faith in Central Banks?*
[59] Kenneth Rogoff, "The Optimal Degree of Commitment to an Intermediate Monetary Target" *Quarterly Journal of Economics* 100(4) (1985): 1169–90.
[60] Fischer, "Modern Central Banking", p. 196.

The reason why central bankers consider strict rules for monetary policy, however, may be found in the rationale for the earlier nostalgia for the gold standard. Monetary rules remove the "inflation tax" from the control of fiscal authorities, can eliminate monetization of government debt and the attendant inflationary effects, and generate sanguine reputational effects that provide a "way out of the dynamic time inconsistency problem."[61]

The time inconsistency paradigm

The time inconsistency problem is the assertion in the economic literature that monetary policymakers have incentives to exploit trade-offs between employment and inflation in the short run (short-term employment and economic output maximization in the domestic economy) through monetary stimulus, even though monetary expansion in itself cannot produce sustainably higher levels of employment and economic growth in the long run. The appellation of the "time inconsistency" paradigm derives entirely from its rational choice theoretic formulation and the *problematique* assumes unintended consequences at time B of rational action at time A. As Sylvia Maxfield formulates it, "[t]he best government policy choice prior to policy implementation is not necessarily consistent with the best policy choice after implementation, because the public responds by anticipating a change in government policy."[62] Here of course we mean a change in monetary policy. This is because consumers, businesses, and financial market actors, according to economic orthodoxy, ostensibly "rationally" adjust their expectations to anticipate the effects of higher levels of money and credit expansion in the economy.[63]

The standard time inconsistency model (TIM) has not passed without criticism, however, even within the economics profession, particularly among academic economists. For example, it is argued that the model is inherently *ahistorical* and cannot, for example, explain the very low levels of inflation in the United States in the 1950s and early

---

[61] *Ibid.*, pp. 196–8.   [62] Maxfield, *Gatekeepers of Growth*, p. 11.
[63] See Finn Kydland and Edward Prescott, "Rules Rather than Discretion: The Inconsistency of Optimal Plans" *Journal of Political Economy* (June 1977): 473–91, and Robert J. Barro and David Gordon, "A Positive Theory of Monetary Policy in a Natural Rate Model" *Journal of Political Economy* (August 1983): 589–610.

1960s, assuming, as it does, a predisposition for central bankers to accommodate politicians with loose monetary policy. Moreover, the model simply assumes a desire for governments to sustain a level of economic output that exceeds what is achievable with a constant rate of inflation, even though it has really been well understood since the 1970s by central bankers that this is unobtainable. Contemporary central bankers now expect that adjustments of expectations by economic actors to looser monetary conditions will defeat the intended effects of greater monetary stimulus in the long term,[64] by, for example, engaging in speculative activity that inflates asset prices, inflation-indexing wage contracts, and passing on the costs of those wage contracts on to consumers.

Rule-based monetary policy frameworks, or "operating systems," are seen by many analysts to have the advantage of policy predictability and to generate a way out of this problem. It is not difficult, however, to find former central bankers who find no validity whatever in the TIM problem or framework.[65] A rule-based monetary policy framework is not only a very strong and credible commitment mechanism, but if executed consistently "it would be seen as a prospective policy pre-commitment . . . [thus advocates argue that] . . . appropriate rules contribute to policy *transparency* as well as to policy *credibility*."[66] As will be argued at length in chapter 7, transparency is a "monetary policy multiplier." It permits businesses, consumers, and transnational financial market actors to anticipate the likely direction of monetary policy and to plan and transact their business in anticipation of future moves in interest rates. Transparency permits central banks to potentially exert a much greater influence on the "long" end of the yield curve, where rates of interest charged on long-term maturity sovereign and corporate debt instruments are determined by the bids of investors in the bond market. Credibility, in this context, is the

---

[64] Freedman, "Central Bank Independence," p. 95.

[65] Freedman quotes three recent central bankers who are quite dismissive of the TIM paradigm, including Alan Blinder and Lawrence Meyers in epigraphs in *ibid.*, p. 94.

[66] Manuel Guitán, "Rules or Discretion in Monetary Policy: National and International Perspectives" in Tomás J. T. Baliño and Carlo Cottarelli (eds.) *Frameworks for Monetary Stability: Policy Issues and Country Experiences* (Washington DC: International Monetary Fund, 1994), p. 22. The emphasis is original.

metric of the belief that market actors demonstrate that the promise of the central bank, to uphold the current value of its currency, is valid. Thus, as a corollary, the government's promise to repay its debt in "sound money" is also deemed valid.

Irrational expectations and shared understandings in the bond markets

The gold standard's system of par values was both transparent and credible, and a significant argument of this book is that current moves toward central bank independence and transparency are an attempt to re-establish something resembling the gold standard's rule-based credibility, by creating the political and institutional conditions under which price stability will be restored to the paramount position of the agenda of every central bank. Work on historical bond market activity indicates that political events that might lead to a suspension of the gold convertibility rule were matters that occasionally shook the confidence of bond investors in the nineteenth century. Ferguson suggests, with classic British understatement, that this movement of historical bond prices with political crises of various forms "presents an awkward problem for economic theory, in that investors do not rely purely on economic data when forming their expectations of future policy...it is at least suggestive that every major jump in yields coincided with a major domestic or international political crisis."[67] Ferguson's statistical evidence suggests that rate movements by the Bank of England (21 percent of the sample) were historically the most frequent source of movements in bond yields between 1845 and 1900, while a broad range of determinants in the price of British government debt securities may be identified, with war (15.7 percent) and foreign political events and crises (8.9 percent) accounting for nearly a quarter of these between them.[68] Bond investors abhorred, and continue to abhor, "wars and rumors of wars." It is by no means fanciful to deduce that the threat of suspension of gold convertibility that could so often attend a major foreign war was a significant source of these sudden demands for a significant risk premium by investors in government debt.

[67] Feguson, *Cash Nexus*, p. 177.   [68] *Ibid.*, table 7, p. 184.

As Ferguson suggests, with all the normal caveats for those who insist on convergence to statistical significance before they are willing to consider a relational inference, his statistics "do offer some insight into the way [nineteenth-century] contemporaries thought, and hence into the way that expectations were formed."[69] It appears that "rational expectations" in the bond markets can be as often based on speculative panic as on cold calculation of the meaning of economic data. In constructivist terms, "the way" nineteenth-century bond market investors "thought" constituted a system of intersubjectively shared beliefs and social meanings. Wars and rumors of wars for these nineteenth-century bond market actors meant a probability (and if it is my money at risk even a possibility will suffice) that the Bank of England would suspend gold convertibility at worst, or the British government would hike taxes, engage in fiscal shenanigans, and drive up the price of any number of commodities by requisitioning them to a war effort at best, thus diminishing the credibility of sustained convertibility. The resulting intersubjectively shared expectations of these nineteenth-century bond investors might even be written as a constitutive rule of the nineteenth century bond market:

"Wars and rumors of wars" count as "possibility that gold convertibility will be suspended" in the context of "lending to the government in a political crisis that portends hostilities."

Recall the form of constitutive rules is "X counts as Y in context C." A regulative rule that followed logically from this constitutive rule was:

"demand a high risk premium" in the context of "lending to the government in a political crisis that portends hostilities."

Regulative rules are of the form "do X in context C."

Importantly, what is salient in the manner in which these market mechanisms actually function is not that economic actors individually pursue rational expectations, that generate collectively suboptimal outcomes, but that they act with economic consequence on intersubjectively shared social understandings. In this case, bond investors act with economic consequence. They sell holdings of previously purchased government bonds at a discount and/or demand hefty risk

---

[69] *Ibid.*, p. 183.

premiums in order to make any further purchase whatsoever of current government debt security offerings. They act on the social meaning, shared between them, that war or rumors of war means that the government's promise to pay its debt, in money whose purchasing power is constant from the time of debt issue, is less credible than that of a government at peace, or of a government experiencing no conflict-threatening crisis. The social understanding that the bond market investors share intersubjectively, in fact, is that the war or crisis has diminished the moral agency of the government, and its promise to pay in stable money. These actors respond to this changed social relationship by discounting that promise through the market mechanisms of selling bonds at a discount, and demanding a greater risk premium as a *quid pro quo* for agreeing to provide the government with fresh financing.

Discretionary and rule-based monetary operating systems

In more contemporary times the alternative to the rule-based formulation of monetary policy is the discretionary view. This is the Keynesian view that supposes that monetary stimulus can shield a national economy from exogenous shocks, provide countercyclical monetary accommodation, and generate full employment. But experience with the Great Inflation of the late 1960s through the early 1980s demonstrated that monetary policy alone could not solve the unemployment problem without generating significant and persistent inflation. Central banking wisdom then swung back from discretion to rules with a brutal experiment in Friedmanite monetary targeting under the Volcker Fed. This experiment did help "wring out inflation" by letting interest rates gyrate wildly, and ultimately changed the long-standing expectations of consumers, businesses, and financial markets that prices would always continue to rise. It did so, however, at exorbitant short-term cost to the economy.

Another problem with monetarist operating systems is the problem of identifying monetary aggregates and velocities (the rate at which money changes hands). The utility of monetary targeting is predicated on the assumption that you should target what you can count. Financial innovation, generating a looser relationship between monetary aggregates and prices, has consequently significantly diminished the capacity of central banks to "count" (to account for) monetary aggregates and velocities in the real economy. This problem generated a trend back toward more discretionary monetary operating systems focused on more diffuse policy aims (such as "price stability" variously defined, and "financial system stability"). Central banks, particularly in industrialized countries, have consequently more often employed policy frameworks and operating systems that employ a "hybrid" between rules and discretion in monetary policy formulation and execution.[70]

While Friedman's "monetarist rule" is transparent and easily understood by the public, as well as effective at containing price inflation, fluctuations in the public's demand for money, and the rule's failure to provide it when demanded even in the absence of inflationary pressures, does not meet the requirements of a healthy, growing economy for an adequate money supply. Interest rates under monetary targeting are permitted to spiral wildly with market conditions and demand for money can fail to be met in an environment of non-inflationary growth. Ultimately the incapacity of central banks to quantify, or even to unambiguously define, the quantity of monetarily usable financial vehicles circulating in the economy at any given time, generates an insurmountable intersubjective problem between the central bank and the financial system. These actors cannot share intersubjectively a socially or economically salient understanding of the answer to the question "what is money?" The answer to this crucial question varies, given the incapacity of central banks to anticipate the next market moves, or the capacities for financial innovation of economic actors in the "real economy."

Problems of intersubjectivity in monetary operating systems

But the question cannot be allowed to vary if monetary aggregates are to be targeted to constrain monetary growth. The problems are clear in considering, as a useful example, the historical changes in operating systems of the US Federal Reserve system. Prior to October 1979 the Fed targeted the Federal Funds rate, which is the rate of interest banks charge one another for overnight, interbank loans. Banks that lack sufficient reserves to meet their reserve depository requirements with the Federal Reserve system will borrow at the Federal Funds rate the

---

[70] Guitán, "Rules or Discretion," p. 6.

difference between their required reserve level and their actual reserve level at their reserve maintenance period. By targeting the Federal Funds rate, the Fed's objective was to control the growth of monetary aggregates.

The OMD at the Federal Reserve Bank of New York, which effects open market transactions to execute the FOMC's monetary policy directives, would implement monetary policy under the pre-1979 operating schema by adjusting the non-borrowed reserves (NBR) in the Federal Reserve system. NBR are the "total reserves [in the system] (member bank deposits in the Federal Reserve banks, plus vault cash, less funds borrowed [borrowed reserves])."[71] Borrowed reserves are "funds loaned to a bank generally on a short term basis by another bank" which can include bills payable, eurodollars, federal funds, rediscounts of promissory notes and paper at the Federal Reserve banks, and repurchase arrangements.[72] Commercial banks are charged a penalty by the Fed for failing to meet their reserve requirements;[73] it is sufficiently stiff for it to serve as an inducement for the bank to bear the opportunity costs of placing and keeping on deposit with a Federal Reserve bank their required reserves, for which they are paid no interest.

When the Fed targeted the Federal Funds rate (a market rate set by commercial banks with spare funds to lend) they did so by ordering the OMD to confine the Federal Funds rate to a narrow range. The OMD would buy or sell securities and repurchase arrangements (repos) on the open market as required to keep the Federal Funds range within the target until the next meeting of the FOMC.[74] While targeting the Federal Funds rate the Fed "relied on the influence that changes in the fed funds rate would have on other interest rates and the influence

---

[71] Finch, *Barrons*, p. 316. [72] *Ibid.*, p. 65.

[73] Reserve requirements on member institutions vary by the number of checkable dollar deposits that a depository member institution holds. From 1996 banks holding fewer than $4.3 million in such deposits were exempt from reserve withholding requirements. Member institutions holding more than $4.3 million but less than $52 million in checkable deposits must maintain 3 percent of those deposits with the Federal Reserve system, and member banks with over $52 million in checkable deposits must maintain 10 percent of deposits at their regional Federal Reserve Bank. See Federal Reserve Bank of New York, "Understanding Open Market Operations," http://www.newyorkfed.org/education/addpub/omo.html, figure 3–1, p. 16.

[74] R. Anton Gilbert, "Operating Procedures for Conducting Monetary Policy" *Bulletin: Federal Reserve Bank of St. Louis* (February 1985): 15.

of interest rates on the quantity of money demanded in the future. Money demand was assumed to be influenced by lagged values of interest rates."[75] But the operating procedure was highly dependent on Fed staff economist estimates of current levels of available NBR, and consequently attempts to stabilize the Federal Funds rate to the range targeted. Thus underestimates by the Fed staff of NBR could generate excess money supply "long enough to affect total spending in the economy."[76] An absence of shared understandings between the Fed staff and the commercial banking industry regarding the level of NBR generally available, as well as the financial vehicles available as NBR, may have led to a chronic underestimate of NBR by the Fed staff in this period, leading to persistent monetary excess.

In October 1979 the Volcker Fed embraced open monetarism and changed the Fed's operating system to target NBR. Rather than constraining the Federal Funds rate to a narrow range, under the new operating system "the objective of open market operations was to supply the amount of reserves consistent with their [the FOMC's] objectives for money growth, while permitting larger fluctuations in the fed funds rate."[77] In other words the Fed fixed the growth of monetary aggregates, and when demand for money by commercial lending institutions exceeded that supply, commercial banks were required to bid against one another for a limited supply of those monies strictly limited by the Fed. This procedure caused the Federal Funds rate to spiral when the demand for funds dramatically exceeded the level of monetary aggregates that the Fed was willing to supply. The latter were strictly limited and specified at the previous FOMC meeting by a resulting statement of the FOMC, which stated the Fed's objectives "as a specified percentage growth rate for each monetary aggregate from month to month before the meeting to some future month."[78]

Money supply growth was then absolutely limited, by category of money. Demand for more money by commercial lending institutions, as a matter of FOMC policy, was not met under the new operating system. Member institutions were forced, if they wanted it badly enough, to bid up the Federal Funds rate to levels as high as 19.8 percent[79] in order to obtain funds to meet their reserve requirements without suffering the reputational consequence of "going to the discount

---

[75] *Ibid.*, p. 17.   [76] *Ibid.*, pp. 16–17.   [77] *Ibid.*, p. 17.   [78] *Ibid.*
[79] Greider, *Secrets of the Temple*, p. 221.

window" for the funds. So while "the prior procedure of targeting the federal funds rate relied on a stable demand function [estimated by the Fed Staff] for money [the] second procedure of targeting on NBR relied on a relationship between reserves and the money stock."[80]

Thus instead of assuming a stable demand for money, and estimating and targeting the rate of Federal Funds that would reduce this demand, the Fed staff estimated the total reserves of the system. Total reserves here are then the sum of borrowed reserves and NBR in the banking system, which constitutes the monetary base of the economy. The Fed staff estimated (assumed) the average level of borrowed reserves that would remain extant in the banking system until the next FOMC meeting, and the OMD "would not increase the level of NBR in response to an increase in demand for reserves; it might actually decrease NBR to keep total reserves near its path level."[81] By targeting and controlling NBR the Fed could place an absolute ceiling on the amount of new money entering the banking system, or actively extinguish existing money in the system. The Fed then permitted the market for Federal Funds to determine what commercial lending institutions would pay for their borrowed reserves, and consequently what business and consumers would pay for loans.

At the onset of instituting the monetarist operating system, the Fed changed its assumptions and altered its operating system rules. As a consequence, the expectations of consumers, businesses, and financial market participants changed. Commercial bankers could no longer go to bed at night with any reasonable certainty of the price that they would be required to pay for Federal Funds to meet their reserve requirements if they had lent out more money during their maintenance period than was consistent with those requirements. Businesses similarly could not rely upon earlier assumptions about the price that they would have to pay for funds to finance their operations. Nor could they assume that they could continue to pass those costs along to consumers, who began to extinguish (pay off) their debts.

---

[80] Gilbert, "Operating Procedures," p. 18.

[81] Excess reserves are the "surplus balances above what banks are legally required to hold to meet reserve requirements. Excess reserves can be held as vault cash, reserve account balances in a Federal Reserve Bank, or in a pass-through account at a correspondent... Banks sell excess reserves to one another in the Federal Funds market." Finch, *Barrons*, p. 169.

When the public was persuaded that the Fed would permit the Federal Funds rate (and consequently, rates for loans to businesses and consumers) to rise to any level without satisfying the demand for money, and when the costs of borrowing began to exceed the compensation of any reasonable expectation of return on such costly capital, the Federal Funds rate finally stopped spiraling upwards and began falling. When the Federal Funds rate finally began falling, it fell over 6 percent within a couple of weeks.[82]

This monetary targeting can certainly be credited for purging the Great Inflation from the United States and global economy. The cost to the economy was high, however. Because interest rates were allowed to rise to punishing levels under this operating system, massive business liquidations resulted, particularly with smaller businesses that faced higher borrowing costs, and a serious recession with significant increases in unemployment resulted. Much larger amounts of money were extinguished in the processes, as consumers rushed to pay off high-interest debts when rates finally began falling, extinguishing money from both sides of the balance sheets of banks and financial institutions which count outstanding loans as assets. Recall that "credit is money too." Both constitute promises to pay.

One former Federal Reserve official diplomatically claims that the Fed's decision to suspend monetary targeting in October 1982 was "precipitated ... [by the] ... maturity of a large volume of all-savers certificates ... [which had a] ... temporary effect on money demand."[83] However, it is clear that monetary targeting was too difficult to continue because excess reserves in the banking system were impossible for the Fed staff to estimate, and the monetary aggregates fluctuated too wildly to account for, let alone control. The money supply essentially defied definition. You cannot target what you cannot count, or even define. Years after the Volcker Fed's abandonment of a monetarist operating system, Alan Greenspan responded to monetarist enthusiasts in the Reagan administration, such as the budget chief, Richard Darman, with his own view "that the Fed had been unable to control or even to accurately measure the money supply for years. The notion that it was possible was outdated."[84] This is not a simple "information deficit" or a problem of

---

[82] Greider, *Sercrets of the Temple*, p. 201.
[83] Gilbert, "Operating Procedures," p. 19.   [84] Woodward, *Maestro*, p. 88.

"asymmetric information" in the rationalist sense in which neoclassical economics employs the terms. These intersubjective challenges of the monetarist operating system were insurmountable. In order to successfully target monetary aggregates the central bank and markets must share understandings regarding the demand for money in the economy, as well as assumptions regarding which financial instruments will be employed as money (e.g. the identity of money in the economy). The Fed and market actors could establish neither of these shared understandings during the Fed's monetarist experiment in the early 1980s. The resulting suspension of short-run objectives for M-1 meant that the Fed's operating system had to change. While the monetarist experiment was deemed successful in its primary goal of ending inflation expectations, its costs and operational difficulties also served as a harsh reminder that "in no market economy can the central bank control the inflation rate or the price level directly."[85]

Since October 1982 the Fed's current operating procedure has targeted borrowed reserves and the Fed supplies NBR at a rate highly dependent, again, on Fed staff estimates of total reserves in the system. This is a return to the pre-monetarist experiment of attempting to influence the Federal Funds rate, and ultimately to influence the demand for money, rather than to directly control its supply. It "depends upon the influence of policy actions on interest rates and the quantity of money demanded."[86] As with the pre-1979 operating system, the current system permits the Federal Funds markets to determine the demand for money, and the Fed supplies that level of money up to a level consistent with a specified (but wider than the pre-1979) range in the Federal Funds rate. If the rate exceeds this wider range, the OMD, to execute the FOMC's directive, will not purchase the securities or contract the repos to supply the monetary levels demanded by the markets. As was the case with the monetarist operating system that targeted NBR, the current system, targeting borrowed reserves, permits a wide range in the rate the markets will charge for Federal Funds, but no longer targets monetary aggregates directly, and is a more discretionary than rule-based operating system.

---

[85] William Poole, "Monetary Policy Rules?" *Review: Federal Reserve Bank of St. Louis* (March/April 1999), p. 11.
[86] Gilbert, "Operating Procedures," p. 21.

Inflation targeting: "rules" or frameworks?

Inflation targeting regimes are becoming more popular rule-based monetary regimes that still permit some discretion in monetary policy. There is a bit of a rift in the literatures on monetary economics and central banking regarding whether inflation targeting regimes should be treated as a "rule" in the same fashion as the gold standard or strict targeting of monetary aggregates,[87] or whether they should be treated conceptually as a monetary policy "framework." Inflation targeting regimes tend to offer instrument independence to the central bank without goal independence. In other words the central bank is free to choose its open market or other instruments for executing monetary policy, while it is constrained by statute or pre-announced settlement with the government – normally in the guise of the finance minister – regarding the goal, or range of acceptable annual inflation rates. These are normally quantitatively defined as a percentile increase over a fixed time period. The goal may be adjusted with some ease, as is the case of the United Kingdom, where the Exchequer may adjust the inflation target, or in New Zealand where the inflation target is pre-negotiated between the head of state and the Governor of the Reserve Bank of New Zealand. Or else it can be nearly impossible to adjust, as in the case of the ECB, whose 2 percent "over the medium term" inflation target is enshrined in the international treaty language of the Treaty of the European Union, and is thus an integral component of the monetary union, requiring a two-thirds majority ratification of EU states to be adjusted.

Thus as a "commitment" mechanism, inflation targeting regimes on the whole (with the possible exception of the ECB's inflation targeting regime) are too "discretionary" and "contingent" in the hands of the government to be treated as a formal monetary rule of the stringency of a metallic standard, or rigid monetarism.[88] It may be doubted whether inflation targeting regimes, while intended as alternative commitment mechanisms, "will ever attain the credibility associated with

---

[87] See e.g. Benjamin F. Friedman and Kenneth Kuttner, "A Price Target for US Monetary Policy? Lessons from the Experience with Money Growth Targets" *Brookings Papers on Economic Activity* 1(1996): 77–146.

[88] See e.g. Ben S. Bernanke, Thomas Loubach, Frederic S. Mishkin, and Adam S. Posen, *Inflation Targeting: Lessons from the International Experience* (Princeton, NJ and Oxford: Princeton University Press, 1999), pp. 21–2.

a gold convertibility rule."[89] Inflation targeting "does not provide simple, mechanical operating instructions to the central bank . . . inflation targeting as it is actually practiced confers a considerable degree of discretion on policy-makers."[90] In terms of our institutional analytic framework, inflation targeting regimes confer on the government the deontic power to decree, in specific terms, an "acceptable" rate of loss of purchasing power of money over a known and pre-announced period of time. Such regimes confer on the central bank the deontic power to adjudicate when that government-decreed target has been breached, and when and how to act to correct it. Constitutive and regulative rules of central bank action in inflation targeting regimes may thus be trivially derived.

Rules for reserve requirements

One means of constraining the money supply is to adjust reserve requirements directly. Within the context of a domestic legal system the central bank has the deontic power (often in consultation with the government's executive and/or legislative authorities) to alter by fiat the proportion of checkable deposits that commercial banks must place and keep on reserve with the central bank. Raising these reserve requirements is a very direct, effective, and obviously rule-based, mechanism by which the supply of money circulating and credit extended in the economy may be reduced, or more dangerously for financial system stability, raised. These real effects on the economy are effected, as are so many causal effects in the monetary realm, by deontic fiat. In constructivist terms, they are constitutive rules with causal effects.

Reserve requirements were levied in developing countries in no small measure in response to the bank runs of the Great Depression. The central bank could always be certain it could then show up at a bank suffering such a run with an armored car full of currency to meet and ostensibly stem the demand for cash withdrawals by panicked depositors. But reserve requirements can also be employed, not only as a tool in limiting commercial bank extension of credit (remember that credit is money too), but also to help smooth volatility in overnight

[89] Ferguson, *Cash Nexus*, p. 333.
[90] Bernanke *et al.*, *Inflation Targeting*, p. 22.

interest rates (by lengthening averaging periods for commercial banks to meet reserve requirements). This can be valuable in less developed countries with inadequately liquid capital markets. As no or low interest is paid on reserve deposits, reserve ratios also impose a government seigniorage tax on banks to compensate the government for the cost of providing central bank liquidity lending, payment settlement, and regulatory services.[91] So reserve requirement rules have a variety of causal effects on money and credit creation and the "real" economy.

Data on the rules on required reserves of banking systems from 2003 indicate required reserve ratios that vary between nothing and 40 percent. Hong Kong SAR, Australia, Sweden, Switzerland and the United Kingdom appear to privilege banking as an industry, imposing no reserve requirements, while in 2003 Argentina imposed reserve requirements varying between 22 and 40 percent. Most national central banks pay no interest on reserves, while the Philippines paid 4 percent on up to 40 percent of commercial bank reserves. Averaging periods to meet reserve requirements varied between a few days and a month. Some central banks permit commercial clients to apply their vault cash in addition to deposits in various forms of securities with the central bank to meet reserve requirements. Some do not.[92] But all of these reserve rules and stipulations tend to be stricter for developing countries, which face more significant challenges to the stability and transnational perceptions of the credibility of their banking systems and currencies alike.

Yet it is clear that though reserve requirements in the developing world, "play more diverse roles than in industrialized countries, there are clear signs of convergence to lower levels and less active reliance on them."[93] A major impetus behind this institutional isomorphism is the perceived requirement to lower the operating costs of bank intermediation relative to the costs of disintermediated securitization of credit arrangements in the bond market.

---

[91] John Hawkins, *Globalisation and Monetary Operations in Emerging Economies*, BIS Papers 23 (Basle: Bank for International Settlements, 2005). See annex A, "The demand for, and supply of, bank reserves," pp. 68–71.

[92] *Ibid.*, table A1, "Rules on banks' required reserves (as of late 2003)."

[93] Jozef Van 't dack, *Implementing Monetary Policy in Emerging Market Economies: An Overview of Issues*, BIS Papers 5 (Basle: Bank for International Settlements, 1999), p. 39.

Significant risks to national banking and financial system stability can arise from this policy, however, as the Mexican experience with this policy move in the late 1980s and early 1990s has demonstrated.[94] In the developing world reserve requirements also serve the sanguine purpose of automatically sterilizing flows of portfolio capital in an age of hyper-capital mobility.[95] Money that is deontically designated by statute to sit on deposit with the central bank with no interest compensation cannot be employed to create new money and credit in the domestic economy. The effect on domestic money supply of the portion of the portfolio flows relegated to reserves is consequently "sterilized." Yet, as will appear as a continuing theme in this book, financial innovation can ultimately defeat even statutory controls such as reserve requirements. These reserve requirements have been employed in the developing world to help to sterilize the effects of portfolio flows on domestic money supply, yet "the effectiveness...tended to decline over time as investors found other channels, not subject to reserve requirements, through which to conduct their transactions."[96]

Rules, discretion and governance

The literature essentially distinguishes rule-based vs. discretionary monetary policy regimes by whether central banks are constrained by rules or enjoy discretion in the formulation of monetary policy. Note that all four of the operating systems that have been most commonly employed in industrialized countries since the collapse of the Bretton Woods system are entirely consistent with monetary policy formulation by central banks which have been granted instrument and (in nearly all cases) goal independence by the government. Instrument independence permits central banks discretion (but for some inflation targeting regimes) of the choice of operating systems and instruments by which monetary policy, even if dictated or strongly influenced by the government, is executed. Goal independence permits central banks not only to determine which monetary instruments to target and to employ to affect desired levels of money, credit and their cost in the economy, but what the goals of monetary policy are. Goal independence permits central banks to determine what "price stability" means, what "financial system stability" means, what its responsibilities as a "lender of

[94] *Ibid.*   [95] *Ibid.*, p. 40.   [96] *Ibid.*

last resort" to ensure "financial system stability" are in the context of the domestic economy. And for central banks whose currencies serve as or support major reserve currencies, goal independence permits the central bank to determine what its responsibilities for "global financial stability" are, and what this means as well. In this context, goal independence provides central banks with deontic powers to generate many constitutive rules of the domestic monetary system and in some cases, the international monetary system as well.

But what this literature on discretionary vs. rule-based monetary policy frameworks misses is the question of governance. To whom is authority granted in determining (or helping to determine) the supply and cost of money and credit? The rules of operating systems designate authority (governance functions) not only to independent central banks. However, the act of generating independent central banks and thus removing government governance functions (and to varying extents, government accountability) from the decision-making processes frees central banks and governments to hand governance capacity to private market actors.

6 | *Central bank independence as credibility*

Not all Germans believe in God, but all believe in the Bundesbank.

Jacques Delors

You know, Bill, I'm having my gallbladder out. You wouldn't do it [raise interest rates] while I'm having my gallbladder out, would you?

Lyndon Baines Johnson to William McChesney Martin

. . . the worst episodes in monetary history – the great inflations – have been marked by the subjection of central bankers to overriding political pressures.

R. S. Sayers

Subsequent to the demise of the classical gold standard, the debate over rules-based vs. discretionary monetary systems can be traced back at least as far as the inter-war period to a famous essay by one of the leading liberal lights of the Chicago School of economics. In an exposition that appears curious to contemporary eyes, Henry Simons argued passionately for a rule-based system to defend democracy and capitalism against what he regarded to be the "immanent danger" that democratic free enterprise would be subverted and lost by "delegation of legislative powers and the setting-up of authorities instead of rules."[1]

I will employ Simons's oft-cited essay as an early exploration of the continuing debate within monetary economics between "rules" and "discretion" in monetary policy. This debate exemplifies some of the liberal commitments that still shape the debate, and have resulted in a turn toward central bank independence and transparency strategies as the means to recapture the price stability and credibility of the classical gold standard, while retaining the benefits of "discretion," at least a form of contingency. Simons actually shared with Keynes a conviction

[1] Simons, "Rules Versus Authorities," p. 2.

that there could be no return to the "rules of the game" of the gold standard, to whose deflationary nature he attributed the economic depression in which his nation and the world were firmly mired as he wrote in 1936. Simons argued:

the worst financial structure is realized when many nations, with similar financial practices and institutions and similar credit pyramids (and narrowly nationalist commercial policies) adopt the same commodity as the monetary standard . . . it seems almost beyond diabolical ingenuity to conceive a financial system better designed for our economic destruction. . . . it is to the writer a source of continued amazement that so many people of insight should hold unwaveringly to the gold standard as the best foundation of national policies. The worship of gold, among obviously sophisticated people, seems explicable only in terms of our lack of success in formulating specifications for a satisfactory, independent national currency.[2]

But Simons was no Keynesian. He bitterly criticized "many irresponsible proposals for indefinite inflation, based on the notion that our ills are traceable to deficiency of consumer-purchasing power."[3] He mistrusted both the motives and the competence of central bankers in exercising authority delegated to them by congressional or parliamentary bodies, and he criticized the motives of "radicals" such as the disciples of Keynes because "[t]hey define programs in terms of ends, with little discussion of appropriate means; they call for an authority with a considerable range for discretionary action, and would require much intelligence and judgment in their administration."[4]

Simons was not without cause in suspecting both the competence and motivations of the central bankers of his day. The contribution of rigid adherence to gold in the early years of the Great Depression, irrespective of its highly deflationary impact on an already deflated economy, is well documented in the standard accounts of political economists and economic historians.[5] The competence of Great Depression era central bankers in adhering to gold under such harrowing circumstances might be questioned without rehearsing the well-known consequences for economic output and employment. It is worth noting in this context, however, that in the United States the

---

[2] *Ibid.*, pp. 11–12.   [3] *Ibid.*, p. 12.   [4] *Ibid.*

[5] See e.g. Eichengreen, *Golden Fetters*, and Charles P. Kindleberger, *The World in Depression: 1929–1939* (Berkeley, CA: The University of California Press, 1986).

money supply shrank in volume by more than a third from late 1929 to early 1933[6] with only very limited Fed action to inject liquidity into a collapsing banking system. US President Herbert Hoover might be forgiven for suggesting that the US Federal Reserve "was indeed a weak reed for a nation to lean on in time of trouble."[7] Milton Friedman, the heir to Simons's early monetarist impulses, has famously chronicled with Anna Schwartz his view of the Depression era Fed's incompetence in some detail.[8]

Simons can also be forgiven for his suspicions of the motives of his Depression era Fed governors and Treasury officials. While his essay betrays his own commitments to an untrammeled liberalism, the ideological commitments of Simons's contemporary monetary and fiscal authorities have been revealed to constitute a devastating mixture of extreme *laissez-faire* commitments bordering on liberal Puritanism. This was a commitment shared by the business leaders of the day. Those in charge of US monetary, fiscal and business decision-making regarded the market crash of 1929 and the subsequent liquidation of affected business to be a "normal correction to excess."[9] Alan Meltzer relates that "[t]he prevailing belief was that the depression was purgative. Business leaders argued that 'a depression was a scientific operation of economic laws' and could not be interfered with."[10] Unfortunately, Hoover's Fed and Treasury wholly concurred. William Greider reports that ten months after the 1929 market crash, President of the Philadelphia Federal Reserve Bank, George W. Norris, argued to his Fed colleagues that:

The consequences of such an economic debauch [as the excesses of the "roaring twenties"] are inevitable ... We are now suffering them. Can they be corrected or removed by cheap money? We do not believe that they

[6] Greider, *Secrets of the Temple*, p. 299.

[7] Herbert Hoover, *The Great Depression: 1929–1941.* Vol. III of *The Memoirs of Herbert Hoover* (New York: Macmillan, 1952), p. 212.

[8] Milton Friedman and Anna Jacobson Schwartz, *A Monetary History of the United States, 1867–1960* (Princeton, NJ: Princeton University Press, 1963).

[9] Greider, *Secrets of the Temple*, p. 300.

[10] Allan H. Meltzer, *A History of the Federal Reserve*, Vol. I: *1913–1951* (Chicago, IL: University of Chicago Press, 2003), p. 464. Meltzer quotes Roosevelt's Chairman of the Board of Governors of the US Federal Reserve, Marriner Eccles, from Eccles's memoir *Beckoning Frontiers: Public and Personal Recollections* (New York: Alfred A. Knopf, 1951).

can. We believe that the correction must come about through reduced production, reduced inventories, the gradual reduction of consumer credit, the
liquidation of security loans and the accumulation of savings through the
exercise of thrift.[11]

This "harsh medicine" prescription of liquidation, austerity, and
thrift will sound rather familiar to developing world recipients of IMF
prescriptions subsequent to modern financial crises. Norris's prescription was wholly consistent with the advice provided to Hoover by his
Treasury Secretary, Andrew Mellon:

The way out of the Depression, he [Mellon] confided to President Hoover,
was more failure, and unemployment, more liquidation. "Liquidate labor,
liquidate stocks, liquidate the farmers, liquidate real estate," Mellon
declared. The Treasury Secretary believed, and many other Fed officials
agreed, that panic and recession were good for people. "It will purge the
rottenness out of the system," Mellon explained. "People will work harder,
live a more moral life. Values will be adjusted and enterprising people will
pick up the wreck from the less-competent people."[12]

And there is significant evidence that the US Federal Reserve system during the Great Depression experienced a conflict of interest
whose origins were not entirely dissimilar to those experienced by the
Bank of England in the nineteenth century, with the effect that like its
nineteenth-century British progenitor, the Fed acted in a perverse fashion rather at odds with its public charter as (in this instance) a lender
of last resort. Recall that the nineteenth-century Bank of England often
yielded to a temptation to raise (rather than lower) the discount rate to
attract gold in order that it might issue more notes when the domestic
demand for money exceeded its reserves. This behavior was in clear
contravention of the "rules of the game" which suggested that the
British central bank should lower the discount rate and let gold flow
abroad in response to a balance of payments surplus. And the Bank of
England would often fail to raise the discount rate to attract gold in
response to a balance of payments deficit for fear that, as a private concern with an obligation to pay dividends to its shareholders, it would
lose loan business to competing discount houses.

Members of Hoover's Fed opposed reflation on the grounds that
the lower rates on Treasury securities that monetary accommodation

---

[11] Morris is quoted in Greider, *Secrets of the Temple*, p. 300.   [12] *Ibid.*

generated hurt the balance sheets of their member banking institutions. Having taken a bath in red ink from non-performing loans, US banks invested in bonds, and when the market in corporate bonds turned down and more losses resulted they had cast about for a safe haven and lit upon short-term US Treasury securities. These constituted nearly half of bank earnings from portfolio assets by 1933.[13] What monetary stimulus the Fed provided had resulted in a decline in the rate paid on three-to six-month Treasury bills from 3.4 percent in November 1929 to 0.34 percent in June 1932.[14] Depository institutions of the US Federal Reserve system complained bitterly to their regional Fed Governors and presidents of the negative impact on their bottom lines of the reduced Treasury yields. These forms of earnings were particularly important to balance sheets of banks in the Chicago and Boston districts in 1932, and Chicago District Fed Governor James McDougal argued for scaling down the size of Fed open market purchases of US Treasury securities to alleviate the impact of the attendant lower rates on member institutions.[15] The prevailing attitude toward monetary accommodation and reflation in the banking industry is indicated from a quote during this period from one of the leading trade journals:

These artificially low rates are of no benefit to anyone ... the banks are no longer able to employ their funds to advantage, and hence get no proper compensation for their services. Such rates are, in fact, ruinous, and inasmuch as they do not allow banks to earn an adequate profit, must in the end impair the stability of the banks if not actually involve them in ruin.[16]

Thus the 1932 monetary expansion was halted, a wave of bank failures followed anyway, and the credibility of the US Federal Reserve was demolished as Franklin Roosevelt was swept into office on a wave of despair.[17] One of Roosevelt's first actions in office was to close the gold window, effectively devaluing the dollar by 40 percent relative

---

[13] Gerald Epstein and Thomas Ferguson, "Monetary Policy, Loan Liquidation, and Industrial Conflict: The Federal Reserve and the Open Market Operations of 1932" *Journal of Economic History* 44(4) (1984): 969–70.

[14] *Ibid.*, 970.   [15] *Ibid.*, 977.

[16] *Commercial and Financial Chronicle*, July 9, 1932, quoted in Gerald Epstein and Thomas Ferguson, "Answers to Stock Questions: Fed Targets, Stock Prices, and the Gold Standard in the Great Depression" *Journal of Economic History* 51(1) (1991): 190.

[17] Greider, *Secrets of the Temple*, p. 303.

to the currencies of gold bloc countries, creating the US dollar as a nationally administered currency.

It is against this background that Simons outlined the Chicago School's endorsement of rules over discretionary monetary policy. The bitter experience of the United States (as well as that of the United Kingdom in the post-WWI period)[18] with the deflationary consequences of gold left Simons quite certain that a return to gold could not provide a monetary rule to avoid the indefinite continuation of what he regarded to be the dangers of "managed currency [which] (along with protectionism) is the prototype of all current 'planning' schemes – in the sense of all the illiberal connotations of planning . . . in the movement for central banking."[19] Simons flirted with the concept of monetarism, well before Friedman's rediscovery of it. In the context of his concern about placing administrative authority for a managed currency in the hands of unaccountable central bankers he argued that it at least avoided "reliance on discretionary (dictatorial, arbitrary) action by which an independent monetary authority and [*sic*] defines a statutory rule which might be enacted by the competent legislature without substantial delegation of its powers."[20]

But Simons recognized the theoretical difficulties that were empirically validated by the Volcker Fed in the early 1980s, namely that the "obvious weakness [of monetarism] lies in the danger of sharp changes on the velocity side, for no monetary system can function effectively or survive politically in the face of extreme alternations of hoarding and dishoarding."[21] And he recognized that monetarism might just generate and legitimate the creation of new financial vehicles and quasi-currencies that he deemed to be so fatal to financial stability, and was concerned that "fixing of the quantity of circulating media might merely serve to increase the perverse variability in the amounts of 'near-moneys' and in the degree of their general acceptability, just as the restrictions of bank notes presumably served to hasten the development of deposit (checking-account) banking."[22]

In surveying the boom and bust cycle economy with which Simons's contemporaries were so distressingly familiar, a rule-based monetary system to limit the destructive volatility of the cycles they were

---

[18] See e.g. John Maynard Keynes, *The Economic Consequences of Mr. Churchill* (London: Hogarth Press, 1925).
[19] Simons, "Rules Versus Authorities," p. 3.   [20] *Ibid.*, p. 5.
[21] *Ibid.*   [22] *Ibid.*

suffering, without surrendering sovereign authority over monetary policy to a technocracy, was a highly enticing prospect. Thus Simons considered monetarism. But having rejected both a return to gold parities and monetarism, Simons and the Chicago School cast about for a workable rule to avoid the foibles of the planned economy that they feared would come hand in hand with "discretion" and "managed money." Simons argued that

In a free enterprise system we obviously need highly definite and stable rules of the game, especially as to money . . . Once established . . . they should work mechanically, with the chips falling where they may . . . so that, hereafter, we may hold to it unrationally – on faith – as a religion, if you please. The utter inadequacy of the old gold standard, either as a definite system of rules, or as the basis of a monetary religion seems beyond intelligent dispute.[23]

Unfortunately for Simons, in the absence of gold parities or monetarism as a viable rule, he was constrained to a rather puerile plea for some *deus ex machina* mechanism that did not then exist, nor yet has been discovered, as the basis for a "blind faith."

While calling for "the establishment of a simple, mechanical rule of monetary policy"[24] he was yet powerless to supply it. Seemingly aware of his dilemma, his famous essay, however briefly, gazes wistfully back to the monetarism he had once advocated, but having thought through was later compelled to reject. He suggested that his:

earlier persuasion as to the merits of the rule of a fixed quantity of money was fundamentally correct, although the scheme is obviously too simple as a prescription under anything like the present conditions. Its limitations, however, have to do mainly with the unfortunate character of our financial structure – with the abundance of what we may call "near-moneys" – with the difficulty of defining money in such a manner as to give practical significance to the conception of quantity.[25]

The passage does not put Simons's best intellectual foot forward. First, he essentially repeats his earlier (1933) defense of monetarism, then says that it would work if only the conditions of the financial system (namely financial innovation) in a free-enterprise economy were not precisely what they actually are. In order to address this, Simons seemed to advocate regulation to hobble financial innovation. Paradoxically, the Chicago School liberal, Simons advocated so regulating

---

[23] *Ibid.*, p. 13.   [24] *Ibid.*   [25] *Ibid.*, p. 16.

banking in order to make monetarism work that he would have all but
abolished banking as we know it, and he said so:

This would mean, above all, the abolition of banking, i.e., of all special
institutional arrangements for large-scale financing at short term. Demand-
deposit banking would be confined (in effect, at least) to the warehousing
and transferring of actual currency.[26]

Unfortunately, as Niall Ferguson's work suggests, the arrangements
that Simons would have abolished were precisely those that had made
it possible, for example, for merchant Britain to finance its shipping
operations through letters of credit and the development of proto-
checking-generated economic work-arounds of shortages of specie at
critical times. It is somewhat cognitively dissonant to see a clearly committed liberal advocate that his government regulate away precisely
the innovative capacities of capitalism that had historically turned it
into an engine of economic growth. Revolving lines of credit and the
financing perquisites of corporations were also on the chopping block
as needed adjustments to financial reality in order to make monetarism
work, so far as Simons was concerned.[27] So attractive was the chimera
of a *deus ex machina* rule to resolve the monetary problem, that if God
would not come out of the machine, the government had to create the
machine from which God would emerge. If banking as we understand
it – in spite of its crucial role in generating the innovations that brought
about modern capitalism – was in the way of this machine, then banking as we know it, argued Simons, must go.

Fortunately for capitalist political economy, banking was not abolished, and monetarist rules were not implemented in the depths of
the Great Depression. Liberal panaceas were set aside and moderate reforms of the banking system were instead pursued. The United
States, for example, implemented the Glass–Steagall Act, which separated brokerage lending and functions from the banking system so
that it could not place its solvency at risk by margin call lending.
The Act also forbad interest payment on checking (demand) deposits
and limited to 3 percent the rate of interest that could be paid on time
deposits to limit banking competition for deposits to alleviate pressures
on the frail banking system. Unfortunately the Act also generated an

[26] *Ibid.*   [27] *Ibid.*

inducement for the public to hoard currency.[28] The Banking Act of 1933 expanded the responsibility of the Federal Reserve system for surveillance and regulation of the banking system, provided for the regular examination of member banks, fixed the percentage of the amount of a bank's capital that could be out on loan, and created the Federal Deposit Insurance Corporation to insure bank deposits.[29]

Recent literature on the question of rule-based vs. discretionary monetary orders revisits many of these early themes explored by Simons. Contemporary central banker Otmar Issing endorses Simons's call for central banking with a clear and limited mandate as a "set of rules that constrain the discretionary use of power by the government and the central bank."[30] But in addressing the question of whether we should have faith in central banks, Issing provides us with a more nuanced discussion than Simons's call for the development of some *deus ex machina* monetary rule that subsequently we "may hold to it unrationally – on faith – as a religion, if you please."[31] Issing's more nuanced treatment of the question implicitly if not explicitly bows deeply to the social character of money. Whereas Simons would see us ascribe trust to a monetary rule as a "theological belief . . . or more generally 'belief founded on authority'"[32] Issing reminds us quite correctly that "trust must be earned."[33] Addressing himself to the example of the comparatively novel ECB, Issing does advise "faith" in it, but faith as "used in everyday language as a synonym for 'belief', 'reliance', and 'trust.'"[34] As we discussed in chapter 2, money is a promise, and the promiser represents himself as a moral agent. Issing envisions the bond between the central bank and the public as a form of "credit relationship" and reminds us that in Latin, *credit* means "he believes."[35] The Latin Mass features in the liturgy the *credo* ("I believe") in which the congregation recites the Nicene Creed of core Christian beliefs. In the absence of belief, there is no money. It is a pure deontology, whose

---

[28] Donald R. Wells, *The Federal Reserve System: A History* (Jefferson, NC and London: McFarland & Co., 2004), p. 62.

[29] The Act is reproduced in Frederick E. Hosen, *The Great Depression and the New Deal: Legislative Acts in Their Entirety (1932–1933) and Statistical and Economic Data (1926–1946)* (Jefferson, NC and London: McFarland & Co., 1992), pp. 153–93.

[30] Issing, *Trust in Central Banks*, p. 13.

[31] Simons, "Rules Versus Authorities," p. 13.

[32] Issing, *Trust in Central Banks*, p. 17.   [33] *Ibid.*

[34] *Ibid.*   [35] *Ibid.*, p. 19.

existence, let alone utility, is predicated on intersubjectively shared social understandings and the collective assignment of status function.

Benjamin Cohen defines trust in money in this context as "the reciprocal faith of a group of like-minded transactors in a money's general usefulness and future acceptability."[36] Issing similarly reminds us that "the very nature of money ... [is] ... built on trust, on a promise" and that the designation of a bank note as legal tender "imposes an obligation to accept the note in settlement of contracts, and highlights the fact that money derives its value ... from the willingness of other economic agents to accept it to settle transactions ... Thus money is a social achievement."[37] This is particularly true of fiat money but "even commodity money [such as a metallic standard] requires trust and a well-founded expectation that it will be accepted for a wide range of transactions."[38]

Trust and authority in the era of fiat money

In the era of fiat money, the social achievement that money constitutes is thus even more impressive, and more demanding. Herbert Simons and his latter-day followers hoped for a simple, mechanical rule, given by nature, with a little help from man's ingenuity, in which we might trust blindly. Most contemporary monetary economists, however, have accepted the dearth of such a rule, and have focused their intellectual efforts on constructing monetary systems in which they argue that we may still trust, even if less blindly. The system of trust that they suggest we might construct without the aid of a belief in the intrinsic value of a metallic standard for money (the gold standard), or a rigid administrative curtailment of the supply of money (monetarism), and the deflationary consequences of such "rules" which have been employed in the past, is trust in monetary authorities and in systems of monetary governance.

In orthodox monetary theory the global capitalist economy cannot function without reliance upon the price mechanism to adjudicate value, and to permit market-based decision-making to allocate capital and the distribution of its returns, without a stable "unit of account." Trust in this context means that actors must trust that national

---

[36] Cohen, *The Geography of Money*, p. 147.
[37] Issing, *Trust in Central Banks*, pp. 20–1.   [38] *Ibid.*, p. 21.

monetary authorities, and the systems of governance they manipulate, will maintain the stability of that unit of account. At the domestic level of analysis this entails public trust in the promise of price stability. At the international level of analysis, prices may vary somewhat as the FOREX markets adjudicate the relative purchasing power parities of various national currencies. The goal of global price stability would only be possible with the development of an international currency unit to fix a global "store of value" as a universal "unit of account." No such universal currency unit has been constituted, thus the international monetary system is instead characterized by currency competition.[39]

Thus at the international level, to the extent that we "trust" in global monetary arrangements, we trust them to generate global financial stability rather than global price stability. That this trust can be shaken by huge regional disruptions, such as the Asian financial crisis of 1997 and its aftershocks, has generated an intellectual growth industry in search of a new international financial architecture[40] that its proponents hope will deliver global financial stability. We are to trust that the value of money will not collapse internationally, and that a system of international payments will continue to function, and that currently employed currencies will continue to be accepted for international settlements. We are to trust that while the relative purchasing power parities of these currencies will vary, international payments will, regardless of the terms (exchange-rate parities) on a given day, continue to clear.

---

[39] See e.g. Cohen *The Geography of Money*; Benjamin J. Cohen, *The Future of Money* (Princeton, NJ: Princeton University Press, 2004), and Jonathan Kirshner, *Currency and Coercion: The Political Economy of International Monetary Power* (Princeton, NJ: Princeton University Press, 1995).

[40] See e.g. Leslie Elliott Armijo, "The Political Geography of World Financial Reform: Who Wants What and Why?" *Global Governance* 7 (2001): 379–96; Padma Desai, *Financial Crisis, Contagion, and Containment: From Asia to Argentina* (Princeton, NJ: Princeton University Press, 2003); Barry Eichengreen, *Toward a New International Financial Architecture* (Washington, DC: Institute for International Economics, 1999); Peter B. Kenen, *The International Financial Architecture: What's New?, What's Missing?* (Washington, DC: Institute for International Economics, 2001); Steven Radelet and Jeffrey D. Sachs, "The East Asian Financial Crisis: Diagnosis, Remedies, Prospects" *Brookings Papers on Economic Activity* 1 (1998): 1–98; Joseph Stiglitz, "Must Financial Crises Be this Frequent and this Painful?" McKay Lecture, Pittsburgh, Pennsylvania, September 23, 1998; Joseph Stiglitz, *Globalization and Its Discontents* (New York: Norton, 2002).

In order for this system to work at all, we must trust central banks and international financial market actors. We must trust central banks because they control the domestic and influence the international supply of money, and thus the domestic value of money directly (through monetary policy) and the international value indirectly (by influencing fiscal and exchange rate policy – though some central banks, particularly in the developing world, also control these directly). We must trust international financial markets for the system to work because we have collectively assigned to them the deontic power to adjudicate the transnational value of money in the FOREX markets, the transnational cost of money in the global bond markets for corporate, municipal, and sovereign debt instruments, and the value of the returns of productive capital in the international equities markets.

Significantly, if the international financial markets (particularly the FOREX market) do not "trust" a particular national government (to rein in fiscal policy) and/or its central bank (to engage in appropriately tight monetary policy) to maintain the currency as a "store of value," market actors will take it into their own hands to adjust the value of that national currency as an international "unit of account" so that it may continue to provide a serviceable "medium of exchange" that reflects fundamental economic realities in the global economy. This is so in theory. In practice, exchange rates overshoot and undershoot dreadfully what fiscal, trade, and monetary "fundamentals" suggest are reasonable exchange-rate realignments.[41] However, this observation takes us, for the time being, away from our purpose.

What are the bases of this trust that permit the contemporary system of competitive fiat monies to reproduce the utility of orthodox monetary theory's three functions of money? Issing argues that in the end having "faith" in central banks means that we have faith in central bankers, and this in turn rests upon "the technical competence and professional skills of the central bankers" and in the institutions that central banks constitute, inasmuch as institutions are considered by the public to be "more reliable and more durable carriers of trust and reputation than individuals alone."[42] Trust may also be lodged in networks of social and economic relationships among economic actors,

---

[41] Ferguson, *Cash Nexus*, p. 327.
[42] Issing, *Trust in Central Banks*, pp. 29–30.

such as networks of central bankers, finance ministers, and financial market actors.

In exploring the social preconditions for currency crises, for example, Peter Aykens draws upon the sociology of embedded business networks and argues that our perceptions of risk are strongly influenced by whether or not we have established relations of trust with other actors. In a network of such relations "[u]nder conditions of declining trust, state and market actors redefine what constitutes risk, decrease their time horizons and resort to more coercive modes of compliance to influence the behavior of others in the network."[43] The development of relationships of trust influences perceptions of risk in a manner that is at variance with the expectations of rationalist theory. Quite usefully, Aykens develops three distinct social forms of ensuring compliance with expectations that reveal three distinct forms of relations of trust among actors. Put most simply, mutual relations of distrust require coercive mechanisms to ensure compliance with expectations, while we can be persuaded to trust another actor if s/he has a reputation for consistently meeting expectations over the long term. To trust another actor without reservation, or to generate "affective" relations of trust, we must regard that actor or institution as constituting an authority that unreservedly deserves our trust. To develop these concepts somewhat:

Where there is distrust (no faith that the other party will perform as expected), exchanges only occur when the vulnerable party is coerced... Gradually, actors involved in exchanges develop *reputations* for competence and consistency in their area of responsibility... trust is based on reputation and "reputation" has ultimately to be acquired through behavior over time in well understood circumstances.[44]

Early modern monarchs, who had a dreadful record of repayment, were thus required to coerce financiers and wealthy merchants into loaning them money to finance their wars and projects. As Niall Ferguson reports of royal treatment of early modern financiers, "Sir George Carew had said of [French King] Henry IV that he 'wringeth them... like sponges and ransometh every three or four years.'"[45] The

---

[43] Peter Aykens, "(Mis)trusting Authorities: A Social Theory of Currency Crises" *Review of International Political Economy* 12(2) (2005): 312.

[44] *Ibid.*, p. 318. Emphasis added. [45] Ferguson, *Cash Nexus*, p. 141.

practice of first coercing subjects with money to lend it, and then defaulting on the debt, was continued by the French crown well into the modern period. Ferguson reports that the French "defaulted wholly or partially in 1559, 1598, 1634, 1661, 1648, and 1698, and again in 1714, 1721, 1759, 1770, and 1788."[46] Persuading people that institutions have been properly designed, and then demonstrating this through their consistent performance, so that institutions "become carriers of reputation as a function of their past behavior"[47] is one way in which actors can be persuaded to trust.

The sort of trust that monetary economists and central bankers wish to instill in money, with their searches for various rule-based mechanisms and schemas, however, is an even stronger form than reputational trust. Issing, in addressing the question of whether the European public should place trust in the novel (at the time of writing) ECB notes that trust "is deepened and reputation is built when it is tested in difficult circumstances and when it is maintained over an extended period."[48]

The Volcker and Greenspan Feds earned the trust of the US public and the global financial markets in precisely this way. Volcker kept on the monetary brakes until expectations that further inflation was normal and expected were demolished. Subsequently, Volcker's status rose enough to permit him to "loosen up a bit in public, even joking about his reputation as the hardhearted central banker. 'Central bankers are brought up pulling the legs off of ants,' he quipped at one Washington party."[49] His long and distinguished public service, at significant personal cost, and his unwillingness to compromise in the face of enormous pressure to slack off the monetary breaks during the steep recession that the monetarist experiment had generated, until public inflationary expectations had been tamed, lent him an enormous personal credibility that opened doors for him in corporate boardrooms after he left the Fed:

Volcker was the stiff, inflexible man of integrity, deliberately unfashionable and irascibly honest as he had always been. Somehow, get Volcker on your team and money would come. They believed that on Wall Street and it proved to be true... the attraction among potential employers lay in a deep

---

[46] *Ibid.*   [47] Issing, *Trust in Central Banks*, p. 35.
[48] *Ibid.*   [49] Greider, *Secrets of the Temple*, p. 556.

sense that the mere association of his name with a financial enterprise would lift its prospects.[50]

Support for Issing's assertion in the case of former Fed Chairman Alan Greenspan is provided in two newspaper headlines over a decade apart during his tenure. The first of these appeared very shortly after Greenspan's appointment, when the financial markets had begun to recover after the October 1987 crash. The *Wall Street Journal* ran a headline that read "Passing a Test: Fed's New Chairman Wins a Lot of Praise on Handling the Crash."[51] The second appeared on 4 March 1999 when the *New York Times* ran an editorial headlined "Who Needs Gold When We Have Greenspan?" in which the Fed Chairman was given credit for acting to mitigate the consequences of the Asian financial crisis, along with US Treasury Secretary Robert Rubin, and his deputy Lawrence Summers. This trio were collectively eulogized by *Time* magazine as "the committee to save the world."[52] Niall Ferguson suggested, while Greenspan was still in office, that "[s]o high is the esteem in which the Chairman of the Federal Reserve [is] held . . . that he is absolved from explicit targets, instead dispensing occasional Delphic utterances."[53] Add to these continuing expressions of credibility with the establishment political and financial press over a decade apart from the fact that the book on Greenspan's career that recounts them is entitled *Maestro*, and we get a picture of the enormous credibility of the institution of then US central bank, and the person of its chairman. And as an epigram to this chapter announces, the Deutscher Bundesbank has a reputation as an institution with unshakable credibility in combating inflation; EU architect Jacques Delors has quipped that "not all Germans believe in God, but all believe in the Bundesbank."[54]

The credibility with which earned reputational trust provides an economic agent like a central bank is a "utility" (in the language of rationalism) of a very high order. This is because:

The trusted need not resort to intensive forms of persuasion to compel action, because the trusting finds their prior behavior persuasive enough. In turn, actors begin to withhold judgment (at least temporarily) in the face of what [under conditions of reputational trust] would otherwise appear

[50] Joseph B. Treaster, *Paul Volcker: The Making of a Financial Legend* (New York: John Wiley & Sons, 2004), p. 187.
[51] Woodward, *Maestro*, p. 49.   [52] *Ibid.*, p. 214.
[53] Ferguson, *Cash Nexus*, p. 161.   [54] Issing, *Trust in Central Banks*, p. 35.

to be violations of trust. For example, investors do not immediately sell a currency when inflation rates rise and policy officials do not immediately intervene in financial markets when capital flows become more volatile. They withhold these actions because they put stock in the other party's reputation for rightful action.[55]

Anecdotal evidence abounds that central bankers are intensely conscious of reputational considerations. During most of the years of the Greenspan Fed, for example, the directive to the OMD that concluded each FOMC meeting included a "bias" statement to indicate, irrespective of whether the FOMC had acted to raise rates, lower them, or leave them unchanged, the direction in which the committee was leaning for possible action at the next meeting. Woodward recounts an FOMC meeting in which the Governor of the New York Fed, Gerald Corrigan, asked for a directive with a bias toward a rate increase, arguing "I think institutionally that it makes us look better." Federal Reserve Board Vice-Chairman David Mullins agreed "[we] can only look good."[56]

Reputational trust may be as good as it gets for central banks and central bankers. However, a more powerful, "affective" bond of trust between a public and the central bank, whose outlines we can perceive in Delors's tribute to the pre-EMU Bundesbank, is the aim of the current architects of the movement toward ever greater, and increasingly universalized, central bank independence, and newly transparent communications strategies. Because while government coercion is required to induce the public to employ printed money or purchase government debt when there is no trust, and persuasion is required when trust is based on reputation, "affective" relations of trust (or authority) obviate the requirement for the recipient of trust to obtain it. As the social philosopher, Hannah Arendt once observed:

authority always demands obedience... Yet, authority precludes the use of external means of coercion; where force is used authority itself has failed. Authority... is incompatible with persuasion, which presupposes equality and works through a process of argumentation. Where arguments are used authority is in abeyance... If authority is to be defined at all... it must be in contradistinction to both coercion and persuasion through arguments.[57]

[55] Aykens, "(Mis)trusting Authorities," p. 318.

[56] Woodward, *Maestro*, pp. 106–7.

[57] Hannah Arendt, "What was Authority?" in Carl J. Friedrich (ed.) *Authority* (Cambridge, MA: Harvard University Press, 1958), p. 82, quoted in Aykens,

The form of trust that central bankers hope to develop is that of "affective trust." This form of trust "restricts the range of interpretations the trusting party imposes on the behavior of those they trust by providing actors with an internally guaranteed sense of security about the other's motives."[58] Aykens points out that unlike the calculative rationalist approach to trust as "the probability that an actor we depend on will disappoint our expectations causing us to lose something we place at risk with them (such as money)"[59] we can instead "conceptualize trust not as a product of calculation but as an *intersubjective* condition that gives a particular social context meaning."[60] Trust is a social phenomenon that fundamentally relies upon intersubjectively shared social understandings between the trusted and the trusting.

While we normally reserve this form of trust for loved ones and close friends and associates, it can be granted to those with exceptional expertise that, when employed, consistently generates sanguine outcomes. In earlier work on private authority and global governance, I argued along with Thomas Biersteker that such expertise is a form of moral authority that we have labeled the authority of expertise or of "authorship."[61] While we and our collaborators had explored explicitly private (non-governmental) forms of authority as mechanisms of global governance, the typology developed in that work is quite applicable to public forms as well. As one our contributors, A. Claire Cutler, noted in her contribution to the volume, legitimacy and authority can accrue from

the respect accorded to "an authority," such as a specialist, a scholar, or an expert whose authority derives from specialized knowledge and practices that render such knowledge acceptable, and appropriate, as authoritative. It also involves the respect accorded those "in authority," such as political leaders, generals, or representatives who possess an explicit or implicit grant of authority from the state.[62]

"(Mis)trusting Authorities," p. 363. This passage from Arendt is also extensively quoted in Cohen, *The Geography of Money*, p. 143.

[58] Aykens, "(Mis)trusting Authorities," p. 318.   [59] *Ibid.*, p. 315.

[60] *Ibid.*, p. 318. Emphasis added.

[61] Thomas J. Biersteker and Rodney Bruce Hall "Private Authority in Global Governance" in Rodney Bruce Hall and Thomas J. Biersteker *The Emergence of Private Authority in the Global Governance* (Cambridge: Cambridge University Press, 2002), p. 215.

[62] A. Claire Cutler, "Private Regimes and Interfirm Cooperation" in *ibid.*, p. 28.

Barnett and Finnemore have recently applied this distinction between being "an authority" and "in authority" to international organizations as well. The theoretical insights that here derive from the study of bureaucracies as rational-legal authorities may thus be generalized and applied to monetary institutions. Bureaucracies proscribe action for actors, generate rules that "define, categorize and classify the world... [and] create or constitute the world" so that bureaucracies can interact with it.[63] As authorities, bureaucracies are authorities by definition. They are "rational-legal authorities in their domain of action... [and enjoy] moral standing [and] expertise [and employ] discursive institutional resources to get other actors to defer to them."[64] Actors who are an authority "derive standing from expertise demonstrated by credentials, education, training and experience."[65]

Biersteker and I have argued that these are forms of "moral authority"[66] which has its source in these as well as other attributes of actors. We developed these observations inductively from studies of private authorities, but they can clearly be applied to public authorities like central banks as well as private authorities (like markets, as I shall shortly argue):

Some... actors possess moral authority because of their capacity to provide expertise on an important issue. Others claim moral authority because of a combination of their possession of expertise and the plausibility of their claims to neutrality on a controversial issue. Still other private actors claim moral authority because of more general normative claims that they are socially recognized to represent progressive or, in some instances, morally superior, transcendent social and political positions.[67]

Much of the authority that central bankers and monetary economists glean is a result of their expertise, and their claim to master and expertly orchestrate that which is not even comprehensible to the average citizen. It is a form of clericalism that separates the initiated from the uninitiated behind a veil of mystery. William Greider has explored the nickname of the US Federal Reserve as "the temple" in this context:

[63] Barnett and Finnemore, *Rules for the World*.
[64] *Ibid.*, p. 20.   [65] *Ibid.*, p. 25.
[66] For an extended development of this concept related to power in the international relations literature see Rodney Bruce Hall, "Moral Authority as a Power Resource" *International Organization* 51(4) (1997): 591–622.
[67] Hall and Biersteker, *Emergence of Private Authority*, p. 215.

Its mysterious powers of money creation, inherited from priestly forebears, shielded a complex bundle of social and psychological meanings. With its own form of secret incantation, the Federal Reserve presided over awesome social ritual, transactions so powerful and frightening they seemed to lie beyond common understanding... [such that]... The money process... still required a deep, unacknowledged act of faith, so mysterious that it could easily be confused with divine powers.[68]

The links between faith (authority), money, and banking are long standing and sometimes consciously invoked by central bankers:

"It is a truism that public confidence is important to banks," an editorial in *The Wall Street Journal* observed. "That's why early Hebrews did their banking in temples and the later American and European banks built banks that looked like temples." Officials of the Federal Reserve themselves were the ultimate rationalists – economists who analyzed numbers, constructed scientific theories to explain economic behavior and tested the theories against reality – yet they too unconsciously invoked the sacred aura of the institution... describing the confidential fraternity that economists entered into when they joined the Fed Staff... [as]... "taking the veil," the expression that describes nuns entering a convent. A chairman of the House Banking Committee sometimes referred derisively to the Fed's senior economists as "the monks."[69]

Sacral images and historical institutional sacral progenitors aside, the modern faith of science and the self-consciously "scientific" artifice constructed around modern economics, to the extent that people buy into the new faith, ensures that the monetary economists who staff modern, contemporary central banks enjoy the status of high priests of the secular, scientific revolution:

The public's confusion over money and its ignorance of money politics were heightened by the scientific pretensions of economics. Average citizens simply could not understand the language, and most economists made no effort to translate for them... Most economists, regardless of their particular ideological biases... cloaked their observations in dense, neutral-sounding terminology that was opaque to non-scientists. The neutral language masked the political content of economics and the social rituals of capitalism – as if all economic players were simple molecules destined to behave according to the same natural order.[70]

[68] Greider, *Secrets of the Temple*, p. 53.   [69] *Ibid.*, p. 54.
[70] *Ibid.*, pp. 55–6. For an extended analysis of the less than scientific consequences of this obscurantist language of economics see Dierdre N.

Since the monetary policy actions of central banks are ostensibly the result of rigorous scientific analysis of vast amounts of data, the judgments of central bankers have come to be accepted by publics as the result of (morally) neutral, sober analysis of the monetary medicine that is the best prescription for what currently ails the economy. This is so at least to the quite limited extent that monetary policy can serve as a corrective for macroeconomic problems that may actually have their sources in structural deficiencies in the economy, fiscal, or trade policy, or result from some exogenous shock to the economy.

Of course monetary policy can rarely provide such a panacea in practice. But to the extent that publics are persuaded that central bankers apply neutral, scientific analysis to correctly guide monetary policy from their ostensibly vast store of expertise that is wholly inaccessible to the layperson, central banks enjoy the moral authority of neutrality and of expertise, or "authorship."[71] To the extent that publics have come to believe that market-based decision-making is superior to politically based decision making,[72] either in terms of maximizing economic utility, and/or in normative terms (of "fairness" or a "level playing field" depicted in liberal ideology as the sanguine results of economic competition) then central banks, and the open market operations through which they implement monetary policy, can also enjoy what Biersteker and I have designated "normative" moral authority.[73] This is particularly so in societies in which neoliberal ideas and policy initiatives have been successfully embedded in popular thinking.

Individual central bankers can also build up enormous personal authority through leadership with sanguine outcomes during difficult times, as indicated previously, and even through personal integrity and self-sacrificial behavior. Former Fed Chairman Paul Volcker was particularly admired, even by his many enemies, for his self-denying

---

McCloskey, *The Rhetoric of Economics* (2nd edn) (Madison, WI: University of Wisconsin Press, 1998).

[71] See our taxonomy of forms of "private" authority in Hall and Biersteker, *Emergence of Private Authority*, p. 218. See also Rodney Bruce Hall, "Private Authority: Non-State Actors and Global Governance" *Harvard International Review* (summer 2005): 69.

[72] Rodney Bruce Hall, "Explaining 'Market Authority' and Liberal Stability: Toward a Sociological-Constructivist Synthesis" *Global Society* 21(3) (2007): 319–45.

[73] Hall and Biersteker, *Emergence of Private Authority*, p. 220.

personal habits and the significant personal sacrifices he made in order to serve as Chairman of the Federal Reserve. As Martin Mayer has reported:

Volcker was the first chairman of the Fed for whom the job was a personal sacrifice. His salary as president in New York was almost double what he would be paid in Washington...His wife could not move to Washington: for his eight years as chairman, Volcker maintained an apartment in New York and lived all week in a studio on Capitol Hill. He smoked cheap cigars because he couldn't afford good ones. The son of a public servant, he was and is a man of extraordinary probity and dignity, setting high standards for himself and all around him, unimpressed by the rank, title, or income of the people with whom he does business...[74]

Unfortunately Volcker's undisputed personal integrity reputedly could not dissuade Reagan Treasury Secretary James Baker, who had lobbied against reappointing Volcker to a third term as Fed Chairman, from the celebratory exclamation that "[w]e got the son of a bitch"[75] upon learning that Volcker had decided not to seek reappointment. With little put away in the way of savings at the age of sixty after a life of public service, Paul Volcker had decided he could not financially afford reappointment to another term. Paul Volcker would likely have been surprised to learn that he had been "got." But the authority of the Fed Chairman had discommoded more than one Treasury Secretary loyal to a president who needed monetary accommodation to keep the polls from closing in on his re-election prospects. Presidents could even be found pleading with Fed Chairmen to avoid or at least delay rate rises. Former Fed Chairman William McChesney Martin recounts an instance in an October 1965 meeting with President Lyndon Johnson:

In October, I was hauled over to the White House by Johnson, just when I was ready to go [raise the discount rate]. He said, "You know, Bill, I'm having my gallbladder out. You wouldn't do it [raise interest rates] while I'm having my gallbladder out, would you?" All I could say was, "I've had my gallbladder out. It isn't so bad." But I went home to my wife and I said, "Well, suppose the President is in the hospital and I raise the discount rate and he dies . . ."[76]

[74] Mayer, *The Fed*, p. 192.   [75] Woodward, *Maestro*, p. 24.
[76] Mayer, *The Fed*, p. 176.

The anxious reader will be pleased to learn that Martin delayed the discount rate hike until early December when Johnson was safely back in the White House, minus a gallbladder.

Social actors can also act in social settings from within which they are in authority. Actors who are "in" authority are those "whose authority derives from the institutional roles they occupy."[77] Martin experienced this pleading from a US president precisely because he was "in" authority on the topic of monetary policy, delegated to him and his FOMC colleagues by statute to decide, independent of Johnson administration officials. As officials and institutions "in" authority, central bankers and central banks exercise authority delegated to them by the government. This delegated authority arises from collective assignment of the status functions that I developed as deontologies in chapter 3. Barnett and Finnemore, in application of the concept of "delegated" authority to international organizations, suggest that bureaucratic institutions that enjoy delegated authority are "authoritative because they represent the collective will of their members."[78] International organizations, argue Barnett and Finnemore, must be autonomous at some level in order to fulfill their remits, as states create international organizations to sort out problems. At some level, being autonomous is part of the mandates of international organizations; thus they go about representing themselves as acting on behalf of the principles agreed upon by their members.[79]

The same may surely be said of central banks that have been granted independence of the government. They are contingently autonomous, however, because delegated authority may always be seized back by the state in a crisis.[80] Both international organizations and central banks, then, exercise deontic powers, though in very different domains, and are thus empowered to generate the constitutive rules of institutions. Recall, from my development of John Searle's institutional philosophy in chapter 3, that constitutive rules arise from, and help to create, intersubjectively shared social meanings between agents, and the assignment of status functions is crucial in generating shared social meanings between subjects. Barnett and Finnemore may be seen to

[77] Biersteker and Hall, *Emergence of Private Authority*, p. 215.
[78] Barnett and Finnemore, *Rules for the World*, p. 22.   [79] *Ibid.*, pp. 22–3.
[80] For an excellent discussion of the contingency of delegated private authority, for example, see Louis Pauly, "Capital mobility, state autonomy and political legitimacy" *Journal of International Affairs* 48(2) (1995): 369–88.

effectively argue, though they do so in very different terms, that this power to generate constitutive rules, from deontic powers, is a generic feature of the power and authority of bureaucratic institutions. This authority entails the "ability to transform information into knowledge, that is, to construct information in ways that give it meaning."[81]

Bureaucracies, like international organizations and central banks, employ their deontic powers and delegated authority to create inter-subjectively shared social meanings. "These meanings are socially constructed, and often are constructed by bureaucracies."[82] Their expert knowledge "not only reflects social reality" as defined by them, "but also constructs that reality . . . [from] . . . the ability to use rules and deploy knowledge in order to change incentives and regulate behavior."[83]

Like international organizations and other forms of bureaucracies studied generically by Barnett and Finnemore, central banks employ their deontic powers and delegated and moral authority to

1) classify the [economic] world, creating categories of problems, actors and action; 2) fix meanings in the social world; and 3) articulate and diffuse norms and rules . . . [because] . . . Problems have to be con-structed . . . [they] . . . are not part of objective reality but are subjectively defined and constituted.[84]

These are constitutive effects of bureaucratic authority resulting from the deontic powers that bureaucracies enjoy, their delegated authority arising from the collective assignment of status functions, and their moral authority arising from their expertise and ostensi-ble normative and political neutrality. Bureaucracies constitute the social reality they then regulate. Barnett and Finnemore argue that international organizations, like the United Nations, determine "not only who is in violation of human rights, but what human rights are."[85] Similarly, fully independent central banks determine not only what price of money is consistent with price stability, but what "price stability" is. Central banks face many challenges, however, in gen-erating and communicating intersubjectively shared social meanings that complicate their own decisions and policy-making processes, as well as their transmission of these decisions and policies to the global

---

[81] Barnett and Finnemore, *Rules for the World*, p. 29.   [82] *Ibid.*, p. 30.
[83] *Ibid.*   [84] *Ibid.*, pp. 31–2.   [85] *Ibid.*, p. 7.

financial markets. I shall explore this in detail in chapter 7 when I explore the "transparency" and communications strategies of modern central banks, which when coupled with central bank independence, are designed, I argue, to generate a system of monetary governance in conjunction with markets that generate a new "nominal anchor" for the international monetary system.

Issing claims that trust in independent central banks, though that trust must be earned, is the foundation of a system of monetary governance that, while discretionary rather than formally rule based, might still anchor international monetary system stability. "It is both economically sensible as well as democratically legitimate to delegate such a limited and well-defined task to an independent central bank," he argues. It is legitimate in the case of the ECB because its authority was formally delegated by treaty law, signed and ratified by the governments of the members of the EMU. It is legitimate elsewhere, he would argue, as the authority is delegated to a national central bank by the national government. To Issing's credit – though he would like to see modern central banks earn an authority approaching the "affective" form of authority explicated by Aykens, through a long and patient process of "reputational" authority acquired along the way – he would not concur with Simons's call for a "money religion." This is so in part because Issing recognizes that no *deus ex machina* mechanical rule is available with which to anchor price stability. At least monetary economists have discovered no rule which, unlike the gold standard and monetary targeting, will not prove highly deflationary with severe economic consequences during times of adjustment. And while all Germans may believe in the Bundesbank, Issing suggests soberly that "if a central bank...acquires prestige and standing that transcend the strict confines of its mandate, and becomes an object of faith or mystical devotion, this suggests that it fills a void left elsewhere" in a society.[86]

Credibility, intersubjectivity, and authority

In the monetary realm, as the term is employed in the literature on monetary economics and central banking, authority is dependent ultimately upon the "credibility" that the central bank will act to ensure

---

[86] Issing, *Trust in Central Banks*, p. 37.

price stability – to back up the "promise" that the money it issues constitutes. There are varying definitions of "credibility" in the literature on central banking. Most of them in current use are tied to the institutional independence of the central bank from government pressure on monetary policy.

For economist Benjamin Friedman "a 'credible' central bank is one that is believed to be firmly committed to low inflation."[87] For political scientist Stephen Bell a "credible central bank is one whose policy commitment to low inflation is not doubted and whose track record in dealing with inflation illustrates this."[88] Having a strong, consistent reputation as an inflation hawk appears to have been the test of credibility for former Fed Chairman Alan Greenspan upon hearing the news that his new incoming Vice-Chairman of the Fed, Alan Blinder, had been thought by some to lack it:

"Don't worry," Mullins said, "it's not like he's a communist or anything. It's just in his early publications he's noticeably soft on inflation." He provided chapter and verse . . . Greenspan quipped, "I would have preferred he were a communist."[89]

Deane and Pringle define credibility in negative terms, inasmuch as a central bank "that has a poor track record, and is then given independence, has to convince the markets that it has given up its old inflationary habits."[90] Thus, for economist Charles Freeman central bank credibility is enhanced by explicit mandates.[91] These mandates are best formalized and enshrined in statute or preferably constitutional or treaty law, but can be informal mandates as well. As one example of informal mandates, President Carter tried to "buy" credibility – subsequent to his failure to signal determination to the financial markets to reduce US budget deficits, and reverse the capital flight and dollar depreciation that resulted from this failure – by appointing

---

[87] Benjamin M. Friedman, "The Use and Meaning of Words in Central Banking: Inflation Targeting, Credibility and Transparency" in Paul Mizen (ed.) *Central Banking, Monetary Theory and Practice: Essays in Honour of Charles Goodhart*, Vol. I (Cheltenham, UK Northampton, MA: Edward Elgar, 2003), p. 120.

[88] Bell, "Limits of Rational Choice," p. 487.

[89] Woodward, *Maestro*, p. 127.

[90] Deane and Pringle, *The Central Banks*, p. 22.

[91] Freedman, "Central Bank Independence," p. 103.

Paul Volcker to chair the Fed to "buy back legitimacy."[92] Volcker's subsequent harsh monetarist venture to reverse inflationary expectations was then heralded as "a monetary shot that echoed around the world."[93] Carter indeed purchased Volcker's credibility and authority, but likely did so at the cost of his re-election.

The search for credibility in monetary policy is at the heart of the passion of those who have historically searched for monetary rules to obviate discretion in monetary policy. And it as at the heart of the movements toward central bank independence and transparency strategies. In the present, post-Keynesian era of nearly untrammeled capital mobility, while there are, to be certain, many domestic determinants of central bank independence and numerous variations of monetary institutions,[94] politicians gain a "credibility dividend" with domestic constituencies and global financial market actors by granting independence to central banks.[95] With the growth of financial markets, nations in a globalizing world economy experience ever greater economic interdependence and it would be odd indeed had political and institutional arrangements not experienced some changes to accommodate the increasing power and preferences of financial market actors. The mounting convergence toward independent central banks has arisen precisely to address the preferences of these market actors.[96] Nor should constructivists hesitate to acknowledge central bank independence as, in part, a causal effect of the increasing "structural power" of financial market actors.[97] In this context, as Stephen Bell argues, independent central banks mediate between the state and the structural preferences of actors in the financial markets. But as we shall see in chapter 7, this is only part of the explanation. A more complete explanation of the sources of this emerging institutional isomorphism attends a constructivist explication of the changing social purposes of monetary institutions, and of the crucial role of central bank transparency in communications strategies in augmenting

---

[92] Helleiner, *States and the Reemergence of Global Finance*, pp. 131–3.
[93] *Ibid.*, p. 135.
[94] See the collection of essays in the special issue of *International Organization* on "The Political Economy of Monetary Institutions."
[95] Bell, "Limits of Rational Choice," p. 487.   [96] *Ibid.*, p. 488.
[97] Bell employs the term "structural power" in a quite different context from Barnett and Duvall, in whose lexicon the form of power to which Bell refers would appear as "institutional power."

central bank independence to bring financial market actors into emerging systems of multilevel financial governance.

Social purposes of monetary policy

However, attempts to construct financial credibility via central bank independence and transparency strategies may not simply be rational policy responses to the "rational expectations" of financial market actors, with the causal effects of taming financial market volatility and structuring financial market outcomes to favor the governments that implement them. They may also constitute ideological and intersubjective strategies, with cognitive and ideational constitutive effects.

Contrary to orthodox monetary theory, money is not a "neutral veil" in the economy, and monetary policy is not simply the realm of highly competent, politically and economically neutral technocrats. Monetary orders and institutions, and monetary policy, are highly political agencies with significant effects on distributional outcomes. Precisely because economic institutions and systems of governance always privilege some actors and disprivilege others, many of us study political economy rather than a reified "science" of economics. The notion of "credibility" itself may then be politicized.

Some analysts charge that the vast literature on "policy credibility" within the extant literature on central banking and monetary economics is itself an attempt to depoliticize monetary policy.[98] Monetary policy has been subject to changing social purposes over the past century. The literature in monetary economics would have us believe that monetary policy has cleaved to an unvarying social purpose of price stability. However, the social purpose of central banks in the early twentieth century was largely to manage the supply of currency consistent with the requirements of backing up the gold standard. Subsequent to its abandonment due to the horrendous deflationary effects on the economy of the gold standard the social purposes of central banking adjusted with the Keynesian revolution to maximizing economic

---

[98] See e.g. Jane Kelsey, "The Denationalization of Money: Embedded Neo-Liberalism and the Risks of Implosion" *Social and Legal Studies* 12(2) (2003): 155–76 and Ilene Grabel, "Ideology, Power, and the Rise of Independent Monetary Institutions in Emerging Economies" in Jonathan Kirshner (ed.) *Monetary Orders: Ambiguous Economics, Ubiquitous Politics* (Ithaca, NY and London: Cornell University Press, 2003), pp. 25–54.

output. The central bank became the (inflationary) engine of finance of the welfare state in the developed world, and of post-colonial development in the developing world. Now, in reaction against the inflationary effects of these experiments, and what monetary economists now call the Great Inflation of the fourth quintile of the twentieth century, the social purposes of central banking in the fifth quintile, and the early twenty-first century, has been given over to price stability.[99]

The social purpose of central banking, in the era of capital mobility and the burgeoning power of transnational financial market actors, according to critical analysts, is to "assure investors that governments will not bend to popular pressures to abandon the 'right policies.'"[100] The preferences and the social purposes of powerful social actors inform the construction and stability of institutions and systems of governance. John Ruggie reminded us of this over two decades ago when he pointed out that the Bretton Woods institutions did not arise merely, as structural realist, hegemonic stability theories of international relations would suggest, to reflect the power capacities of the states that engaged in the construction of this regime. The Bretton Woods framework certainly reflected the liberal preferences of the United States and the United Kingdom. But more importantly, the regime's coherence and stability reflected a fusion of power with social purpose thought to be legitimate by a preponderance of powerful actors.[101] To meet the preferences of financial market actors, and put in place strategies for "importing" credibility as we have defined it earlier in this section, various countries have constructed rule-based systems, such as "dollarization" and currency substitution, currency boards as well as adoption of the operating systems of Western central banks, and even ascriptions to IMF orthodox stabilization and structural adjustment programs, to constrain central bank operations in the developing world.[102] A grant of statutory independence to the central bank, preferably constitutionally enshrined, is increasingly the developing world's bid to purchase "credibility" as conventionally defined, ultimately, by financial market actors. And "credibility" is defined by financial market actors precisely

---

[99] See e.g. Deane and Pringle, *The Central Banks*, p. 318.
[100] Grabel, "Ideology, Power," p. 34.
[101] John Gerard Ruggie, "International Regimes, Transactions and Change: Embedded Liberalism in the Postwar Economic Order" *International Organization* 36(2) (1982): 378–415.
[102] Grabel, "Ideology, Power," p. 32.

because these private actors have been granted deontic power to adjudicate credibility in the emerging multilevel system of governance.

Monetarism, another rule-based system whose parameters we have previously explored, has largely been removed from the "play books" of central banks due to the realization that central banks have limited capacity, in practice, to distinguish money from credit. As Ingham puts it "the practical consequences of the . . . untenable distinction between money and credit became more apparent, but not before myriad forms of credit – money supply had given rise to new measures of the money supply. M_2 led to M_3 and so on to M_{17}."[103]

Both the monetarist and central bank independence doctrines seek a commitment mechanism to provide a "nominal anchor" to generate a monetary system characterized by price stability. Monetarism, however, arose from orthodox monetary theory – particularly the "quantity" theory of money that I have developed in chapter 2 – while the "time inconsistency" paradigm that informs the literature on central bank independence is a product of the "rational expectations" revolution in neoclassical economics. The rational expectations hypothesis essentially suggests that "[p]eople's economic behavior . . . [is] . . . shaped by their [rational] expectations of the future, rather than past experience."[104] Rational expectations theory is a "micro-foundational" account of economic behavior that assumes that "causal accounts of the behavior of aggregates – for example income and investment – must be grounded in convincing causal accounts of the behavior of individuals."[105] The assumptions that underpin the rational expectations hypothesis as applied to monetary economics are essentially that:

If governments can create a credible commitment to low and stable inflation, then rational agents will not be tempted to engage in a self-defeating round of wage increases . . . The forging of "rational expectations" is seen to be the responsibility of governments whose fiscal policies are the major determinants of the money supply, and therefore, inflation. To this limited extent, the rational expectations approach to money is consistent with orthodox

---

[103] Ingham, *Nature of Money*, p. 30.
[104] Kelsey, "Denationalization of Money," p. 158.
[105] Mark Blyth, *Great Transformations: Economic Ideas and Institutional Change in the Twentieth Century* (Cambridge: Cambridge University Press, 2002), p. 142.

ideas that the quantity of money affects prices and that the money supply is exogenously determined.[106]

Thus the time inconsistency paradigm arises from the rational expectations hypothesis rather than orthodox neoclassical monetary theory, while at the same time remaining a product of neoclassical theory as it manifests itself today in the rational expectations hypothesis.

Critical theorists argue that a significant amount of ideological content, replete with normative claims, may be found in the scientific claims and pretensions of this rational expectations revolution. It tends, according to some analysts, to reify monetary theory to the status of an "'objective science' ... [while the] ... discourse of 'rational expectations', 'sound monetary policy', 'fiscal discipline', and 'economic fundamentals' ... [is] ... 'imbued with neutrality and virtue.'"[107] Critics argue that the tendency of the discursive terms of neoclassical debates over monetary policy, particularly those informed from a "rational expectations" perspective, is to "eliminate politics and power from view."[108] Ilene Grabel is quick to suggest that to argue that there are ideological aspects to neoclassical rational expectations theory is not the same as arguing that the theory can be reduced to pure ideology. It is, however, she argues, certainly self-insulating at a minimum, because, according to neoclassical theory and the rational expectations hypothesis, policies based on them "are rational, after all, so they would not possibly choose the wrong theory [*sic*]. How elegant, wonderfully convenient, and irreducibly ideological!"[109]

Perhaps. We might say the rational expectations literature in monetary economics is at a minimum rather teleological, self-referential, and self-insulating. Having set up a world in which neoclassical rational expectations theory will yield the promised outcomes:

policy failure is explained by the presence of all manner of distortions that characterize the economy, by political uncertainty, by the public lack of confidence in the longevity of technocrats, by the failure to guarantee operational ... independence of policymaking institutions, and so on. Credibility theory therefore precludes any substantive empirical refutation of the case for institutional independence ... [in order to] preserve the theoretical case for independence despite the empirical record ... advocates of CBI [central

---

[106] Ingham, *Nature of Money*, p. 31.
[107] Kelsey, "Denationalization of Money," p. 160.
[108] Grabel, "Ideology, Power," 36.   [109] *Ibid.*

bank independence] can always invoke the gap between legal and operational independence.[110]

Price stability is privileged (by assumption) over all other social or economic outcomes in the literature informed by the rational expectations hypothesis, and is consistently and self-consciously treated as a public good. The transmission of authority by governments to an insulated technocracy is axiomatically treated as a noble act of responsibility on behalf of governments as a contribution toward that public good. And thus "[h]aving transferred public authority to the guardians of the common good, governments could disclaim responsibility . . ."[111] The domestic benefit of disclaiming responsibility for unpopular monetary decisions is tangible enough in political terms. And it is tangible enough to lend credence to Grabel's claim that "credibility plays an important role in neoclassical theory" as it dispenses with the distributive effects of policies derived from its strictures.[112] Significantly, in constructivist and institutional terms, to the extent that central bank independence arising from rational expectations theory has become the only language in which central bankers and monetary economists may "credibly" speak, the theory itself has become a social convention.

Intersubjective expectations vs. rational expectations

There is an extremely important point to be drawn out of this discussion for the institutional and constructivist analysis of applications of rational expectations theory in economic and monetary affairs. Put most simply, it is that intersubjective expectations rather than rational expectations *per se* generate stable, predictable, and cooperative outcomes between market actors and those who seek to affect market outcomes.

As Mark Blyth has already pointed out, Keynes understood, and some (particularly theorists of rational expectations) have chosen to forget, market actors are non-rational and myopic as often as they are rational and calculating. They look to one another for signals to inform their own market transactions.[113] Markets react adversely

---

[110] *Ibid.*, pp. 39–40.   [111] Kelsey, "Denationalization of Money," p. 160.
[112] Grabel, "Ideology, Power," p. 39.
[113] Mark Blyth, "The Political Power of Financial Ideas: Transparency, Risk, and Distribution in Global Finance" in Jonathan Kirshner (ed.) *Monetary Orders:*

against information and signals (such as signals from the central bank)
if the information or signals are contrary to the conventional expectations (not the rational expectations) of market actors. In this context:

> conventions are intersubjective understandings shared by market actors that
> specify how markets are supposed to behave...they are sociological con-
> structs...Market behavior therefore rests on the coordination of agents,
> expectations through the maintenance of conventions. So long as intersub-
> jectively held conventions regarding the economy are adhered to, then the
> economy will perform within the parameters of the expected "conventional
> judgment". In sum, there is no truth about markets "out there" apart from
> the prevailing wisdom markets have about themselves.[114]

Thus not only are the expectations that coordinate market behavior based upon intersubjectively shared social understandings, rather
than "rational" expectations, these intersubjective expectations have
constitutive effects, per Alexander Wendt's lexicon.[115] Wendt distinguishes constitutive from causal effects and argues that "[i]deas or
social structure have constitutive effects when they create phenomena –
properties, powers, dispositions, meaning, etc. – that are conceptually or logically dependent on those ideas or structures that exist
only 'in virtue of' them." Because market actors so often act on
the basis of the "truth" of their intersubjective understandings and
expectations, what the markets believe to be the case on the basis
of these expectations is indeed the case. Market stability (read here
as market "reality") then relies upon intersubjectively held conventions, and "change occurs when expectations diverge and conventions
falter."[116]

We see countless examples of the reliance on intersubjectively shared
cognitive conventions in the literature across topical areas of economics to explain how the behavior of market participants diverges
(and it diverges frequently) from the behavior predicted by rational
expectations theory. A decade ago, for example, in an early contribution to a now burgeoning literature on investor psychology, Yale
economist Robert Shiller, however unconsciously, invoked intersubjectively shared cognitive conventions to explain speculative booms
(or "manias") and crashes in quite similar terms:

Ambiguous Economics, Ubiquitous Politics (Ithaca, NY and London: Cornell
University Press, 2003), p. 257.
[114] *Ibid.*   [115] Wendt, *Social Theory*, p. 88.   [116] *Ibid.*

Now it should be recognized that if market participants think that investor psychology is the cause of stock market movements, then that is the view that informs their actions, and then, indeed, market psychology *is* the cause of stock price movements.[117]

What the markets believe has a causal effect on market behavior. And what the markets believe can be quite unrelated to their analysis of the "fundamentals" of the "real economy." Markets participants rely on "confidence" in intersubjectively shared conventional understandings that the present is understood and the future may be predicted. As economist Charles Kindleberger has suggested, "a change in expectations from a state of confidence to one lacking confidence in the future is central."[118] This is how "manias" or "booms" or "asset bubbles" so quickly become "panics," "crashes," or "busts." A rising tide of wholly irrational expectations about future rewards can carry along investors, many of whom look to one another's behavior for signals rather than performing fundamental cost/benefit or risk/reward analyses of their own to guide their investment decisions. When does a mania become a panic and a crash? Kindleberger answers simply, "[s]omeone sells."[119] No great amount of high-powered, rational, technical, or quantitative analysis has been conducted by any market actor to reverse market fortunes:

> *causa proxima* is some incident that snaps the confidence of the system, makes people think of the dangers of failure, and leads them to move . . . back into cash. In itself, *causa proxima* may be trivial: a bankruptcy, a suicide, a flight, a revelation, a refusal of credit to some borrower, some change of view that leads a significant actor to unload. Prices fall. *Expectations* are reversed.[120]

Changing expectations generate major market reversals. Had the earlier expectations that generated the mania or bubble been based upon "rational expectations" no "market correction" would be required or observed. The operative terms that have a "causal" effect in bursting asset bubbles, in Kindleberger's study, are loss of confidence

---

[117] Robert Shiller, "Speculative Booms and Crashes" in Forrest Capie and Geoffrey E. Wood, *Monetary Economics in the 1990s: The Henry Thornton Lectures*, 9–17 (London: Macmillan, 1996), p. 71.
[118] Charles P. Kindleberger, *Manias, Panics, and Crashes: A History of Financial Crises* (New York: Wiley, 2000), p. 91.
[119] *Ibid.*, 101. [120] *Ibid.*, 100. Emphasis added.

and changing expectations. In a more recent work Shiller describes the "amplification mechanisms" that lead to investor overconfidence entirely in terms that point to wholly irrationally expectations of investors, as "naturally occurring Ponzi processes."[121] No "rational expectations" may be found here!

Market intersubjective expectations regarding central bank behavior change in a similar fashion, and with similar results. In this context, Blyth relates an account of how the markets were persuaded that the Volcker monetarist program was the only means by which inflation could be tamed and their conventional expectations of the economy restored:

> financial markets jumped upon the regime of monetary targeting as the sole benchmark of economic performance... As such, the new conventions of monetarism became a self-fulfilling prophecy for both the Fed and the financial markets... According to monetarism, the only way inflation can arise is by the state pumping up the money supply... The very act of accepting monetarism as the true definition of the crisis created a self-fulfilling dynamic... What was important... was that the markets believed monetarism was true, since by coordinating expectations through this new convention, monetarism became self-fulfilling... Monetarism became the governing convention of both the Fed and the markets.[122]

When the markets believed that only monetary targeting would wring out inflation and reduce market volatility, it became a social fact that only monetary targeting would do so. It became an institutional fact with the constitutive effect that market intersubjective expectations, that had never been formally "rational", were changed, and with the causal effect that markets would only respond positively to the application by the Fed of bitter monetarist medicine. In generating economic reality in the markets it mattered not, then as now, what the markets could calculate about the meaning of what was going on in the economy. Nor did it matter what the markets could rationally expect the future to bring on the basis of those calculations. What mattered was what the markets believed was required to restore healthy growth to the economy, and a stable return on investment.

---

[121] Robert Shiller, *Irrational Exuberance* (New York: Broadway Books, 2000), pp. 44–68.
[122] Blyth, *Great Transformations*, pp. 170–1.

And what the markets believe remains significant in explaining the behavior of financial market actors. Layna Mosely reports that despite the fact that the robustness of the link between central bank independence and lower inflation rates has not been well established, and "given market participants' tendency to accept the conventional central bank-inflation wisdom [she expects] that governments with more independent central banks will pay lower government bond rates, as they will have some success in changing market participants' expectations regarding inflation."[123]

More recently, with the retirement of Alan Greenspan as Chairman of the Federal Reserve, Wall Street and the bond markets clearly did not know what to make of the utterances and behavior of Greenspan's successor, monetary economist Benjamin Bernanke. Thus one read assertions from bond strategists that in his early days at the Fed's helm, they did not understand Benjamin Bernanke's policy approach, in large measure because the approach to monetary policy of Bernanke – an advocate of inflation targeting – was a more data driven, wait and see approach. The financial markets had understood conventionally that the Fed under Greenspan would always approach a rate-tightening cycle in regular, quarter-point (25 basis point) steps and then stop; perhaps tightening one quarter point beyond what the data suggested was necessary to halt inflationary pressures in the economy, before halting rate rises for a prolonged period of time.

This pattern of Greenspan Fed behavior had conventionalized expectations in the bond and equities markets. It permitted market actors to place fairly safe bets that they could call the end of a tightening cycle, and place reasonably safe bets on a bond market rally, as they conventionally expected that a loosening cycle in quarter-point increments would follow a long pause in Fed action at the top of the tightening cycle. These were, then, the intersubjective expectations of market actors regarding Fed behavior toward the all-important cost of money. There was nothing particularly "rational" about expecting a Bernanke Fed to continue this trend, given the high historical dependence of Fed behavior on its chairmen. This expectation was particularly irrational given Bernanke's well-documented proclivity toward inflation targeting operating procedures. Under inflation targeting, market actors

[123] Layna Mosley, *Global Capital and National Governments* (Cambridge: Cambridge University Press, 2003), pp. 205–6.

would need to know what quantitative annualized inflation rate the central bank intended to keep inflation at or below.

Precisely because financial market actors lack the capacity to base their decisions upon "rational expectations" in a highly contingent political and economic world, they base them on intersubjectively shared expectations. When these intersubjectively shared understandings are challenged by disconfirming events, markets panic. They sell off. One reads confirmation of the actual, intersubjective, conventional, "psychological" (according to some literatures) bases of actual market behavior in the banalities of the financial press – such as "the markets hate surprises." The unpredictability of the social and economic worlds are the well-understood reason for market volatility. They are among the principal reasons for the development of "hedging" instruments such as financial derivatives. They are the reasons for constant searches for a "new international financial architecture" to quell the market volatility that is a quintessential artifact of an inability to base investment decisions on "rational expectations" in what former Treasury Secretary Robert Rubin refers to as "an uncertain world."[124]

There exists no "Mr. Market" who always, collectively, gets it right. Theories built upon the rational expectations hypothesis expect institutions such as independent central banks to "coordinate expectations 'as if'" market rationality and infallibility were actually consistent with actual market behavior. This emperor cannot be demonstrated to be fully clothed. There is a system of global financial governance, however, in which the current institutional isomorphisms of central bank independence and increasingly sophisticated transparency strategies, in constant communication with market actors, are allocated the major roles. The following chapter will elaborate these communications strategies, and sketch out this system of global financial governance.

[124] Robert E. Rubin and Jacob Weisberg, *In an Uncertain World: Tough Choices from Wall Street to Washington* (New York: Random House, 2003).

7 | *Transparency and intersubjectivity in central banking*

You mean to tell me that the success of the [economic] program and my reelection hinges on the Federal Reserve and a bunch of [expletive deleted] bond traders?

William Jefferson Clinton

I used to think if there was reincarnation, I wanted to come back as the President or the Pope or a 400 baseball hitter. But now I want to come back as the bond market. You can intimidate everyone.

James Carville

"The word honor in the mouth of Daniel Webster," said Senator John Randolph of Virginia (on the Senate floor, too) "is like the word love in the mouth of a whore." I have some of that feeling when I hear a central banker recommend "transparency."

Martin Mayer

Banking is a pervasive phenomenon, not something to be dealt with merely by legislation directed at what we call banks. The experience with the control of note issue is likely to be repeated in the future; many expedients for controlling similar practices may prove ineffective and disappointing because of the reappearance of prohibited practices in new and unprohibited forms. It seems impossible to predict what forms the evasion might take or to see how particular prohibitions might be designed in order that they might be more than nominally effective.

Henry C. Simons

Transparency in systems of monetary governance

Having developed the relationship between trust and authority as pertains to central banking, I now turn to the relationships between trust and authority that are applied to the other major actors engaged in

189

the specification of money's "functions" in the domestic and global economies. In this concluding chapter I will develop the monetary systems of governance that relationships of trust between these market actors and central banks together constitute.

Recall that we have developed the deontic powers of central banks, and the authority relations constituted by those deontic powers. We have also noted that relations of trust between central banks and market actors are critical for establishing the central banks as authorities. This is so even as collective assignment of status functions and delegation of those functions by governments are sufficient to establish independent central banks in authority. In a globalizing economy under conditions of capital mobility, domestic deontologies resulting from the assignment of status functions to institutions like central banks by domestic collectivities are necessary but not sufficient conditions to establish trust in the integrity of a currency as a stable store of value, medium of exchange, or unit of account. Adjudication of the credibility of money in these contexts is a process that results from additional deontologies.

Decision-making authority to generate these social facts – as the judgments of market actors regarding the creditworthiness of borrowers clearly constitute – has been delegated in no small measure to actors in the bond markets, and in the FOREX markets. Assessments of "creditworthiness" are social and institutional facts. The consequence for financial governance is that decision-making authority to determine access to credit, and the price that a country will pay to borrow internationally to finance its governmental operations, is delegated to the international disintermediated bond markets. Actors in these markets, in this system of governance, enjoy deontic power to adjudicate the credibility of the monetary and fiscal policy of every government on the planet with a convertible, or tradable, currency whose value is not set entirely by official administrative controls. But these critical deontologies are clearly passed over in the governance literature in international relations, as are the private deontologies that delegate decision-making authority, and thereby governance functions, to these markets. Examples follow.

While domestic interest rates, and thus the cost as well as the supply of money, is controlled by a public deontology of central bank decisions, central bank operating system rules can, as we saw in chapter 5, allocate authority and governance functions to market actors.

Floating exchange-rate regimes assign to the FOREX markets the power of exchange-rate determination. However, the cost and price, as well as the supply (should bond investors choose to limit it) of funds to finance government operations, and of funds for firms to finance investment and production, is collectively assigned to actors in the bond markets.

Disintermediation and governance

This assignment of these deontic powers to the bond markets is in no small measure a result of the accelerating process of disintermediation. In conventional lending, banks intermediate between lenders (depositors) and borrowers and profit from the differential the bank charges its creditors (the depositors) and debtors (its borrowers) less operating costs. The securitization of debt through bond issuance cuts bank intermediation out of the process of credit creation and extension; thus securitized debt bond issuance generates disintermediated debt instruments. This process of disintermediation has a huge impact on the capital formation process, and places decision-making authority for this process firmly in the hands of private, individual, and institutional bond investors. Timothy Sinclair describes the impact of these arrangements on the costs and conditions of capital formation for firms, municipalities, and nations, as a "change in the location of judgments about who gets credit,"[1] and on what terms they receive it, if at all.

Transparency and intersubjectivity

Having consigned deontic power to adjudicate the credibility of fiscal and monetary policy to market actors, central bankers are anxious to "signal" their credibility (and thus national creditworthiness, as Sylvia Maxfield suggests) to those markets. Central banks have deontic power to create or destroy "high powered money" primarily through their control of the supply and price of credit to the commercial banking system, at extremely short-term rates. But due to disintermediation, the supply and cost of long-term credit is increasingly determined by

[1] Sinclair, *New Masters of Capital*, p. 3.

actors in the bond markets, and less frequently by commercial banks, whose lending practices monetary policy can immediately impact.

Thus in order to drive the supply and costs of longer-term credit (recall that credit is money too) central banks are anxious to communicate the current and future directions of their monetary policy to actors in the bond markets, as well as to the investment community at large. Bond market actors can be more easily employed as a vehicle by which the direction of monetary policy may be transmitted to the economy when the direction of monetary policy is "transparent" to the markets. If the markets are unambiguously appraised of what to expect, the central bank may thus recruit the bond markets as an ally in transmitting its monetary policy decisions to the economy.[2] It will attempt to employ the bond markets as a monetary policy force-multiplier. By such devices market actors are recruited as a mechanism of financial governance in the service of central bank policy, rather than an antagonistic mechanism of purely private governance.

The meaning of "transparency" in the contemporary literature on monetary economics and central banking arises, as did the emphasis on "credibility," from the rational-expectations theoretic literature on the time inconsistency problem.[3] Economist Benjamin Friedman takes a candid swipe at the ostensible "scientific neutrality" of the rhetoric of economics[4] in this context by reminding us that the "meaning attached to ordinary words in any specific context often depends on the prior evaluation of how that word has been used in that context."[5] Friedman assures us that the current emphasis on central bank credibility and transparency "did not emerge in a vacuum."[6] The common usage of central bank "credibility," as we have seen in the previous chapter, arises in the context of advocacy of central bank independence in the

---

[2] Lars E. O. Svensson, "Inflation Targeting as a Monetary Policy Rule" *Journal of Monetary Economics* 43 (1999): 609–11.

[3] See e.g. Petra M. Geraats, "Central Bank Transparency" *The Economic Journal* 112 (November 2002): F532-F565; Georgio Chartareas, David Stasavage, and Gabriel Sterne, *Does it Pay to be Transparent? International Evidence From Central Bank Forecasts* Working Paper: Bank of England, 2001; Frederic S. Mishkin, *Inflation Targeting in Emerging Market Countries,* NBER Working Paper 7618, 2000; A. Sibert, "Monetary Policy Committees: Individual and Collective Reputation" *Review of Economic Studies* 70 (July 2003): 649–65; Robert J. Barro, "Reputation in a Model of Monetary Policy with Incomplete Information" *Journal of Monetary Economics* 17(1) (1986): 3–20.

[4] McClosky, *Rhetoric of Economics.*

[5] Friedman, "Use and Meaning of Words," p. 118.   [6] *Ibid.,* p. 119.

literature on monetary economics and on central banking. Similarly the common usage of central bank "transparency" is tied to the advocacy of inflation targeting regimes. Central bank transparency is advocated to enhance credibility.[7] The forms of transparency that are advocated regard transparency about central bank goals, methods, and decision-making procedures.[8]

The meaning of "transparency" is socially constructed in this literature, and intersubjectively shared between monetary economists and central bankers. As we shall see, central banks which have embraced transparency as a monetary policy force-multiplier engage in elaborate communications strategies to transmit and teach the social meanings of their goals, methods, and decision-making procedures so that these meanings may be intersubjectively shared with market actors. Thus, in the language of theories of international regimes in the literature on international relations theory, central banks have an "epistemic function"[9] to "teach" market actors how to interpret their goals, methods, and decision-making procedures. In this context, Alan Blinder and collaborators argue that a central bank "is transparent when it provides at all times sufficient information to the public to understand the policy regime, to check whether the bank's actions match the regime and to pass judgment on its performance."[10] Saying that the "public" must have enough information to pass judgment on the central bank's performance is another way of saying that transparency cooperates with market actors' deontic power to adjudicate the credibility of the central bank's monetary policy and the money it issues.

Transparency of central bank goals, methods of inflation forecasting, and decision-making procedures in the formulation of monetary policy are practiced by increasing numbers of central bankers – especially those that have acquired inflation targeting regimes. They have chosen "transparency" strategies because of another failure of rational expectations theory. This is the failure of the "expectations

---

[7] See e.g. J. Faust and L. E. Svensson, "Transparency and Credibility: Monetary Policy with Unobservable Goals" *International Economic Review* 42(2) (2001): 369–97.

[8] Alan S. Blinder, *The Quiet Revolution: Central Banking Goes Modern* (New Haven, CT: Yale University Press, 2004), p. 14.

[9] See e.g. Peter M. Haas (ed.) *Knowledge, Power, and International Policy Coordination*. Special issue of *International Organization* 46(1) (1992).

[10] Blinder *et al.*, *How Do Central Banks Talk?*, p. 10.

theory of the term structure"[11] of interest rates. According to this theory investors are supposed to react rationally to demand a risk premium "to compensate them for the higher risk or lower liquidity of longer-dated instruments . . . [and these rates] . . . should depend mainly on [rational] expectations of future central bank policy."[12] These "rational" expectations by investors are then the major vehicle of transmission of monetary policy – which immediately impacts only a short-term rate structure – to the long-term end of the yield curve. Bond investors are theoretically supposed to be able to compute "implied forward rates" from algebraic equations derived from the rational expectations theory of the term (maturity) structure. But Princeton monetary economist and former central banker Alan Blinder points out that:

> implied interest rate forecasts (expectations) that can be deduced from the yield curve bear little resemblance to what future interest rates actually turn out to be . . . Suffice it to say that the *abject empirical failure* of the expectations theory of the term structure of interest rates is a *well-established fact*.[13]

No shrinking violet in his criticism of rational expectations theory, Blinder argues forcefully that it fails over both moderate and longer time horizons and the theory constitutes "a mutually agreed self-delusion" between central bankers and market actors to which each cleave "as an act of desperation."[14] In speculating as to what then does determine long-term rates in the bond market, Blinder offers two speculative suggestions. The first, plausible enough, is that due to the depth and breadth of the secondary markets for securitized debt instruments, bond investors who make the initial purchase of a bond are simply treating long-term securities as short-term investments. In this view investors are expecting to hold long-term maturity bonds for a short time and then sell them on the secondary market, thereby transferring the risk of holding a long-term bond at a short-term rate to another investor.

His second speculative suggestion, more daring – and of more salient theoretical interest to our analysis – is that market actors simply do not make investment decisions on the basis of rational expectations.[15] Blinder suggests that the empirical data better fit an "adaptive expectations" model and that "actual human behavior put[s] far too much

[11] Blinder, *The Quiet Revolution*, p. 11   [12] *Ibid.*, p. 76.
[13] *Ibid.*, p. 77. Emphasis added.   [14] *Ibid.*, p. 80.   [15] *Ibid.*, p. 81.

weight on current market conditions" as a guide to future conditions.[16] This is another way of saying that "rational expectations" of the future based on extrapolation of past and current action fail, and that market actors actually "adapt" to better information that serves as a basis for "intersubjective expectations" to inform investment decisions. As central banks have deontic power to determine the size of the monetary base, and its liquid (short-term) price, markets actors naturally look to central banks first for such information. Thus Blinder and his collaborators in evaluating central bank communications strategies feel that it is absurd for central banks to ever become captured by the existing intersubjective expectations of markets. Because "[f]or bond markets, central banks hold the key to current and future interest rates. This gives them the ability to strongly influence the [bond, and FOREX and equity] markets, therefore, they need not be concerned to go against them."[17] This observation is surely at the heart of the oft-heard market wisdom "don't fight the Fed."

The short-term money markets are driven by central banks rather than the converse. All of Alan Greenspan's public and private musings over the shape of the bond yield curve essentially amounted to his puzzling over how Fed policy could impact or alter the private deontology assigned to the bond markets, and why the flat yield curve he bemoaned indicated that investors were not demanding the risk premiums that rational expectations theory would predict. Deontic power to adjudicate the credibility of central bank monetary policy, and government fiscal policy, has been, after all, assigned to market actors. The interesting question for constructivist monetary theory is, assigned by whom? Who assigns to markets these status functions, empowering these private deontologies?

The *causa proxima* of this deontology (to the very limited extent that a causal lexicon can be applied to the collective assignment of status functions) is that the central bank does so when it relies upon "open market operations" instead of administrative controls to directly dictate the rate structure on the short-term end of the yield curve. The finance ministries (such as the US Treasury and UK Exchequer) did so when they began offering for public bid longer-term debt securities (ranging out to thirty-year maturities for US Treasury bonds and even 50-year maturities for UK "gilts"). The market participants have

---

[16] *Ibid.*, p. 82.   [17] Blinder *et al.*, *How Do Central Banks Talk?*, p. 16.

compliantly arrogated to themselves some of this deontic power in the process of creating a vibrant market for disintermediated debt. This began when investment banks began underwriting corporate, municipal, and even sovereign debt securities, and offering them for public tender bids. The assignment of status functions that generated these deontologies arose from both public and private collective actors, and the public ratifies them every time it makes an investment in a financial concern that holds such investment vehicles in its portfolio.

Central bank transparency as governance

Thus the communications strategies of central banks and their moves to "transparency" constitute negotiations over governance capacities. To the extent that these governance capacities and the systems of governance that they constitute are contested among public and private deontologies, these are struggles over deontological power – the power to assign status functions and generate deontologies as a basis for authority over, and governance of, international monetary arrangements. Yet many central banks seek to deploy transparency, and inflation targeting regimes employ inflation reports, in order to impact decisions that are made by the bond markets regarding, for example, the risk premium that is appropriate for bond investors to charge in order to be willing to purchase long-term sovereign debt. These risk premiums constitute a metric of the credibility of monetary (and fiscal) policy of the note issuer, in the case of sovereign debt, and the credibility of the business outlook and balance sheet of the note issuer in the case of private (corporate) debt.

When the central bank engages in such transparency and communications strategies, it is not clear that it is necessarily attempting to supplant the deontological agent of adjudication – the private individual or institutional bond investor. This is far from the case. However, the central bank is trying to impact the decision-making process at the location of the deontology. It is trying to alter the decisions of financial market actors by altering their intersubjectively shared expectations of the future direction of rates by intimating the future direction of monetary policy. Of course, government fiscal policy plays a significant role in shaping these expectations as well. In consequence, government fiscal policy is also a target of the central bank's communication strategy in this negotiation over governance capacity. I will explore these strategies below.

For this system of governance to function, the decision-making procedures of the relevant private deontology attend the "expectations" of market participants. However, as we have already observed, the salient expectations of market participants that generate outcomes in the FOREX and the bond markets are often not formally "rational" in the sense that rational choice theoretic approaches assume. This is so precisely because "it is not irrational to trust"[18] an actor who has developed credibility, or a reputation for right action in difficult circumstances, or for whom another actor has developed a sense of "affective trust." Thus central banks wish, speak, and act, above all, to establish and maintain this credibility, to earn continuously this trust. Central banks are also attempting to alter both the rational and intersubjective expectations of the public, and to earn its reputational and affective trust as well. If the central bank can earn this trust from the public the latter will not, for example, collectively demand wage contracts with built in inflation-rider clauses in expectation of future inflationary trends in the economy. The terms of the public's borrowing, however, are generally intermediated by commercial banks, over whose cost of funds central banks have a great deal more control than they do over long-term rates, which are determined by the risk premiums charged in the disintermediated bond market.

Central bankers, in one sense, bow deeply to rational expectations theory. The presumed source and location of decision-making authority – thus of governance capacity at the heart of all these central bank communications strategies, and of the operating systems and their rules devised by central banks – are the expectations of consumers, business enterprises, and financial market participants. Yet in carefully cultivating their reputations and credibility that they will act as they have indicated through their communications strategies with the financial markets and the public, central banks are attempting to construct a system of intersubjectively shared social understandings with these actors, generating a system of intersubjective rather than formally rational expectations. Effectively the "governance negotiation" is played out between central banks, market actors, and the public at the level of ideas. The rules of the operating systems of

[18] Aykens, "(Mis)trusting Authorities," p. 312.

independent central banks, and of government-directed central banks that engage in open market operations, assign authority to markets. Central banks contend ideationally for credibility with domestic publics and global investors regarding what the latter's expectations – both rational and intersubjective – should be.

Once a system of intersubjectively shared social understandings is established between the central bank and the financial markets, financial market actors may consult their acquired knowledge of the system of intersubjectively shared understandings of central bank "signals" in order to make the appropriate market decisions that will earn them profits. In doing so they may send long-term interest rates (in the bond market) and exchange rates (in the FOREX markets) in the direction that the central bank would like to see them go. Thus these transparency policies and communications strategies may, through successful transmission of intersubjectively shared meanings of central bank signals and behavior to market actors, induce informed market actors to become the monetary policy force-multipliers of central banks. As central banks have only very limited and crude tools (deontic power over the level of short-term interest rates) at their disposal to do a very big job, they are anxious to find means to let the bond markets and FOREX markets help them do their work.

In the realm of financial governance, the "negotiation" between central banks and market actors is driven by "credible" (independent and transparent) central banks. One could imagine a script in which the central bank says to private investors in the financial markets, "I'll hand you the authority to adjudicate the credibility, as well as future direction of my monetary policy, but I want you to see it my way. I'll teach you that when I say 'X' it means I'm going to do 'Y,' and I want you to use the understandings I am teaching you about the meaning of my communications and behaviors to meet my goals." To this extent, the communications between central banks and market actors constitute more of a negotiation over monetary and financial governance, and tutorial of what central bank statements and actions mean, than either a "struggle" or "contest" over governance. And we need have no doubt that the international monetary system is managed, in practice, as a system of shared governance between central banks and financial market actors, as well as governments. To a significant extent mismanaged fiscal policy can defeat the monetary policy of the most skillful central banker.

Ratings agencies: deontic power to "Grade" credibility and risk

Bond investors are particularly anxious for access to independent and authoritative judgment of the credibility of monetary and fiscal policy of countries, and particularly of developing countries, about which they know little, irrespective of whether these issue debt in their own currencies or not. Ratings agencies act as "reputational intermediaries" and report on who is violating the prevailing norms of financial and commercial practice.[19] Thus, according to one respected rater, Fitch:

The risk...is that the country may service its debt through excessive monetary creation, effectively eroding the value of its obligations through inflation – when a sovereign nation borrows in a foreign currency there is a more serious risk of outright default since the central bank cannot print the means of servicing its debt. The task of the credit rating agency is to assess the sovereign borrower's ability and willingness to generate the foreign exchange necessary to meet its obligations.[20]

The judgment, or interpretation, of the ratings agency becomes authoritative in spite of the fact that the rating constitutes a judgment rather than the result of a specifically scientific process.[21] Nor do raters appear to claim otherwise. In describing, in quite qualitative and general terms, their risk model, Fitch explains the difficulty of their job, arguing that it is much easier to analyze corporate or banking default risks than sovereign default risks. A small sample size for statistical analysis of sovereign defaults constitutes one difficulty. Nations are very loath to default on their debts for fear of long-term or even permanent foreclosure of access to global capital markets. "So the rating of sovereigns depends more on the art of political economy than on the science of econometrics," admits Fitch.[22]

Statistical studies of the determinants of sovereign credit ratings, however, suggest a short-term logic of market actors. Ratings, which are supposed to take into account "ability and willingness" to pay, or to generate foreign currency to pay, and signs of central bank inflationary finance are clearly scrutinized by ratings agencies according to

[19] Sinclair, *New Masters of Capital*, pp. 51–2.
[20] Fitch, "Sovereign Ratings Methodology"
   (http://rru.worldbank.org/Documents/Toolkits/Highways/pdf/extract/E24.pdf).
[21] Sinclair, *New Masters of Capital*, p. 62.
[22] Fitch, "Sovereign Ratings Methodology."

their own claims. Yet Richard Cantor's and Frank Parker's statistical study found that while ratings were clearly a statistically significant determinant of bond yields (reflecting the risk premiums charged for extending credit to sovereign debt issuers), inflation rates were not. How can this be when they report that inflation rates are statistically significant to within 1 percent in determining sovereign bond ratings in the same study?[23]

One explanation may arise from the fact that this particular study sampled only sovereign debt that was issued in (hard, stable) currencies other than the currency of the debtor nation. In these cases the debtor country had absorbed the foreign exchange risk and pledged to repay in stable money whose short- and medium-term value enjoyed credibility with actors in the bond and FOREX markets. If the debtor subsequently engaged in fiscal or monetary policy practices deemed to be imprudent by market actors, the risk of default might rise, but the resulting market opprobrium and subsequent denial of market access would raise the costs of default to the debtor to levels that would render default less likely. The threat of denial of market access due to default is a heavy inducement for the debtor government to maintain fiscal policies, and the debtor central bank to maintain monetary policies deemed "prudent" in accordance with the intersubjective expectations of global market actors. And given the increased liquidity in the global markets in sovereign debt instruments in recent years by yield-hungry investors in an era of low returns, market actors can always dump the security should the credibility of fiscal or monetary policies of the issuer subsequently decline. Cantor and Packer report in their study that their statistics indicate that generally the market has normally already moved to generate a higher bond yield spread well before the announcement of a rating downgrade, with more impact reported with speculative grade securities than with investment grade securities, and that the markets hit the bonds again subsequent to a downgrade announcement by a ratings agency.[24]

A more recent study by Gregory Sutton at the BIS reinforces the view that bond raters and investors focus on short-term willingness and ability to repay in ratings and investment decisions. In Sutton's

---

[23] Richard Cantor and Frank Packer, "Determinants and Impact of Sovereign Credit Ratings" *FBRNY Economic Policy Review* (October 1996): 43.
[24] *Ibid.*, pp. 45–8.

study the highly statistically significant variables are perceptions of corruption, the time since the last sovereign default, service on public debt against exports, and the maturity structure of international banking claims against the sovereign issuer. Together these four quantitative variables explain 87 percent of the variance in Sutton's study.[25] He concludes that ratings reflect short-term capacity, and to a lesser extent willingness, to pay. But as bonds are bought and sold on the secondary market, an investor can always dump a "loser" which is not actually in default if s/he is willing to take a "haircut" on the original investment, selling the security at a discount to the purchase price prior to maturity, and transferring the risk of default to another investor.

While ratings judgments are necessarily largely qualitative, there is a strong bias within the investment community for hard numbers, and an "intersubjective belief that quantitative data is the only criterion of credit rating."[26] Thus, as we have seen, economists conduct large-N statistical studies to attempt to assess which quantitative indicators of economic performance most strongly correlate with the ratings generated and the yield spread demanded by investors. And as we have also seen, purveyors of such studies are sometimes frustrated when the quantitative correlations they find fail to explain observed variance and outcomes. Yet the ratings generated, however qualitatively or judgmentally, clearly acquire authoritative status among investment professionals and portfolio managers, and are employed as a basis for investment decisions. Announced changes in these ratings move markets, as do even anticipated changes in ratings. How can data-hungry economists and investment professionals – rigorously trained and socialized into an intersubjective understanding that they are to privilege hard quantitative economic data, as a basis for formulating "rational expectations" – instead rely on qualitative judgments alphabetically ranked by external agencies whose methodologies are largely opaque?

Timothy Sinclair reminds us that once generated, these ratings become social, institutional facts. Recall our discussion of the distinction between brute and observational facts and social facts in chapter 3 in this context:

[25] Gregory D. Sutton, *Potentially Endogenous Borrowing and Developing Country Sovereign Credit Ratings* Occasional Paper no. 5 (Basle: Bank for International Settlements, 2005), p. ix.

[26] Sinclair, *New Masters of Capital*, p. 35.

the significance of rating is not to be estimated like a mountain or national population, as a "brute" fact that is true (or not) irrespective of shared beliefs about its existence, nor do the "subjective" facts of individual perception determine the meaning of rating . . . What is central to the status and consequentiality of rating agencies is what people believe about them and act on collectively, even if those beliefs are demonstrably false.[27]

Thus we are back to taking seriously "what the markets believe" and to analysis of "intersubjective" expectations rather than "rational" expectations among market actors to explain their observed behavior. The deontic powers assigned to ratings agencies to "grade" the creditworthiness of sovereign borrowers endows them with a constitutive capacity. Just as international organizations are empowered to constitute the social reality they consequently regulate, ratings agencies go about "creating an interpretation of the world."[28] The social and institutional facts they generate become accepted as knowledge and this "knowledge comes to be 'objectified' and acquires 'authority' in the process of its creation."[29] Sinclair argues that fiscal and financial "crises" among borrowers they have previously rated are similarly social facts[30] generated by ratings agencies, leading to "downgrades" in the ratings of borrowers, with very serious impact on the costs and availability of credit for these borrowers. Because these social facts are understood and acted upon by market actors as "brute" or "observational" facts, authoritatively issued by a neutral expert,[31] ratings agencies have deontic power with constitutive effect to help constitute the identities of borrowers and market agents.[32] Thus ratings agencies constitute an enormously important agency of transnational private authority in the system of global financial governance emerging in the present era of "capital" mobility, in which capital simultaneously issues forth as fiat money.

The case for central bank transparency

Investors act not only on ratings, but on their own intersubjective expectations of market movements and returns on capital investments. Naturally they look to the source of high powered money, central bank money, which provides the monetary base of the domestic economy,

---

[27] *Ibid.*, p. 54.   [28] *Ibid.*, p. 61.   [29] *Ibid.*, pp. 35–40.   [30] *Ibid.*, p. 88.
[31] *Ibid.*, p. 84.   [32] *Ibid.*, p. 69.

for signals regarding the future supply and cost of money. Alan Blinder and his collaborators argue that the "link is market expectations working through a term structure of rates. The link from short rates to long rates acts like a dog's leash, transmitting the owner's (the central bank's) command to the dog (the economy)."[33] They argue that in the period 1996 to 1999 the bond markets began to anticipate the Fed's actions, and while the Fed left rates comparatively flat the bond market moved interest-rate premiums on sovereign, corporate, and municipal debt rates up somewhat when it had inflation concerns and down somewhat when it did not, so that "It was said at the time that the bond market was 'doing the Fed's work for it' – that is, acting as a macroeconomic stabilizer."[34]

While markets have been delegated authority to adjudicate the credibility of monetary and fiscal policy, markets look to central banks for a basis for the intersubjective expectations that guide their investment decisions. Governments which have delegated deontic power and authority for monetary policy to central banks are relatively happy with this outcome as it absolves them of responsibility for bouts of monetary tightening that are unpopular both with financial market actors, and with the public at large. Jane Kelsey argues that:

> markets conferred political authority on the central bankers, and policy makers conferred authority on the financial markets . . . Having transferred public authority to the guardians of the common good, governments could disclaim responsibility . . .[35]

However, Kelsey does not get the delegation of deontic powers quite right. Authority for independent monetary policy is delegated to central banks by governments, not market actors. Deontic power to adjudicate the credibility of monetary policy is delegated to markets by central banks and private investors, who rely upon the markets to assess risks and the price of long-term credit through a disintermediated, open market procedure. But the trappings of power, without the responsibilities and burdens of exercising the genuine article, accrue to governments which step aside from the process (and thus the consequences) of monetary policy formation. Governments increasingly appear to regard this arrangement as rather a good bargain.

---

[33] Blinder, *How Do Central Banks Talk?*, p. 9.   [34] *Ibid.*
[35] Kelsey, "Denationalization of Money," p. 160.

If central banks are adequately independent and adequately credible with the public and with financial market actors, then their monetary policy will be credible, and market actors will expect that government fiscal policy will be constrained and ultimately be driven back to fiscal equilibrium by independent monetary policy. In such an arrangement, the means by which central banks maintain credibility is "transparency."[36] Jacqueline Best suggests that transparency is a neoliberal strategy for managing "ambiguity." However, she argues, this strategy provides purely technical solutions and generates a normative claim[37] that all players will play their cards correctly for optimal economic outcomes provided only that they can see the cards. There is much to recommend this observation. An IMF dominated by neoclassically trained economists has always relied upon data-driven macroeconomic models to generate its policy prescriptions and advice. This insistence that inadequate "transparency" of developing country macroeconomic performance is the cure for its policy errors during the Asian financial crisis currently drives the IMF's passion for signing up all of its subscribers to provide economic data formatted according to its special data dissemination standards.[38]

However, while ostensibly attempting to impact rational expectations of market actors, central bank transparency strategies in general, and inflation targeting regimes in particular, clearly aim to establish intersubjective expectations among market actors to drive market decisions regarding the long-term cost of credit that are consistent with central bank preferences and the direction of their monetary policy. Consistent with Best's description, transparency policies of central banks are strategies for limiting ambiguity, but they are more than this. Economist Benjamin Friedman suggests that:

Inflation targeting is a way of manipulating private sector decision makers' expectation about future inflation. It removes from explicit discussion whatever objectives the central bank may hold for output, employment, or other real outcomes over the long run ... It achieves "credibility" in the specific sense of making a commitment to low inflation believable by keeping out of the discussion those considerations that would reveal that

---

[36] Deane and Pringle, *The Central Banks*, p. 125.
[37] Jacqueline Best, *The Limits of Transparency: Ambiguity and the History of International Finance* (Ithaca, NY: Cornell University Press, 2005), p. 12.
[38] Best, "Bringing Power Back In."

commitment to be qualified and hence not completely credible in the usual sense.[39]

Friedman is asserting that independent central banks, and especially those with inflation targeting regimes, create a commitment device to buy credibility for monetary policy. Inflation targeting regimes commit to act to avoid permitting price inflation to climb above a specified, pre-announced inflation rate. Whether or not central banks employ an inflation target, or target money supply, borrowed reserves, non-borrowed reserves, or some other identifiable or quantifiable metric, they assert the largely fictional notion that their preferences are entirely indifferent to real economic outcomes. They manipulate the expectations of the public and market actors through a fiction that submerges the more complex preferences of central banks.

Thus central bank transparency, while ostensibly oriented toward removing ambiguity, can be an example of what Best calls "creative ambiguity"[40] that permits resolution of issues that more rigid, transparent rules could not accommodate. Central bank transparency is transparent "in that it holds a part of what the central bank is doing before a clear glass while obscuring other parts behind a logical partition … 'Transparency' is one dimensional. It is so in order to achieve credibility."[41]

Otmar Issing argues that transparency in monetary policy-making generates both democratic accountability and more credible and effective monetary policy.[42] The fact that the "clear and limited mandate" of the ECB, for example, is enshrined in the Treaty law of the European Union provides the democratic accountability required for the ECB to operate as an independent central bank.[43] The European polity has thus delegated authority for a European monetary policy to a supranational European institution, the ECB. Similarly Alan Blinder and his collaborators argue that transparency

is based on both policy effectiveness and democratic accountability. Monetary policy is more effective when the central bank is better able to *condition*

---

[39] B. Friedman, "Use and Meaning of Words," p. 120.
[40] Best, *The Limits of Transparency*, p. 25.
[41] B. Friedman, "Use and Meaning of Words," p. 121.
[42] Issing, Otmar, *The Euro Area and the Single Monetary Policy* Osterreichische Nationalbank, Working Paper 44 (2001).
[43] Issing, *Faith in Central Banks*, p. 13.

the market expectations that are critical to the transmission of monetary policy ... The essential message that any central bank must convey to the public is its policy regime, what it is trying to achieve, and how it goes about doing so, and its probable reactions to likely contingencies.[44]

Significant empirical evidence has been generated to establish the link between central bank transparency and central bank credibility, and the importance of transparency-related factors in establishing central bank credibility. Some of this survey research is summarized by Jakob de Haan and his colleagues in a recent work on the credibility and transparency of the ECB in an account that features extensive, large-*N* survey studies by Fry and collaborators, by Alan Blinder, and some of their own survey research into these questions.[45] They report that in a comprehensive survey of central bankers worldwide by Fry and collaborators[46] 74 percent of respondents considered transparency to be a very important element of their monetary policy.[47] In Blinder's 2000 survey of 127 central bankers[48] (with a 66 percent response rate) the respondents on average ranked the importance of transparency for central bank credibility at 4.13 on a scale of 1 to 5 (5 is highest), with a standard deviation of 0.71. The importance of central bank independence for credibility was only slightly higher with an average response of 4.51 with a standard deviation of 0.63. Reputational considerations "a history of fighting inflation" weighed in at 4.15 with a standard deviation of 0.67. Notably, by contrast, central bankers appear to have abandoned Henry Simons's passion for rule-based systems. The importance of being constrained by a rule (such as a metallic standard or monetarism, or even a currency board in the era of fiat money) weighed in at an average of only 2.89 with a larger standard deviation of 1.01.[49]

---

[44] Blinder *et al.*, *How Do Central Banks Talk?*, p. xix. Emphasis added.

[45] Jakob de Haan, Sylvester E. W. Eijffinger, and Sandra Waller, *The European Central Bank: Credibility, Transparency, and Centralization* (Cambridge, MA and London: MIT Press, 2005).

[46] M. Fry, D. Julius, L. Mahadeva, S. Roger, and G. Sterne, "Key Issues in the Choice of Monetary Policy Framework" in L. Mahadeva and G. Sterne (eds.) *Monetary Policy Frameworks in a Global Context* (London: Routledge, 2000).

[47] De Haan *et al.*, *The European Central Bank*, p. 114.

[48] Alan S. Blinder, "Central Bank Credibility: Why Do We Care? How Do We Build It?" *American Economic Review* 90(5) (2000): 1421–31.

[49] Blinder's results are summarized in De Haan *et al.*, *The European Central Bank*, table 4.7, p. 115.

That is what central bankers believe. And when we recall the importance of intersubjective expectations in generating economic as well as social outcomes, we want to pay close attention to what central bankers believe, just as we have earlier paid close attention to the intersubjective expectations of market actors ("what the markets believe") in explaining their behavior. What do private sector economists believe about central bank transparency and credibility?

De Haan and his collaborators surveyed not only central bankers but private sector economists and repeated Blinder's survey with a somewhat different ranking scheme in May 2000, and again in October 2001. The May 2000 survey yielded responses from over 200 individuals (a response rate of 45 percent for this survey). Respondents were asked to rank determinants of central bank credibility from 1 to 7, with 1 being the highest. The response of private sector economists to central bank independence as a determinant of central bank credibility was 1.80 on average with a standard deviation of 1.32. The importance of transparency for credibility on average was 3.13 with a standard deviation of 1.46. Reputational considerations of a history of fighting inflation were ranked on average 3.70 with a standard deviation of 1.36, and rule-based constraints ranked on average only 4.86 with a standard deviation of 1.47.

These results are in line with Blinder's survey results, but they indicate that private sector economists tended to place more reliance on central bank independence and transparency, over other determinants of credibility, than did the central bankers and academic economists surveyed by Blinder. If market actors hold intersubjective expectations that lead them to believe that central bank independence and transparency are crucial to the credibility of monetary policy, they will behave accordingly. Central bankers will then ignore these intersubjective expectations of private sector economists (and the market actors they represent) at their peril. Increasingly, central bankers by no means ignore these private sector preferences for independence and transparency.

Strategies for central bank transparency

In a much later study of central bank transparency strategies, Blinder and a team of collaborators have studied the transparency and communications strategies of seven OECD central banks: the US

Federal Reserve, the ECB, the Bank of Japan, the Bank of England, the Bank of Canada, the Swedish central bank (*Sveriges Riksbank*) and the Reserve Bank of New Zealand.[50] Their study expands an earlier important foray into the single transparency and communications strategy of central banks that explicitly have adopted inflation targeting regimes focusing on the effectiveness of the inflation reports issued by the central banks of Australia, Brazil, Canada, Chile, the Czech Republic, Hungary, Iceland, Israel, Mexico, New Zealand, Norway, Peru, the Philippines, Poland, South Africa, South Korea, Sweden, Switzerland, Thailand, and the United Kingdom.[51]

In their study of the inflation reports of inflation targeting regimes, Fracasso, Genberg, and Wyplosz argue that "monetary policy is more efficient the more the central bank can shape market expectations."[52] Recognizing that inflation reports are only one means of central bank transparency, they argue that a good inflation report that contributes to this goal of shaping market expectations must address three areas of particular interest to financial market actors. First it must engage in a comprehensive analysis of current economic conditions. Second it must forecast future inflation rates along with associated uncertainties. This forecast "must also present forecasts or assumptions, concerning... key macroeconomic variable and an explanation of how these different forecasts logically fit together."[53] Note that the financial markets want to understand the operating assumptions of central bank monetary policy committees regarding the direction of key macroeconomic variables, whose unpredictability can skew the performance of the macroeconomic models upon which economists rely to forecast future inflation rates.

This is another way of saying that market actors want to understand the intersubjectively shared expectations of monetary policy makers. They want to know "what the central bank governors believe" about macroeconomic trends that determine future inflation rates, as well as the central bank's expectations regarding future inflation rates. If their own, private forecasts are based on very different assumptions, market

---

[50] Blinder *et al.*, *How Do Central Banks Talk?*

[51] Andrea Fracasso, Hans Genberg, and Charles Wyplosz, *How Do Central Banks Write? An Evaluation of Inflation Targeting Central Banks* Geneva Reports of the World Economy 2 (Geneva: International Centre for Monetary and Banking Studies, 2003).

[52] *Ibid.*, p. 37.   [53] *Ibid.*

actors may adjust their own expectations regarding these macroeconomic variables and act on the basis that the central bankers are correct, and that they as private forecasters suffer an information deficit. Or they may discount the central bank's assumptions and make investment decisions designed to profit on their expectation of the central bank's error, which they would expect to be corrected when the central bank discovered the error. But instead of these two options, provided that the central bank has established credibility with market actors, they are more likely to take the central bank's forecast and assumptions, irrespective of whether they share those expectations, as a signal of the direction in which the central bank is likely to move, and make their investment decisions on this basis alone.

Finally, in this context, Fracasso and her collaborators argue that the inflation report "needs to explain how the MPC [monetary policy committee] interprets the current evidence and the forecasts, including present and future uncertainties."[54] The concern with the central bank's interpretation is a clear expression of the anxiety of the market actors to intersubjectively share, as rigorously as possible, the central bank's understanding of the meanings of the economic data, trends, models, and forecasts available to it. The economic meanings that these data and trends hold for central bankers are the key to predicting their future policy actions. As constructivist theorists of international relations have argued, people act toward things and one another on the basis of the meanings that these things and individuals hold for them. When they share intersubjectively social (and economic) understandings they more easily coordinate their actions.

"Rational" secrecy and surprise?

Much of the basis for the long-standing secrecy with which central banks operated prior to quite recent times stems from the assumptions and predictions of rational choice theoretic approaches to monetary economics and to central banking. The old thinking was that only unanticipated monetary policy movements could be effective. However, according to Alan Blinder and his collaborators:

This assumption, which lies at the heart of the rational choice revolution, holds that rational markets see through the veil of money and promptly

[54] *Ibid.*

adjust all prices ... leaving money to be neutral in the short run. Under that view, to be effective, monetary policy has to be unanticipated ... Despite its considerable weight in theoretical work, the empirical evidence does not support the assumption that only unanticipated money matters. Nor do central bankers report trying to create surprises.[55]

It cannot be sufficiently emphasized that the burgeoning literature on inflation biases – which according to the standard time inconsistency model which springs from the rational choice theoretic tradition sees central bankers springing "inflation surprises" on unwitting publics – is consistently disavowed as devoid of utility by central bankers. British central banker John Vickers points out "there is a large literature on inflation bias, but it is simply not applicable to the MPC. We have no desire to spring inflation surprises to try to bump output above its natural rate (whatever that may be)."[56] Former Fed Governor Laurence Meyer reports similarly that "I have never found the literature on time inconsistency particularly relevant to central banks."[57]

Meyer's apostasy from the rational choice tradition in this instance is particularly troublesome for adherents to the rational choice revolution in economics (and in political science) because Meyer is a Washington University of St. Louis, rational choice economist. He was a leading advocate for taking seriously other theoretical constructs derived from rational choice economic theory, such as the NAIRU in monetary policy decision-making in the Greenspan Fed while Greenspan and others in the FOMC were rather agnostic of the existence of the NAIRU. In this theory NAIRU is "the minimum sustainable unemployment rate – the lowest unemployment rate that can be sustained without lifting inflation."[58] While the reality of NAIRU has been debated in much-read, distinguished journals of economics by economists such as John Kenneth Galbraith, Joseph Stiglitz, and others,[59] Meyer reports

---

[55] Blinder *et al.*, *How Do Central Banks Talk?*, p. 14.

[56] John Vickers, "Inflation Targeting in Practice: The UK Experience" *Bank of England Quarterly Bulletin* 38(4) (1998): 369.

[57] Laurence H. Meyer, "The Politics of Monetary Policy: Balancing Independence and Accountability," remarks delivered at the University of Wisconsin, LaCrosse, Wisconsin, October 24, 2000.

[58] Meyer, *A Term at the Fed*, pp. xvi–xvii.

[59] See e.g. Joseph Stiglitz, "Reflections on the Natural Rate Hypothesis" *Journal of Economic Perspectives* 11(1) (1997): 1–10; James K. Galbraith, "Time to Ditch the NAIRU" *Journal of Economic Perspectives* 11(1) (1997): 93–108; Olivier Blanchard and Lawrence F. Katz, "What We Know and Do Not Know

that he was "surprised" by the challenges to the concept of a natural rate of unemployment by his FOMC colleagues.[60] Due to his consistently strong advocacy of this rational choice theoretic construct, Meyer became known by his FOMC colleagues as "the NAIRU guy."[61]

And, not surprisingly, Princeton economist and former Fed Vice-Chairman Alan Blinder reports that "As an academic, I found this [time-inconsistency] analysis unpersuasive. And what I learned as a central banker strongly reinforced this view."[62] Charles Freedman suggests that the standard time inconsistency model's "inability to explain the onset of a period of high inflation" results from its "ahistorical" nature and "a series of simplifying assumptions" including the assumption that an inflation bias is "inherent" resulting in "important disconnects between the model and the reality faced by those responsible for monetary policy."[63] The model posits by assumption an inflation bias from a "desire of the authorities to achieve a level of output greater than that consistent with the natural rate of inflation."[64] Central bankers clearly deny they attempt to do this, and many of them deny they know what the natural rate of inflation is, let alone NAIRU.

Nor does the model take into account other "institutional facts" found to have causal significance in the economic realm, such as the fact that the fixed wage contracts that industrial workers sign are about twice as long as the lag between monetary policy actions and inflationary phenomena.[65] Goodhart and Huang[66] adjusted the model to reflect some of these institutional facts, with limited enhancement in explanatory power. The problem here is obviously intersubjective. Wage contracts are constructed with very different inflation expectations in mind than those assumed by the central banks that are allegedly anxious to spring "inflation surprises" on workers according to rational choice theoretic models. Even neoliberal economist Stanley Fischer

---

about the Natural Rate of Unemployment" *Journal of Economic Perspectives*, 11(1) (1997): 51–72.

[60] Meyer, *A Term at the Fed*, p. 38.   [61] *Ibid.*, p. 40.

[62] Alan S. Blinder, *Central Banking in Theory and Practice* (Cambridge, MA: MIT Press, 1998), p. 40.

[63] Freedman, "Central Bank Independence," p. 95.

[64] *Ibid.*   [65] *Ibid.*, p. 96.

[66] Charles A. E. Goodhart and Haizhou Huang, "Time Inconsistency in a Model with Lags, Persistence, and Overlapping Wage Contracts" *Oxford Economic Papers* 50(3) (1998): 378–96.

finds some place for intersubjective factors in his discussion of modern
central banking when he writes of the significance of the social fact of
public "beliefs" about inflation. While he notes that empirically inflation results in wealth redistribution from the old to the young, and
from creditors to debtors, he argues that

> such an enumeration does not capture the very strong feelings about
> inflation that are evident even in the less-inflation-adverse industrialized
> economies... [which]... must derive from the belief that inflation unfairly
> takes away the fruits of inflation-caused nominal income increases that peo-
> ple incorrectly attribute to their own merit and hard work.[67]

At this writing, for example, people in the United States and
the United Kingdom believe they have grown wealthy through the
inflation-induced appreciation of residential property. Unfortunately,
OECD central banks have been printing money at unprecedented rates
since the global equities bubble burst in 2000 to pump liquidity into the
global economy to keep it afloat. Globalization has dampened general
inflationary pressures in domestic economies by intimidating workers into limiting their wage claims lest their jobs be exported. Alan
Greenspan argues in his memoirs that the deflationary effects of high
skilled, cheap labor from the former communist world are also under-
appreciated.[68] Thus inflation now tends to appear in the form of asset
bubbles. With the bursting of the equities bubble and with the accommodative monetary policy generated to limit its effects, this liquidity
has flowed into tangible assets like residential and commercial property, oil, and metals. Thus from 2000 or a little earlier, people have
been buying badly overpriced property with sadly debased currencies.
I will predict that as general inflationary pressures build in the global
economy as a result of increased demand for oils and metals from
China and the developing world, these new asset bubbles will either
burst or slowly deflate, and this imaginary "wealth" will dissipate,
and be revealed to have been the effects of asset-selective inflationary
finance. Unfortunately when equities bubbles burst, largely surplus
capital is extinguished, somewhat limiting long-term economic effects.
When property bubbles burst, a surfeit of deflating property assets,
purchased with largely borrowed money, floods the markets, resulting

[67] Fischer, "Modern Central Banking," pp. 182–3.
[68] Alan Greenspan, *The Age of Turbulence: Adventures in a New World*
(London: Penguin, 2007), pp. 382–3.

in defaults. The stability of the banking system can consequently be severely challenged. The best result that might arise from such a scenario is a prolonged period of stagnant nominal property prices that only result in real losses after inflation, ignoring opportunity costs, rather than nominal losses that can generate panic selling and foreclosures. Of course I would be delighted to be proven wrong about these scenarios.

People do fear inflation, given their past bitter experience with its effects. But due to its rational choice theoretic foundations – and the assumptions that permit complex human behavior to be reduced to that of economist Amartya Sen's "rational fool" whose one all-important preference ordering renders him a "social moron"[69] in order that his motivations might be modeled mathematically – the time independence model constructs an empirically non-existent, secretive central banker who plots inflation surprises. But as Charles Freedman points out, and as central bankers aver, the time inconsistency model does not explain the acceleration of inflation in the 1960s that resulted in the Great Inflation, and the "assumptions underlying both of its key equations do not seem to be based firmly in reality."[70] Central bankers seem not to know that they are expected to be especially secretive in the processes of monetary policy formation in order that they may spring "inflation surprises" on unsuspecting publics and market actors.

But as my analysis of even the most recent manifestations of inflationary finance illustrates, market actors have plenty of reasons to attempt to establish intersubjectively shared understandings with central bankers. And central bankers, whose preferences are actually not at all indifferent to economic outcomes or their effects, have plenty of solid reasons to accommodate market actors' thirst for enlightenment, precisely because:

the financial markets constitute the channel through which monetary policy actions are transmitted to the economy... Since this channel is dominated by expectation "convincing the markets" is part and parcel of monetary policy-making... [thus] ... central bank communication is largely, sometimes exclusively, directed at the financial markets.[71]

---

[69] Amartya K. Sen, "Rational Fools: A Critique of the Behavioral Foundations of Economic Theory" *Philosophy and Public Affairs* 6(4) (1997): 336.

[70] Freedman, "Modern Central Banking," p. 96.

[71] Blinder *et al.*, *How Do Central Banks Talk?*, p. 25.

"Rational" central bankers, according to rational choice theory, may be secretive, but successful central bankers – those who get market actors to do their work for them – appear conversely to be transparent and communicative. Successful central banks appear to work to establish intersubjective expectations rather than rational expectations in the bond markets.

Changing norms and intersubjectivity in central bank communications

This can be seen in recent changing norms in two very different central banks. The US Federal Reserve has a dual mandate to ensure price stability and maximize economic output and employment, while the Bank of England, since granted operational independence by the Exchequer in 1997, is an inflation targeting regime whose mandate is largely limited to ensuring price stability. Until February 1994 the Fed remained rather non-transparent, and did not even acknowledge that the FOMC had voted to change the discount rate until well after the fact. It had been a normative taboo to provide any forward looking information about future rate decisions to the markets or the public. On 31 January 1994, for the first time in its history, the FOMC announced a change in the Federal Funds rate simultaneously with its vote to raise the rate. Bob Woodward's chronicle of the Greenspan Fed indicates clearly the rationale for the procedural norm change. "No more covert moves subject to misinterpretation."[72] Similarly, until May 1999 the Fed had kept its "bias" (the indication of its inclination for action or inaction at the following meeting) issued in its policy directive to the OMD at the New York Fed secret until after the following FOMC meeting.[73]

The Fed and the Bank of England both formerly delayed release of the minutes of their FOMC and MPC meetings until after the subsequent meeting for fear that

the commentators and the market would concentrate unduly on what it [the content of the minutes] could imply for the next meeting's decision, paying less attention to the economic arguments. Views have shifted, however, and the Bank of England now aims at conditioning market expectations.[74]

---

[72] Woodward, *Maestro*, p. 121.
[73] Blinder, *How Do Central Banks Talk?*, pp. 36–7.   [74] *Ibid.*, p. 52.

So does the Fed, with different operating procedures. These procedural norm changes indicate both the Fed and the Bank of England have moved toward more transparency of their decisions and proceedings to condition market expectations.

While before February 1994 "the FOMC made only brief and often cryptic explanations when it changed [monetary] policy" it found it expedient to abandon this policy so that by February 1995 the policy of immediate announcement of monetary policy changes was formalized. But the Fed at the same time rejected the recommendation of a Fed subcommittee chaired by Blinder that the FOMC issue "fuller, more frequent statements" when voting to change monetary policy. Blinder pointed out that the Fed has done so, nonetheless, since May 1999.[75]

Financial journalist Martin Meyer reports that:

Normal expectation in the Federal Open Market Committee is that a rise in the Fed Funds rate will reduce the gap between the short-term rate and the long-term rate, if only because the central bank's willingness to raise short term rates encourages investors in longer-term paper to believe that inflation will be kept in check.[76]

But for reasons pertaining to the intersubjective, rather than rational expectations of market actors, a February 1994 rise of 25 basis points had the opposite effect. Meyer reports:

Though he has denied it, I will argue that this experience was the push that moved Greenspan to a belief in "transparency" – in letting the money markets know much more about what the Fed was doing and wanted to do, and about what the banks were doing and its impact on the value of their portfolios.[77]

Another important change in norms directed towards enhancing central bank communications policy has been effected in recent years to resolve problems of intersubjectively shared social meanings both between FOMC members and between the FOMC and financial market actors. This attended norms of FOMC issuance of its "bias" policy statement contained within the monetary policy directives issued subsequent to FOMC meetings. Blinder relates some dialogue that demonstrates that members of the FOMC, at the time when Blinder was a

[75] Blinder *et al.*, *How Do Central Banks Talk?*, pp. 67–8.
[76] Mayer, *The Fed*, p. 223.   [77] *Ibid.*

member of the committee, had their own difficulties in acquiring inter-subjectively shared understandings of the meaning of their bias policy statements. From the transcripts of the FOMC July 1994 meeting, for example, Ms. Kathy Minehan began the following dialogue as a new member of the FOMC, having been appointed President of the Federal Reserve Bank of Boston:

Ms. Minehan: . . . just being new to this whole business, if we go asymmetric [in the bias statement] what does that really mean?
Chairman Greenspan: We don't have a specific formulation. Asymmetry merely means a general sense of the Committee's disposition or the direction of our bias [toward future moves in monetary policy].
Donald Kohn, the director of the Fed's Division of Monetary Affairs, and Greenspan, then both tried to explain the meaning of asymmetry. After some confusing discussion, William McDonough, President of the Federal Reserve Bank of New York, interjected a question:
Vice-Chairman McDonough: Is that fully clear to you?
Ms. Minehan: Yes, I am really clear on this. [Laughter][78]

Blinder then indicates that the FOMC voted nine-to-two to keep interest rates unchanged but included a bias toward future tightening in the FOMC directive. The minutes of the FOMC meeting further indicate that:

At the end of the meeting, Mr. Lindsey indicated to Chairman Greenspan that his dissent . . . was based on a possible misunderstanding of the implications of the bias in the directive. His dissent was from a directive that he perceived as calling for a more or less automatic tightening of policy during the inter-meeting period. On the understanding that any tightening during the inter-meeting period would depend on further indications of inflationary developments, Mr. Lindsey requested that his vote be recorded in the minutes as in favour of this policy action . . .[79]

Blinder and his collaborators urge us to:

Notice the word "automatic" in the preceding passage. Lindsey had been on the FOMC for almost three years at the time, and yet he harboured the misconception that a bias virtually implied an inter-meeting move [on the authority of the chairman alone]. Thus even experienced Committee members were apparently confused about what it meant to issue an asymmetric directive.[80]

---

[78] Blinder *et al.*, *How Do Central Banks Talk?*, 69.   [79] *Ibid.*   [80] *Ibid.*

These "intersubjective ambiguities" over the meaning of bias statements in FOMC directives resulted in a new communications and procedural norm. Until May 1999 the Fed would refuse to announce its bias stance until six weeks after the decision when the directive would be published in order that "the bias could not possibly serve as a signal of the Fed's thinking, except perhaps internally." Subsequent to May 1999 the FOMC added a "balance of risks" statement to the directive to clarify the intersubjective meaning of an asymmetric directive, eschewed the term "bias" as confusing, and announced the "balance of risks" immediately to give the public and financial market actors insight into the likely direction of monetary policy in future FOMC meetings, as well as the likely time horizons.[81] Martin Mayer provides some confirmatory evidence of Greenspan's motivations in this policy norm change in recounting Greenspan's speech to the Economic Club in New York in 2000 in which Greenspan:

celebrated a new willingness to indicate in the public FOMC statement whether or not the group had any bias toward changing rates at its *next* meeting. There might be times when surprise had a value, he said, but as an ordinary matter the Fed would function most efficiently by fulfilling the expectations it had created.[82]

The original May 1999 decision, however, only announced a change in the policy bias when the FOMC regarded the change to be "significant" and Laurence Meyer argues that in consequence:

we tended to make the markets more sensitive and volatile to the news than they were before. When the FOMC announced an asymmetric policy bias, for instance, the markets perceived a rate hike as a virtual certainty, not merely a possibility. The markets also expected the rate change to take place immediately, not over the course of the next few meetings, as the Committee was hoping to communicate.[83]

The intersubjective disconnect with market actors was only resolved by something very much like full transparency. As Meyer reports:

Finally, the Committee decided that it would announce its risk assessment after every meeting, to avoid amplifying the volatility of the market by announcing changes in the risk assessment only when the change was deemed "significant".[84]

---

[81] *Ibid.*   [82] Mayer, *The Fed*, p. 225. Emphasis in the original.
[83] Meyer, *A Term at the Fed*, p. 159.   [84] *Ibid.*, p. 160.

It is worth noting in this context that the expectations the central bank had created in the markets were intersubjective expectations derived from central bank communication of its future intentions, or their absence, not expectations derived from any rational choice logic, or equations derived from rational choice theoretic adventures in monetary economic theory.

This episode is illustration of the less-than-rational behavior of market actors, and the need for full transparency and the establishment of fully intersubjectively shared understandings between central bank signals and market actor interpretations of these signals to avoid market failures and panics. Blinder and his collaborator argue that if central banks "were fully transparent, interest rate changes should merely be the confirmation of all the other signals previously issued."[85] But Laurence Meyer's account of the debacle over partial disclosure in the Fed's attempt to revise the bias statement indicates that market actors were insufficiently clued into the Fed's intentions by less-than-full transparency. They over-reacted to the FOMC's assertion that its bias statement was "significant." Blinder and collaborators suggest that the "downside is that limited transparency makes words unconvincing."[86] Or worse, makes words impart a meaning not at all intended, generating over-reaction. These observations bode ill for the market "rationality", and for the "efficient markets" hypotheses. These over-reactions "could be the symptom of financial market inefficiency, possibly rooted in less than rational behavior of market participants who often react to 'silly signals.'"[87] For Blinder, writing privately, markets react to "silly signals" often enough that he has tongue-in-cheek formulated what he calls "Blinder's law of speculative markets." This asserts that because "markets tend to run in herds and to overreact to almost any stimulus" the result is that "[w]hen they respond to news, the markets normally get the direction right but exaggerate the magnitude by a factor between three and ten."[88]

Tacit norms of central bank behavior are also intersubjectively understood by markets, and some of them remain in force lest the markets misinterpret their meaning. For example, when the FOMC meets, the Fed Chairman is always expected to be on the winning side of a FOMC vote, and to sign the resulting directive. Former Fed Governor Laurence Meyer reports:

[85] Blinder *et al.*, *How Do Central Banks Talk?*, p. 19.
[86] *Ibid.*, p. 20.   [87] *Ibid.*, p. 21.   [88] Blinder, *The Quiet Revolution*, p. 68.

if you were not prepared to support the Chairman . . . you had an obligation to tell him so at the Monday Board meeting. During my term no governor dissented in the vote at an FOMC meeting . . . In my five and a half years on the FOMC, never once did the Chairman fail to secure a vote in favor of his initial recommendation.[89]

The clear rationale for these norms was concern about market interpretations. These norms were so strongly binding that a third dissenting vote against the Fed Chairman's recommendation by an FOMC member:

would be viewed as a sign that the FOMC [was] in open revolt with the Chairman's leadership . . . [thus] . . . the dissents rather than the decision would become the story . . . There were two imaginary red chairs around the table – the "dissent chairs". The first two FOMC members who sat in those chairs were able to dissent. After that, no one else could follow the same course.[90]

Thus dissent by more than a handful of FOMC members is thereby intersubjectively understood by the press, the public, and financial market actors to constitute open revolt against the leadership of the Fed Chairman. If the markets have intersubjectively constructed a constitutive rule of the form "three or more dissenting votes against the FOMC policy directive" counts as "open revolt against the Fed Chairman" in the context of "an FOMC meeting," and take market action consistent with this intersubjectively constructed constitutive rule, then the rule is in effect irrespective of the intention of the dissenting FOMC members. The norm of the "two red chairs" in the FOMC boardroom appears to have been constructed in tacit recognition of the effects of this intersubjectively formulated constitutive rule constructed by market participants. In this manner the FOMC bows to "what the markets believe" and takes action constrained by that belief. This is just one example of how central banks experience the intersubjective expectations of the shared beliefs of market actors (however poorly or irrationally founded) as structural constraints on their behavior.

Changing norms of the behavior of central banks with inflation targeting regimes – vs. the Federal Reserve's more discretionary operating system arising from its dual mandate to ensure both price stability and economic output – also appear driven by attempts to improve intersubjective shared understandings with markets. The ECB, for example,

---

[89] Meyer, *A Term at the* Fed, pp. 50–1.   [90] *Ibid.*, pp. 52–3.

now releases the internal inflation forecasts of the ECB staff. Blinder *et al.* suggest that the markets do not yet quite understand how to "listen to" the ECB, but will become "more sophisticated listeners" over time.[91] Yet it must be noted that while the ECB has an explicit inflation target, the ECB's "two pillars" approach to monetary policy is complex. The first pillar is simple enough to track, namely the M-3 monetary aggregate. However, the second "pillar" taken into account in the process of ECB monetary policy formation comprises a mixed bag of economic indicators. This includes various price indicators in the euro area, indicators for real estate prices, consumer and business confidence indicators, exchange rates with the euro, financial market indicators, and projections and forecasts for both inflation and economic activity.[92] The complexity of the "two pillars" approach has meant that the two pillars "have widely been seen as an attempt at opacity"[93] rather than transparency.

The Bank of England prior to independence from the Exchequer never published its inflation forecast for fear the forecast would differ from that of the Exchequer. Subsequent to a grant of independence from the Exchequer in 1997 the "old lady of Threadneedle Street" publishes forecasts in its quarterly inflation report[94] as well as minutes of the MPC, which "record each individual vote by name . . . with a lag of two weeks" monthly.[95]

During its long climb out of deflation and a nasty "return of depression economics,"[96] and subsequent to obtaining its operational independence from the Japanese Ministry of Finance with the April 1988 New Bank of Japan Law, the Japanese central bank now publishes minutes of its policy board within five weeks of a meeting, and the minutes name names regarding policy positions taken by individual members.[97] Article 3 of the New Bank of Japan Law requires disclosure and transparency "to clarify to the public the content of its decisions, as well as it decision making process, regarding currency and monetary control."[98] Article 20 requires publication of minutes

---

[91] *Ibid.*, pp. 76–7.   [92] De Haan *et al.*, *The European Central Bank*, pp. 12–13.
[93] Blinder *et al.*, *How Do Central Banks Talk?*, p. 75.
[94] *Ibid.*, p. 84.   [95] *Ibid.*, p. 87.
[96] Paul Krugman, *The Return of Depression Economics* (New York: W. W. Norton, 1999).
[97] Blinder *et al.*, *How Do Central Banks Talk?*, p. 78.
[98] Cargill *et al.*, *Central Banking in Japan*, p. 99.

of the policy board and article 54 requires the governors to report at least twice a year to the Diet.[99]

However, no inflation objective or target is stated or quantified, and public interpretation of the term "price stability" is deemed acceptable. These norms arose in the context of extended deflation and the "zero interest rate policy" that pumped liquidity into the Japanese banking system, at no charge to commercial banks, from April 1999 to July 2000, when the Bank of Japan finally raised the uncollateralized overnight call rate to 25 basis points (or one-quarter of 1 percent). Yet during this period the Bank of Japan provided daily information on its reserve balances and provided information four times a day on its open market purchases and sales![100] And Blinder and his collaborators argue that the lack of a specific inflation target and forecast may have frustrated the effectiveness of the Bank of Japan's move to lift the zero interest rate policy by 25 basis points as a signal that the free money era was over, as actors in the Japanese money markets may have incorrectly assumed that having lifted the zero interest rate policy, further rate rises were to come.[101]

Yet upon gaining independence from the finance ministry the Bank of Japan "stopped publishing the monthly data for sectoral bank loans, which it ha[d] been compiling and using as the basis for its credit allocation since 1943 ... [as] ... the core of the window guidance credit allocation process."[102] It is far from clear that the Bank of Japan, let alone developing countries pursing the Asian model of development, have relinquished the deontic power to allocate credit to specific sectors of the domestic economy as a key component of national economic and industrial planning.[103] If we are – as we might well be in the realm of central bank independence – witnessing the emergence of a global institutional isomorphism toward central bank transparency, we may well be seeing variations in the interpretation of "transparency" consistent with what Peter Hall and David Soskice and their collaborators call "the varieties of capitalism."[104]

[99] *Ibid.*   [100] Blinder *et al.*, *How Do Central Banks Talk?*, p. 80.
[101] *Ibid.*, p. 83.   [102] Werner, *Princes of the Yen*, p. 229.
[103] See e.g. Natasha Hamilton-Hart, *Asian States, Asian Bankers: Central Banking in Southeast Asia* (Ithaca, NY and London: Cornell University Press, 2002).
[104] Peter A. Hall and David Soskice (eds.), *Varieties of Capitalism: The Institutional Foundations of Comparative Advantage* (Oxford: Oxford University Press, 2001).

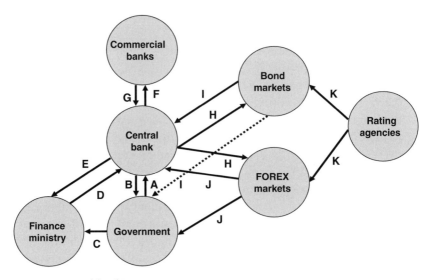

Fig. 7.1 Central banking as governance

Central bank transparency and governance networks

Having developed all of the concepts and power relationships required, we can now outline the emerging system of global financial governance, and the central role played by independent and transparent central banks. Figure 7.1 captures the network of governance relations that the transparency strategies of central banks, and the deontic powers of market actors to adjudicate central bank credibility engender. These relations, and the deontologies that underpin them, will be described by tracing the arrows alphabetized in the figure from A to K.

The first deontology, A, results from the grant of a charter of independence to the central bank by the government. This is a public pronouncement, a speech act with performative effect on the part of the government. This grant of independence may come in many forms, and statutory/constitutional forms are preferred by market actors. It may include operational independence (choice of instruments) and/or goal independence (choice of acceptable rates of inflation). All of the deontic powers (constituted forms of authority) that were described in chapters 2 and 3 accrue to the central bank, including the deontic power to perform all of the others independently of government preferences. I argued at length in chapter 3 that these include the deontic powers to create and to extinguish money, to generate (or refuse to provide) liquidity to distressed financial institutions and to socialize risk, to value or revalue the national product through exchange-rate management, to monetize (or for independent central banks to refuse to monetize) government debt, and for some central banks, the power to allocate credit to specific sectors of the economy. And I would add at this juncture that independent central banks with operational independence in the choice of instruments by which monetary policy is executed have deontic power to delegate subsidiary deontic powers assigned to them to other actors, such as market actors. The importance of the deontic powers allocated in the emerging system of global as well as domestic monetary governance to private market actors was developed at length in chapters 6 and 7.

However, it was argued in chapter 6 that central bank deontic powers that stem from independence are both discretionary and contingent in the sense that independence is revocable by the government with varying degrees of difficulty that are dependent upon institutional arrangements and local political conditions. These deontic powers, and all the subsidiary central bank deontic powers developed in chapters 3 and 4, are legitimated by the collective assignment of this "independent" status by the government, acting in the name of the public, to the central bank. Otherwise, in the absence of a grant of independence, this authority is simply delegated by the government to the central bank. The second deontology, B, is the power of the central bank to influence government fiscal policy through advice, and in the case of independent central banks, through public pressure applied through public judgment pronouncements – normally by the chair of a monetary policy committee – on the prudence of government fiscal policy. The degree of authority of this form available to a given central bank is proportional to both its degree of real independence from the government and to the credibility with which market actors view the central bank's independence, pronouncements, and monetary policy decision-making record.

The government also delegates deontic power, C, to the finance ministry (in many nations an integral part of the government) to determine exchange-rate policy, and often to formulate fiscal policy, or at a minimum to manage the government's debt structure – assessing the forms and mix of maturities of debt instruments to be offered on the markets, or otherwise to be contrived. When central banks are independent, market actors believe that this latter function is less easily accomplished by instructing the central bank to monetize the debt, thereby diluting the real value of the promise of repayment for those investors already holding the government's debt instruments issued previously, as well as the future value of presently issued debt. However, it is important to remember that in countries which have surrendered monetary sovereignty entirely through dollarization or by setting up currency boards, monetary policy has not simply been delegated, it has been surrendered to a foreign central bank, as has exchange-rate policy for dollarized economies, while exchange-rate policy remains in the hands of the government where currency boards have been established. In the latter case the central bank is constrained to issue no more domestic currency than is specified by the government-determined exchange rate, which is supported by central bank holdings of the applicable foreign exchange reserves.

In countries that retain monetary sovereignty, however, the finance ministry exercises deontic power, D, to determine the direction of national exchange-rate policy, and to instruct the central bank to execute its exchange-rate policy by buying and selling the national currency, and instruments denominated in the national currency on the FOREX markets. If the finance ministry wishes to endorse a weaker exchange-rate policy to enhance the competitiveness of national exports, it may instruct the central bank to sell assets denominated in the national currency (most effectively the currency itself). Conversely it may instruct the central bank to buy assets denominated in the national currency if it wishes to strengthen the national currency's international exchange rate. The central bank, if it is independent, may assess independently whether to "sterilize" (neutralize) the effects on the money supply of transactions oriented toward exchange-rate management.

The central bank in turn may exercise deontic power, E, to influence the exchange-rate policy of the finance ministry, again either through advice sought by the finance ministry, or through pressure of public pronouncements on finance ministry exchange-rate policy, for independent and "credible" central banks. This pressure can be very real, because FOREX market actors may, and often do, respond more dramatically to the pronouncements of central bankers than those of the finance minister. The finance ministry is generally believed to be speaking for the government, while an independent central bank speaks for itself, and may refuse to accommodate loose government fiscal policies with loose monetary policy. An independent central bank may also conduct monetary policy in a fashion that contradicts government exchange-rate policy. If the central bank has adequate credibility, the finance minster would be well advised to avoid public disagreement with the governor of the central bank. The result of such a public disagreement with the governor of an independent central bank may well entail a loss of credibility for the finance minister.

Deontic powers of the central bank were well discussed in chapter 3 and will be merely summarized here. The central bank has quite strong deontic power, F, over commercial bank lending and practices through its reserve requirements, its regulatory functions in many countries, and particularly through its control over the issue of currency and intermediated credit. Through its deontic powers as a lender of last resort, it also has the power of financial life or death over distressed commercial institutions as it may agree, or decline, to intervene when a commercial financial institution, particularly a member subject to reserve requirements, is failing. Much of chapters 2 and 3 was devoted to explicating and explaining the deontic powers of central banks on the domestic commercial banking and credit systems.

The major deontic power the commercial banks have with respect to the central bank, G, is the power to induce the central bank, when it chooses to accommodate the commercial bank, to generate money to back the credit that commercial banks extend to private or public sector borrowers. But because "credit is money too" the deontic power of money creation of commercial banking through credit extension has very real economic effects, and not only on commercial banks. As Ingham puts it

it is a central characteristic of capitalism that its financial system is able to continuously devise new forms of credit instruments. These may become a bank's assets and, consequently, form a base for their lending ("broad money") ... when authorities attempt to regulate and control any particular form of credit instrument or "near money" the private capitalist financial system creates new ones that are not covered by the regulation.[105]

---

[105] Ingham, *Nature of Money*, p. 30.

The central bank must respond to such innovation if it wishes to maintain tight control over the monetary base of the domestic economy, and this requirement constitutes one of its major challenges as financial innovation proceeds apace.

The central bank, in its capacity as the executor as well as formulator of monetary policy, assigns (with authority delegated by governments) to actors in the bond markets and the foreign exchange markets the deontic power, H, to adjudicate the credibility of its commitment mechanism and of the money that it generates. This is assigned when open market operations are chosen as the instrument of monetary policy and of exchange-rate policy which the central bank executes on behalf of a finance ministry – or in countries with currency boards, on its own behalf. This authority is delegated by governments to the central bank, which in turn delegates it to the financial markets in choosing open market operations as a vehicle to execute monetary policy. Since governments which are deemed creditworthy by banks have intermediated options to pursue financing of their operations and investments (such as loans from transnational commercial banks, regional development banks, the World Bank, or when in difficulties, the IMF) this deontic power can be somewhat circumscribed. But due to the normally lower cost of financing for "creditworthy" states through disintermediated lending, this deontic power is considerable and it constitutes a burgeoning force in global financial governance. In consequence this "market authority" to adjudicate the credibility of monetary and fiscal policy is a major force behind the considerable energy that central banks increasingly invest in their transparency and communications strategies with market actors.

Investors in both debt securities and currencies will scrutinize both the monetary and fiscal policies of governments issuing debt securities and currencies. As a consequence, when central banks allocate deontic power to market actors to adjudicate the promise that money constitutes (see chapter 2), they delegate that authority simultaneously to both the bond and the FOREX markets. They delegate the power to adjudicate the "prudence" of government fiscal policy as well as central bank monetary policy to these market actors, precisely because these market actors will suspect that government debt will be monetized through pressure on nominally or *de facto* non-independent central banks, and to a lesser extent on independent central banks as well. While the FOREX markets take into account many factors in their currency bids, and while trade-weighted current account figures count heavily among these, monetary policy announcements that are at odds with the intersubjective expectations of market actors generally move the FOREX markets. The distinction between the intersubjective expectations that move markets and the rational expectations of neoclassical economic theory was developed in chapters 6 and 7.

Loose government fiscal policies nearly always drag down the exchange-rate valuations of national currencies issued by governments with large external debts in the FOREX markets. This trend is particularly dramatic as applied to the exchange rates of developing country currencies, but applies to even the most advanced industrialized nations. The US dollar, for example, has at this writing recently traded at historically quite low values against the euro, the yen and the pound sterling as the United States has run simultaneously large current account and budget deficits during the administrations of George W. Bush. US monetary policy was highly accommodative in this period under Former Fed Chairman Alan Greenspan, and during the early months of the term of present Fed Chairman Benjamin Bernanke. Market actors move even more quickly to punish the currencies of developing world nations. Even policy indications in public speeches by heads of state in the developing world that indicate a looser direction for either government fiscal or central bank monetary policy can result in a plunge in the valuation of the currency on the FOREX and the valuation of that nation's sovereign bonds on the secondary market. Significant risk premiums are subsequently demanded to purchase fresh issues of debt securities at large spreads above the rates charged for securities of similar maturity issued by the US Treasury or the UK Exchequer.

Thus actors in the bond market exercise delegated deontic power, I, to adjudicate the credibility of central bank monetary policy and to also signal to the government their judgment of the prudence of government fiscal policy. This authority is exercised in the decision to extend credit to governments through purchases of (or failure to purchase) disintermediated sovereign debt instruments. If the debt is purchased, the interest rate spread over US Treasury securities of a similar maturity provides a metric of the credibility of the promise to repay in money whose value is comparable to the value of the money borrowed. The FOREX markets similarly exercise delegated deontic power, J, to adjudicate the credibility of central bank monetary policy and the prudence of government fiscal policy. An adverse judgment is rendered by a drop in the exchange rate of the currency in question. This adverse judgment can be welcomed or rued by the government, dependent upon the exchange-rate policy formulated by the finance ministry. Governments that wish to see a realignment of exchange rates to lower the exchange rate of their national currency relative to that of their trading partners may welcome a lower exchange rate in the FOREX rate as a boost to their exports, particularly if they are suffering chronic current account (particularly trade) deficits. Similarly governments of highly import-dependent countries concerned about the inflationary effects of a low exchange rate (often in the developing world) on consumer and industrial prices, or whose industrial sectors have large foreign debts denominated in foreign rather than domestic currencies, will fear the domestic inflationary effects of lower exchange rates. These countries will work to maintain tight fiscal and monetary policy to signal the FOREX markets to maintain or raise their exchange rate against those of their trading partners.

Governments which have surrendered their monetary policy to a foreign central bank through a currency board or other hard peg of their exchange rate forgo these anxieties provided they maintain adequate foreign reserves to defend their pegs against speculative attacks by actors on the FOREX markets.[106] However, they can "live and die by hard-pegs"[107] and suffer an exogenous shock to their economies through export decline if the exchange rate of the currency to which they have anchored appreciates significantly against the exchange rate of the currencies of their trading partners in the short or medium term.[108] For these reasons, as well as the temptations toward use of the central bank as an engine of inflationary development finance – with

---

[106] Steve H. Hanke, "On Dollarization and Currency Boards: Error and Deception" *Policy Reform* 5(4) (2002): 202–22.

[107] Augusto de la Torre, Eduardo Levy Yeyati, and Sergio L. Scmukler, *Living and Dying with Hard Pegs: The Rise and Fall of Argentina's Currency Board* (Washington, DC: World Bank, 2003).

[108] See e.g. Michael Mussa, *Argentina and the Fund: From Triumph to Tragedy* (Washington, DC: Institute for International Economics, 2002); Mark Allen, "Some Lessons from the Argentine Crisis: A Fund Staff View" from *The Crisis That Was Not Prevented: Argentina, the IMF, and Globalisation*, FONDAD, January 2003 (www.fondad.org); Maria Matilde Ollier, "Argentina: Up a Blind Alley Once Again" *Bulletin of Latin American Research* 22(2) (2003): 170–86.

long-term consequences inimical to development and national financial stability – some neoliberal economists have recommended that developing countries entirely eschew central banking and surrender monetary sovereignty.[109]

Finally, private ratings agencies exercise delegated deontic power and authority, K, to "grade" the credibility of central bank monetary policy and government fiscal policy and assign this credibility a ranking relative to that of other issuers of debt. The ratings agencies engage in ongoing surveillance and issue ongoing signals to the markets[110] through ratings changes. Ratings downgrades can result not only in higher yield spreads (demands for higher risk premiums by bond investors as a *quid pro quo* to purchase fresh debt) but also may result in a complete suspension of access to the disintermediated global capital markets.

"Clubbing": central banking as global financial governance

The notion of central bank cooperation as an element of the mechanisms of the global financial governance that have been explored in this book has received somewhat spare treatment, largely because the topic of central bank cooperation as global financial governance is in itself worthy of a monograph – that I hope in future to write. And I have neglected the topic partly because those deliberations of central bankers that are not part of a public record of negotiation – such as the Plaza and Louvre Accords that sought to harmonize G-7 exchange-rate policy with mixed success – are entirely private, informal, largely unrecorded, deliberations. The Plaza and Louvre Accords are not, in any event, thought to be particularly successful examples of central bank cooperation.[111] Nor were they particularly good examples, to

---

[109] See e.g. Kurt Schuler, *Should Developing Countries Have Central Banks? Currency Quality and Monetary Systems in 155 Countries* (London: Institute for Economic Affairs, 1996) and Steve H. Hanke and Kurt Schuler, *Currency Boards for Developing Countries: A Handbook* (San Francisco, CA: Institute for Contemporary Studies, 1994).

[110] Sinclair, *New Masters of Capital*, p. 41.

[111] Address by Yutaka Yamaguchi, Former Deputy Governor of the Bank of Japan in Bank for International Settlements, *Past and Future of Central Bank Cooperation: Policy Panel Discussion*, BIS Papers no. 27 (Basle: Bank for International Settlements, 2006), p. 20.

the significant extent that their frameworks were largely driven by the agendas of finance ministers rather than central bankers.

Getting at the facts of informal cooperation among central bankers will require extensive interviews with former central bankers who have now retired to private life, as well as extensive archival research. Economic historian Gianni Toniolo has recently completed a monumental history of the role that that the BIS has played in fostering central bank cooperation since its founding in 1930.[112] But the study ends temporally in 1973, shortly after the collapse of the Bretton Woods gold exchange standard. And Toniolo's study relies – as it must, given the deaths of so many of the principals that Toniolo might wish to have interviewed – much more strongly on BIS archives than any accounts of real discussions that occurred when central bankers put their heads together behind closed doors in Basle. And it recounts events in the history of central bank cooperation that have truly passed into history – namely the BIS's role as the quintessential defender of an international monetary order based upon a metallic standard. Of all the "gold bugs" that have ever lived, the majority of the most avid of these surely held office at the BIS in the forty-three years between the "central bankers' club's" founding, and the final, formal demise of the monetary legacy of Bretton Woods.

Throughout no small part of this history, central bankers were fully subordinated to governments and their finance ministers. This was particularly true of the inter-war period, during the founding of the BIS, throughout the Second World War, when monetary gold was hoarded and currencies were nationally administered. In those times denying access to monetary gold to the enemy was a matter of national security, because monetary gold could always be employed as a means for international settlements by (but never between) belligerents. And throughout all of this history, national administrative controls on the flow of financial capital, as a pillar of international financial stability, was not only a cornerstone of the policy of every nation adhering to the Bretton Woods gold exchange standard, it was required of members of the IMF for precisely the same purpose.[113]

---

[112] Toniolo, *Central Bank Cooperation*.
[113] Rawi Abdelal, *Capital Rules: The Construction of Global Finance* (Cambridge, MA: Havard University Press, 2007).

The BIS in Basle, Switzerland, serves as a forum for a "continuous low-profile exchange of views" among central bankers which "enables policy makers to 'step back' on a regular basis and test their perceptions of economic and financial trends against those of their peers from other countries... it permits a form of 'bonding' among central bankers."[114] Central bankers meet there formally for a weekend of dinners and informal meetings eight times a year, and more frequently in smaller groups for special events sponsored by the BIS. The major charter of the BIS, from article 3 of its statutes, is "to promote the cooperation of central banks and to provide additional facilities for international financial operations."[115] During the heyday of gold the BIS served important functions in helping to organize a "European payments union"[116] to arrange international settlements within Europe during the height of the dollar shortage in Europe after World War II, a "gold pool"[117] to defeat speculation against the gold-backed dollar during the Bretton Woods years. The gold pool had no written rules. It was a gentlemen's agreement between central bankers to help stabilize the price of gold in the London market to help defend dollar/gold parities in the Bretton Woods gold exchange era.[118] The BIS was also instrumental in helping to arrange "swap lines"[119] of foreign currencies for cooperative central bank intervention against currency speculation, and eleven credit arrangements to help "nanny" the pound sterling, while ultimately weak sterling failed to be sustained as a second international reserve currency to the dollar.[120] However, the major, historically continuous function of the BIS in the realm of global financial governance has always been epistemic. During the reign of the gold standard in various forms, the BIS was a consummate champion of the importance of getting on, and staying on, gold as the key to international monetary stability.[121] The BIS has since been reputed to have played a significant role in helping state central banks

---

[114] Address by A. D. Crockett, President of JP Morgan Chase International and former General Manager of the BIS, in *Past and Future of Central Bank Cooperation*, p. 8.

[115] Quoted in Deane and Pringle, *The Central Banks*, pp. 275–6.

[116] Toniolo, *Central Bank Cooperation*, pp. 333–9.

[117] *Ibid.*, pp. 375–81 and 410–23.

[118] Deane and Pringle, *The Central Banks*, p. 279.

[119] Toniolo, *Central Bank Cooperation*, pp. 387–8.

[120] Deane and Pringle, *The Central Banks*, p. 280.   [121] *Ibid.*, pp. 131–6.

formulate the case for their independence from their national finance ministers.[122]

This raises an interesting question of the extent to which the current institutionally isomorphic moves toward central bank independence and transparency are a result of the successful efforts of epistemic communities, like the BIS, or the result of pressures from global financial markets, or some combination of these. While central bank independence is popular with the financial markets, and seen as important to ensuring credibility and price stability with central bankers, it is worth noting that it may also be essential to the stability of the international monetary and financial systems.

These trends permit developing countries to make credible promises of repayment, and they permit developed countries to sustain large fiscal and current account deficits for extended periods of time. For wealthy, industrialized countries dependent on capital imports to finance fiscal and current account deficits, operational independence permits them to essentially monetize government debt for lengthy periods of time at their discretion, even while loosening monetary policy, provided that stable international demand for their sovereign debt issues may be sustained. The credibility attending their independence and transparency may permit them to help their governments to finance sustained fiscal and current account deficits at significantly lower costs than they would face for financing of these deficits on the global bond markets, as market actors would be more concerned that the debts would simply be monetized.

Challenges to the new nominal anchors

Thus the BIS serves as a forum for central bankers to coordinate and converge around independence and transparency, preferably through inflation targeting regimes, as new nominal anchors for an international monetary system comprised nearly entirely of fiat monies. Inflation targeting regimes have been adopted in, for example, New Zealand, Canada, the United Kingdom, Australia, Sweden, Israel, the eurozone, Brazil, Poland, South Korea, Hungary, and Mexico. All of these countries but Brazil had by 2005 been successful in reducing annual inflation rates to roughly 4 percent or below, and all but

---

[122] Deane and Pringle, *The Central Banks*, p. 289.

Brazil, Hungary, and Mexico to below 3 percent.[123] However, continuing trends toward currency competition, disintermediation, and financial innovation provide significant challenges to the efficacy of monetary policy, both in the developing and developed worlds.

The increasing volume of transactions on the FOREX markets provides significant challenges to the stability of the currencies of developing countries, and they can routinely overwhelm the capacity of developing country central banks to intervene to stabilize their currencies. As one result of their brutal experience with the FOREX markets during the Asian financial crisis, Asian central banks in particular have built up huge reserves denominated largely in dollars and euros as a defensive self-insurance mechanism to ensure that they can intervene successfully in the FOREX markets against speculators.

This has resulted in a large transfer of net savings from poorer developing countries to wealthier developed countries. Aside from the opportunity costs to development and investment in Asia, these countries also face opportunity costs of holding these reserves in highly liquid form in Western currencies, as these monies cannot be invested in the domestic economy. As a recent study suggests,

It does not make sense for fast-growing but relatively poor countries to lend cheaply to the richest country in the world. Yet this is effectively what happens when the central bank of an emerging economy builds up dollar reserves beyond what may be required to provide financial security.[124]

As suggested previously, mismanagement of fiscal policy can defeat the monetary policy of the most skillful central banker, and in this case mismanaged fiscal policy by developed economic superpowers like the United States can impose extreme reserve management policies on developing countries when governance capacity is in the hands of market actors. Moreover, central bank coordination cannot by itself overcome such imbalances as these. Exchange rates and global imbalances of central bank reserves cannot be addressed by central bankers while finance ministers are unwilling to address dreadful imbalances resulting from government mismanagement of fiscal policies, or current account deficits resulting from government mismanagement of trade

---

[123] "How to Home in on the Inflationary Range," *Financial Times*, 26 October 2005, p. 17.
[124] Genberg *et al.*, *Reserves and Currency Management*, p. 5.

policy. Resolving these imbalances would no doubt require significant intergovernmental macroeconomic policy coordination.[125]

Currency competition, as previously discussed, has "greatly complicated the task facing governments long-accustomed to the privilege of national monetary sovereignty. Where once states claimed the rights of monopoly, they must now act like oligopolists, vying endlessly for the favor of market agents."[126] This is particularly problematic in developing countries where dollars, euros, and sterling may be strongly preferred for transactions over local currencies. In this context, as Benjamin Cohen has observed "[t]he power of governance, in short, now resides in the social institution we call the market... Governance is provided by whatever may influence market confidence in individual currencies."[127]

Finally, financial innovation from hedge funds and derivatives markets challenges the authority of central banks with a bewildering array of financial vehicles that can leverage astonishing sums of money with incredible destructive potential for global financial system stability. It is unclear that the commercial bankers who increasingly employ financial derivatives to hedge their investments against exchange rate and other forms of market volatility really understand the vehicles upon which they can stake a great deal. And in 1998 the US Fed was required to organize a bail-out of the hedge fund Long Term Capital Management (LTCM) which had parlayed a $2.3 billion capital base into $107 billion in leveraged positions on the derivatives markets in sovereign debt issues, hoping to profit from a "convergence" toward narrowing rate spreads (predicted by rational expectations theory) that never materialized.[128] As "limited partnerships" under US law, hedge funds are exempt from the 1940 Investment Company Act that requires extensive financial reporting from limited liability corporations,[129]

---

[125] William R. Cline, *The Case for a New Plaza Agreement*, Policy Briefs in International Economics no. PB04-4 (Washington, DC: Institute for International Economics, 2005): 6.

[126] Cohen, *The Geography of Money*, p. 167.   [127] *Ibid.*, pp. 146–7.

[128] See e.g. Paul Stoneham, "Too Close to the Hedge: The Case of Long Term Capital Management LP Part One: Hedge Fund Analytics" *European Management Journal* 17(3) (1999): 282–89; and Paul Stoneham, "Too Close to the Hedge: The Case of Long Term Capital Management LP Part Two: Near-collapse and Rescue" *European Management Journal* 17(4) (1999): 382–90.

[129] *Ibid.*, p. 284.

rendering such highly leveraged and destabilizing catastrophes difficult to spot and to stop when they are developing. But so far "responses to the hedge-fund problem have tended to rely more on market discipline than government regulation and more on national than international interests."[130]

In light of these emerging challenges, and their potentially horrific consequences for global financial system stability, I would submit that more than central bank independence and transparency will be required to generate a reliable nominal anchor for an international monetary system characterized by extreme capital mobility in which much of that capital circulates across borders in the form of fiat money to replace lapsed metallic standards. The emerging system of global financial governance is not likely to be complete without a global regulatory component if it is to simultaneously ensure price stability, economic growth, and global financial stability.

---

[130] Barry Eichengreen, "Governing Global Financial Markets: International Responses to the Hedge-Fund Problem" in Miles Kahler and David A. Lake (eds.) *Governance in a Global Economy* (Princeton, NJ: Princeton University Press, 2003), p. 196.

Bibliography

Abdelal, Rawi. *Capital Rules: The Construction of Global Finance* (Cambridge, MA: Harvard University Press, 2007).

Allen, Mark. "Some Lessons from the Argentine Crisis: A Fund Staff View" from *The Crisis That Was Not Prevented: Argentina, the IMF, and Globalisation*, FONDAD, January 2003 (www.fondad.org).

Amsden, Alice H. *The Rise of "The Rest": Challenges to the West from Late-Industrializing Economies* (Oxford: Oxford University Press, 2001).

Andrews, David M. "Money, Power and Monetary Statecraft" in David M. Andrews (ed.) *International Monetary Power* (Ithaca, NY: Cornell University Press, 2006): 7–28.

Armijo, Leslie Elliott. "The Political Geography of World Financial Reform: Who Wants What and Why?" *Global Governance* 7 (2001): 379–96.

Atkins, Ralf and James Politi. "ECB Move to Inject Funds Lifts Markets," *Financial Times*, 23 August 2007.

Aykens, Peter. "(Mis)trusting Authorities: A Social Theory of Currency Crises" *Review of International Political Economy* 12(2) (2005): 310–33.

Bank for International Settlements. *Past and Future of Central Bank Cooperation: Policy Panel Discussion* BIS Papers no. 27 (Basle: Bank for International Settlements, 2006).

Barnett, Michael and Raymond Duvall. "Power in International Politics" *International Organization* 59(1) (2005): 39–75.

Barnett, Michael and Martha Finnemore. *Rules for the World: International Organizations in Global Politics* (Ithaca, NY: Cornell University Press, 2004).

Benoit, Bertrand and Ben Hall. "Sarkozy and Merkel at Odds over ECB," *Financial Times*, 22–3 September 2007.

Bernanke, Ben S., Thomas Loubach, Frederic S. Mishkin, and Adam S. Posen. *Inflation Targeting: Lessons from the International Experience* (Princeton, NJ and Oxford: Princeton University Press, 1999).

Barro, Robert J. "Reputation in a Model of Monetary Policy with Incomplete Information" *Journal of Monetary Economics* 17(1) (1986): 3–20.

Barro, Robert J. and David Gordon. "A Positive Theory of Monetary Policy in a Natural Rate Model" *Journal of Political Economy* (August 1983): 589–610.

Bascom, Wilbert O. *The Economics of Financial Reform in Developing Countries* (New York: St. Martin's, 1994).

Bell, Stephen. "The Limits of Rational Choice: New Institutionalism in the Test Bed of Central Banking Politics in Australia" *Political Studies* 50 (2002): 477–96.

Bernhard, William, J. Lawrence Broz, and William Roberts Clark. "The Political Economy of Monetary Institutions" *International Organization* 56(4) (2002): 693–723.

Best, Jacqueline. "Bringing Power Back In: The IMF's New Constructivist Strategy in Critical Perspective" (manuscript presented at workshop on Economic Constructivism, Radcliffe Institute for Advanced Study, Harvard University, February 2005).

   The Limits of Transparency: Ambiguity and the History of International Finance (Ithaca, NY: Cornell University Press, 2005).

Biersteker, Thomas J. and Rodney Bruce Hall. "Private Authority in Global Governance" in Rodney Bruce Hall and Thomas J. Biersteker *The Emergence of Private Authority in Global Governance* (Cambridge: Cambridge University Press, 2002): 203–22.

Blanchard, Olivier and Lawrence F. Katz. "What We Know and Do Not Know about the Natural Rate of Unemployment" *Journal of Economic Perspectives* 11(1) (1997): 51–72.

Blinder, Alan S. *Central Banking in Theory and Practice* (Cambridge, MA: MIT Press, 1998).

   "Central Bank Credibility: Why Do We Care? How Do We Build It? *American Economic Review* 90(5) (2000): 1421–31.

   The Quiet Revolution: Central Banking Goes Modern (New Haven, CT: Yale University Press, 2004).

Blinder, Alan, Charles Goodhart, Phillip Hildebrand, David Lipton, and Charles Wyplosz. *How Do Central Banks Talk?* Geneva Reports on the World Economy 3 (Geneva: International Centre for Monetary and Banking Studies, 2001).

Blustein, Paul. *And the Money Kept Rolling In (and Out): Wall Street, the IMF, and the Bankrupting of Argentina* (New York: Public Affairs, 2005).

Blyth, Mark. *Great Transformations: Economic Ideas and Institutional Change in the Twentieth Century* (Cambridge: Cambridge University Press, 2002).

   "The Political Power of Financial Ideas: Transparency, Risk, and Distribution in Global Finance" in Jonathan Kirshner (ed.) *Monetary Orders:*

Ambiguous Economics, Ubiquitous Politics (Ithaca, NY and London: Cornell University Press, 2003): 239–59.

Bordo, Michael D. and Finn E. Kydland. "The Gold Standard as a Rule" in Barry Eichengreen and Marc Flandreau (eds.) *The Gold Standard in Theory and History* (London and New York: Routledge, 1985): 99–128.

Cantor, Richard and Frank Packer. "Determinants and Impact of Sovereign Credit Ratings" *FBRNY Economic Policy Review* (October 1996): 37–53.

Cargill, Thomas F., Michael M. Hutchison, and Takatoshi Ito. *Financial Policy and Central Banking in Japan* (Cambridge, MA and London: MIT Press, 2000).

Chartareas, Georgio, David Stasavage, and Gabriel Sterne. *Does it Pay to be Transparent? International Evidence from Central Bank Forecasts* Working Paper (London: Bank of England, 2001).

Cline, William R. *The Case for a New Plaza Agreement*, Policy Briefs in International Economics no. PB04–4 (Washington, DC: Institute for International Economics, 2005).

Cohen, Benjamin J. *The Geography of Money* (Ithaca, NJ: Cornell University Press, 1998).

"Monetary Governance in a World of Regional Currencies" in Miles Kahler and David A. Lake (eds.) *Governance in a Global Economy* (Princeton, NJ: Princeton University Press, 2003): 136–67.

The Future of Money (Princeton, NY: Princeton University Press, 2004).

"The Macrofoundations of Monetary Power" in David M. Andrews (ed.) *International Monetary Power* (Ithaca, NY: Cornell University Press, 2006): 31–50.

"The Transatlantic Divide: Why are American and British IPE so Different?" *Review of International Political Economy* 14(4) (2007): 197–219.

Corden, W. Max. *Too Sensational: On the Choice of Exchange Rate Regimes* (Cambridge, MA: MIT Press, 2002).

Dam, Kenneth W. *Rules of the Game: Reform and Evolution in the International Monetary System* (Chicago, IL: University of Chicago Press, 1982).

Deane, Marjorie and Robert Pringle. *The Central Banks* (London: Hamish Hamilton, 1994).

De Haan, Jakob, Sylvester E. W. Eijffinger, and Sandra Waller. *The European Central Bank: Credibility, Transparency, and Centralization* (Cambridge, MA and London: MIT Press, 2005).

Desai, Padma. *Financial Crisis, Contagion, and Containment: From Asia to Argentina* (Princeton, NJ: Princeton University Press, 2003).

Dessler, David. "What is at Stake in the Agent-Structure Debate?" *International Organization* 43(3) (1989): 441–74.

Eccles, Marriner. *Beckoning Frontiers: Public and Personal Recollections* (New York: Alfred A. Knopf, 1951).

Eichengreen, Barry. *Golden Fetters: The Gold Standard and the Great Depression 1919–1939* (Oxford: Oxford University Press, 1995).

Globalizing Capital: A History of the International Monetary System (Princeton, NJ: Princeton University Press, 1996).

Toward a New International Financial Architecture (Washington, DC: Institute for International Economics, 1999).

"Governing Global Financial Markets: International Responses to the Hedge-Fund Problem" in Miles Kahler and David A. Lake (eds.) *Governance in a Global Economy* (Princeton, NJ: Princeton University Press, 2003): 168–98.

Epstein, Gerald and Thomas Ferguson. "Monetary Policy, Loan Liquidation, and Industrial Conflict: The Federal Reserve and the Open Market Operations of 1932" *Journal of Economic History* 44(4) (1984): 957–83.

"Answers to Stock Questions: Fed Targets, Stock Prices, and the Gold Standard in the Great Depression" *Journal of Economic History* 51(1) (1991): 190–200.

Faust, J. and L. E. Svensson. "Transparency and Credibility: Monetary Policy with Unobservable Goals" *International Economic Review*, 42(2) (2001): 369–97.

Federal Reserve Bank of New York. "Understanding Open Market Operations" (http://www.newyorkfed.org/education/addpub/omo.html).

Ferguson, Niall. *The Cash Nexus: Money and Power in the World, 1700–2000* (New York: Basic Books, 2001).

Financial Times. "How to Home in on the Inflationary Range," 26 October 2005: 17.

Finch, T. P. *Barrons: Dictionary of Banking Terms* (4th edn) (2000).

Fischer, Irving (assisted by Harry G. Brown). *The Purchasing Power of Money: Its Determination in Relation to Credit Interest and Crises* (New York: Macmillan, 1911).

Fischer, Stanley. "Modern Central Banking" in Stanley Fischer, *IMF Essays from a Time of Crisis: The International Financial System, Stabilization, and Development* (Cambridge, MA: MIT Press, 2005): 169–222.

Fitch. "Sovereign Ratings Methodology" (http://rru.worldbank.org/Documents/Toolkits/Highways/pdf/extract/E24.pdf).

Fracasso, Andrea, Hans Genberg, and Charles Wyplosz. *How Do Central Banks Write? An Evaluation of Inflation Targeting Central Banks*

Geneva Reports of the World Economy 2 (Geneva: International Centre for Monetary and Banking Studies, 2003).

Frankel, S. Herbert. *Money: Two Philosophies: The Conflict of Trust and Authority* (Oxford: Basil Blackwell, 1977).

Freedman, Charles. "Central Bank Independence" in Paul Mizen (ed.) *Central Banking, Monetary Theory and Practice: Essays in Honour of Charles Goodhart*, vol. I (Cheltenham, UK and Northampton, MA: Edward Elgar, 2003): 90–110.

Friedman, Benjamin M. "The Use and Meaning of Words in Central Banking: Inflation Targeting, Credibility and Transparency" in Paul Mizen (ed.) *Central Banking, Monetary Theory and Practice: Essays in Honour of Charles Goodhart*, vol. I (Cheltenham, UK and Northampton, MA: Edward Elgar, 2003): 111–24.

Friedman, Benjamin F. and Kenneth Kuttner. "A Price Target for US Monetary Policy? Lessons from the Experience with Money Growth Targets" *Brookings Papers on Economic Activity* 1 (1996): 77–146.

Friedman, Milton. *Money Mischief: Episodes in Monetary History* (New York: Harcourt Brace, 1994).

Friedman, Milton and Anna Jacobson Schwartz. *A Monetary History of the United States, 1867–1960* (Princeton, NJ: Princeton University Press, 1963).

Fry, M., D. Julius, L. Mahadeva, S. Roger, and G. Sterne. "Key Issues in the Choice of Monetary Policy Framework" in L. Mahadeva and G. Sterne (eds.) *Monetary Policy Frameworks in a Global Context* (London: Routledge, 2000).

Galbraith, James K. "Time to Ditch the NAIRU" *Journal of Economic Perspectives* 11(1) (1997): 93–108.

Gavin, Francis. "Ideas, Power, and the Politics of US International Monetary Policy During the 1960s" in Jonathan Kirshner (ed.) *Monetary Orders: Ambiguous Economics, Ubiquitous Politics* (Ithaca, NY and London: Cornell University Press, 2003): 195–217.

Genberg, Hans, Robert N. McCauley, Yung Chul Park, and Avinash Persaud. *Official Reserves and Currency Management in Asia: Myth, Reality and the Future*, Geneva Reports on the World Economy 7 (Geneva: International Center for Monetary and Banking Studies, 2005).

Geraats, Petra M. "Central Bank Transparency" *The Economic Journal* 112 (2002): F532–F565.

Giddens, Anthony. *The Constitution of Society* (Berkeley, CA and Los Angeles: University of California Press, 1984).

The Consequences of Modernity (Stanford, CA: Stanford University Press, 1990).

Gilbert, R. Anton. "Operating Procedures for Conducting Monetary Policy" *Bulletin: Federal Reserve Bank of St. Louis* (February 1985): 13–21.

Goodhart, Charles A. E. and Haizhou Huang. "Time Inconsistency in a Model with Lags, Persistence, and Overlapping Wage Contracts" *Oxford Economic Papers* 50(3) (1998): 378–96.

Grabel, Ilene. "Ideology, Power, and the Rise of Independent Monetary Institutions in Emerging Economies" in Jonathan Kirshner (ed.) *Monetary Orders: Ambiguous Economics, Ubiquitous Politics* (Ithaca, NY and London: Cornell University Press, 2003): 25–54.

Greenspan, Alan. *The Age of Turbulence: Adventures in a New World* (London: Penguin, 2007).

Greider, William. *Secrets of the Temple: How the Federal Reserve Runs the Country* (New York: Touchstone, 1987).

Guitán, Manuel. "Rules or Discretion in Monetary Policy: National and International Perspectives" in Tomás J. T. Baliño and Carlo Cottarelli (eds.) *Frameworks for Monetary Stability: Policy Issues and Country Experiences* (Washington DC: International Monetary Fund, 1994): 19–41.

Haas, Peter M. (ed.). *Knowledge, Power, and International Policy Coordination* Special issue of *International Organization* 46(1) (1992).

Hall, Peter A. and David Soskice (eds.). *Varieties of Capitalism: The Institutional Foundations of Comparative Advantage* (Oxford: Oxford University Press, 2001).

Hall, Rodney Bruce. "Moral Authority as a Power Resource" *International Organization* 51(4) (1997): 591–622.

"The Discursive Demolition of the Asian Development Model" *International Studies Quarterly* 47(1) (2003): 71–99.

"Private Authority: Non-State Actors and Global Governance" *Harvard International Review* (summer 2005): 66–70.

"Explaining 'Market Authority' and Liberal Stability: Toward a Sociological-Constructivist Synthesis" *Global Society* 21(3) (2007): 319–45.

Hall, Rodney Bruce and Thomas J. Biersteker. *The Emergence of Private Authority in the Global Governance* (Cambridge: Cambridge University Press, 2002).

Hamilton-Hart, Natasha. *Asian States, Asian Bankers: Central Banking in Southeast Asia* (Ithaca, NY and London: Cornell University Press, 2002).

Hanke, Steve H. "On Dollarization and Currency Boards: Error and Deception" *Policy Reform* 5(4) (2002): 202–22.

Hanke, Steve H. and Kurt Schuler. *Currency Boards for Developing Countries: A Handbook* (San Francisco, CA: Institute for Contemporary Studies, 1994).

Hawkins, John. *Globalisation and Monetary Operations in Emerging Economies* BIS Papers no. 23 (Basle: Bank for International Settlements, 2005).

Helleiner, Eric. *States and the Reemergence of Global Finance: From Bretton Woods to the 1990s* (Ithaca, NY: Cornell University Press, 1994).

"Below the State: Micro-Level Monetary Power" in David M. Andrews (ed.) *International Monetary Power* (Ithaca, NY: Cornell University Press, 2006): 72–90.

Hosen, Frederick E. *The Great Depression and the New Deal: Legislative Acts in Their Entirety (1932–1933) and Statistical and Economic Data (1926–1946)* (Jefferson, NC and London: McFarland & Co., 1992).

Hooghe, Lisbet and Gary Marks. *Multilevel Governance and European Integration* (Lanham, MD: Rowman and Littlefield, 2001).

Hoover, Herbert. *The Great Depression: 1929–1941.* Vol. III, *The Memoirs of Herbert Hoover* (New York: Macmillan, 1952).

Hughes, Jennifer. "Investors 'Did Not Understand What They Were Buying,'" *Financial Times*, 5 December 2007.

Ingham, Geoffrey. *The Nature of Money* (Cambridge and Malden, MA: Polity Press, 2004).

Issing, Otmar. *The Euro Area and the Single Monetary Policy* Osterreichische Nationalbank, Working Paper 44 (2001).

Should We Have Faith in Central Banks? (London: Institute for Economic Affairs, 2002).

Kapstein, Ethan B. *Governing the Global Economy: International Finance and the State* (Cambridge, MA: Harvard University Press, 1984).

Keeley, Terrence. "Myths About the Sovereign Menace to Treasuries'" *Financial Times*, 29 June 2007.

Kelsey, Jane. "The Denationalization of Money: Embedded Neo-Liberalism and the Risks of Implosion" *Social and Legal Studies* 12(2) (2003): 155–76.

Kenen, Peter B. *The International Financial Architecture: What's New?, What's Missing?* (Washington, DC: Institute for International Economics, 2001).

Keohane, Robert. *After Hegemony* (Princeton, NJ: Princeton University Press, 1984).

Keynes, John Maynard. *The Economic Consequences of Mr. Churchill* (London: Hogarth Press, 1925).

A Treatise on Money (London, Macmillan, 1930).

Kindleberger, Charles P. *The World in Depression: 1929–1939* (Berkeley, CA: The University of California Press, 1986).

A Financial History of Western Europe (2nd edn) (Oxford and New York: Oxford University Press, 1993).

Manias, Panics, and Crashes: A History of Financial Crises (New York: Wiley, 2000).

Kirshner, Jonathan. *Currency and Coercion: The Political Economy of International Monetary Power* (Princeton, NJ: Princeton University Press, 1995).

"The Inescapable Politics of Money" in Jonathan Kirshner (ed.) *Monetary Orders: Ambiguous Economics, Ubiquitous Politics* (Ithaca, NY and London: Cornell University Press, 2003): pp. 3–24.

Kirshner, Jonathan (ed.). *Monetary Orders: Ambiguous Economics, Ubiquitous Politics* (Ithaca, NY and London: Cornell University Press, 2003).

Kratochwil, Friedrich V. *Rules, Norms and Decisions: On the Conditions of Practical and Legal Reasoning in International Relations and Domestic Affairs* (Cambridge: Cambridge University Press, 1989).

"Sovereignty as *Dominium*: Is there a Right to Humanitarian Intervention?" in G. Lyons and M. Mastanduno (eds.) *Beyond Westphalia* (Baltimore, MD: Johns Hopkins University Press, 1995): 21–42.

Krugman, Paul. *The Return of Depression Economics* (New York: W. W. Norton, 1999).

Kydland, Finn and Edward Prescott. "Rules Rather than Discretion: The Inconsistency of Optimal Plans" *Journal of Political Economy* (June 1977): 473–91.

Macleod, H. D. *The Principles of Economical Philosophy*, vol. I (2nd edn) (London: 1872).

Maxfield, Sylvia. *Gatekeepers of Growth: The International Political Economy of Central Banking in Developing Countries* (Princeton, NJ: Princeton University Press, 1997).

Mayer, Martin. *The Fed: The Inside Story of How the World's Most Powerful Financial Institution Drives the Markets* (New York: The Free Press, 2001).

McCloskey, Dierdre N. *The Rhetoric of Economics* (2nd edn) (Madison, WI: University of Wisconsin Press, 1998).

Mercer, Jonathan L. *Reputation and International Politics* (Ithaca, NY: Cornell University Press, 1996).

Meyer, Laurence H. "The Politics of Monetary Policy: Balancing Independence and Accountability." Remarks Delivered at the University of Wisconsin, LaCrosse, Wisconsin, October 24, 2000.

A Term at the Fed: An Insider's View (New York: Harper Collins, 2004).

Mishkin, Frederic S. *Inflation Targeting in Emerging Market Countries* NBER Working Paper 7618 (2000).

Mitchell, Tom. "Hong Kong Committed to Sticking with the US Dollar," *Financial Times*, 2 November 2007.

Moser-Boehm, Paul. "The Relationship Between the Central Bank and the Government" in *Central Banks and the Challenge of Development* (Basle: Bank for International Settlements, 2006): 45–63.

Mosley, Layna. *Global Capital and National Governments* (Cambridge: Cambridge University Press, 2003).

Mussa, Michael. "The Triumph of Paper Credit" in Forrest Capie and Geoffrey E. Wood, *Monetary Economics in the 1990s*, The Henry Thornton Lectures 9–17 (London: Macmillan, 1996): 146–79.

  Argentina and the Fund: From Triumph to Tragedy (Washington, DC: Institute for International Economics, 2002).

Ollier, Maria Matilde. "Argentina: Up a Blind Alley Once Again" *Bulletin of Latin American Research* 22(2) (2003) 170–86.

Pauly, Louis. "Capital Mobility, State Autonomy and Political Legitimacy" *Journal of International Affairs* 48(2) (1995): 369–88.

Poole, William. "Monetary Policy Rules?" *Review: Federal Reserve Bank of St. Louis* (March/April 1999): 3–12.

Radelet Steven and Jeffrey D. Sachs. "The East Asian Financial Crisis: Diagnosis, Remedies, Prospects" *Brookings Papers on Economic Activity* 1 (1998): 1–98.

Resche, Catherine. "Investigating 'Greenspanese': From Hedging to 'Fuzzy Transparency'" *Discourse and Society* 15(6) (2004): 723–44.

Rogoff, Kenneth. "The Optimal Degree of Commitment to an Intermediate Monetary Target" *Quarterly Journal of Economics* 100(4) (1985): 1169–90.

Rosenau, James N. "Governance, Order, and Change in World Politics" in James N. Rosenau and Ernst-Otto Czempiel (eds.) *Governance Without Government: Order and Change in World Politics* (Cambridge: Cambridge University Press, 1992).

Rubin, Robert E. and Jacob Weisberg. *In an Uncertain World: Tough Choices from Wall Street to Washington* (New York: Random House, 2003).

Ruggie, John Gerard. "International Regimes, Transactions and Change: Embedded Liberalism in the Postwar Economic Order" *International Organization* 36(2) (1982): 378–415.

Schuler, Kurt. *Should Developing Countries Have Central Banks? Currency Quality and Monetary Systems in 155 Countries* (London: Institute for Economic Affairs, 1996).

Searle, John R. *The Construction of Social Reality* (New York: The Free Press, 1995).
"What is an Institution?" *Journal of Institutional Economics* 1(1) (2005): 1–22.
Sen, Amartya K. "Rational Fools: A Critique of the Behavioral Foundations of Economic Theory" *Philosophy and Public Affairs* 6(4) (1997): 317–44.
Shiller, Robert. "Speculative Booms and Crashes" in Forrest Capie and Geoffrey E. Wood, *Monetary Economics in the 1990s* The Henry Thornton Lectures, 9–17 (London: Macmillan, 1996): 58–74.
Irrational Exuberance (New York: Broadway Books, 2000).
Sibert, A. "Monetary Policy Committees: Individual and Collective Reputation" *Review of Economic Studies* 70 (July 2003): 649–65.
Simons, Henry C. "Rules Versus Authorities in Monetary Policy" *Journal of Political Economy* 44(1) (1936): 1–30.
Sinclair, Timothy J. *The New Masters of Capital: American Bond Rating Agencies and the Politics of Creditworthiness* (Ithaca, NY and London: Cornell University Press, 2005).
Solomon, Steven. *The Confidence Game: How Unelected Central Bankers are Governing the Changed Global Economy* (New York: Simon & Schuster, 1995).
Soros, George. *The Alchemy of Finance: Reading the Mind of the Market* (New York: Wiley & Sons, 1987).
Stiglitz, Joseph. "Reflections on the Natural Rate Hypothesis" *Journal of Economic Perspectives* 11(1) (1997): 1–10.
"Must Financial Crises Be this Frequent and this Painful?" McKay Lecture, Pittsburgh, Pennsylvania, September 23, 1998.
Globalization and Its Discontents (New York: Norton, 2002).
Stoneham, Paul. "Too Close to the Hedge: The Case of Long Term Capital Management LP Part One: Hedge Fund Analytics" *European Management Journal* 17(3): 282–9.
"Too Close to the Hedge: The Case of Long Term Capital Management LP Part Two: Near-collapse and Rescue" *European Management Journal* 17(4): 382–90.
Sutton, Gregory D. *Potentially Endogenous Borrowing and Developing Country Sovereign Credit Ratings* Occasional Paper no. 5 (Basle: Bank for International Settlements, 2005).
Svensson, Lars E. O. "Inflation Targeting as a Monetary Policy Rule" *Journal of Monetary Economics* 43 (1999): 607–54.
Swedberg, Richard. *Max Weber and the Idea of Economic Sociology* (Princeton, NJ: Princeton University Press, 1998).

Tett, Gillian, Richard Milne, and Krishna Guha. "ECB Injects €95bn to Aid Markets," *Financial Times*, 10 August 2007
  "Money Markets Squeeze: Sense of Crisis Growing Over Interbank Deals," *Financial Times*, 5 September 2007.

Toniolo, Gianni. *Central Bank Cooperation at the Bank for International Settlements, 1930–1973* (Cambridge: Cambridge University Press, 2005).

Torre, Augusto de la, Eduardo Levy Yeyati, and Sergio L. Scmukler. *Living and Dying with Hard Pegs: The Rise and Fall of Argentina's Currency Board* (Washington, DC: World Bank, 2003).

Treaster, Joseph B. *Paul Volcker: The Making of a Financial Legend* (New York: John Wiley & Sons, 2004).

Truman, Edwin M. and Anna Wong. *The Case for an International Reserve Diversification Standard*, Working Paper WP 06–2 (May 2006) (Washington, DC: Institute for International Economics, 2006).

Turccille, Jerome. *Alan Shrugged: Alan Greenspan, the World's Most Powerful Banker* (New York: John Wiley & Sons, 2002).

Van 't dack, Jozef. *Implementing Monetary Policy in Emerging Market Economies: An Overview of Issues* BIS Papers no. 5: *Monetary Policy Operating Procedures in Emerging Market Economies* (Basle: Bank for International Settlements, 1999): 3–72.

Vickers, John. "Inflation Targeting in Practice: The UK Experience" *Bank of England Quarterly Bulletin* 38(4) (1998): 368–75.

Wade, Robert and Frank Veneroso. "The Asian Crisis: The High Debt Model Versus the Wall Street-Treasury-IMF Complex." *New Left Review* no. 228 (March/April 1998): 3–24.

Walter, Andrew. "Domestic Sources of International Monetary Leadership" in David M. Andrews (ed.) *International Monetary Power* (Ithaca, NY: Cornell University Press, 2006): 51–71.

Waltz, Kenneth. *Theory of International Politics* (Boston, MA: Addison-Wesley, 1979).

Weber, Max. *Economy and Society: An Outline of Interpretive Sociology* (Berkeley, CA: University of California Press, 1978).

Wendt, Alexander. "Anarchy is What States Make of It" *International Organization* 46(2) (1992): 391–425.
  Social Theory of International Politics (Cambridge: Cambridge University Press, 1999).

Werner, Richard A. *Princes of the Yen: Japan's Central Bankers and the Transformation of the Economy* (Armonk, NY and London: M. E. Sharpe, 2003).

Widmaier, Wesley W. "The Social Construction of the 'Impossible Trinity': The Intersubjective Bases of Monetary Cooperation" *International Studies Quarterly* 48 (2004): 433–53.

Wolf, Martin. "Central Banks should not Rescue Fools from their folly," *Financial Times*, 28 August 2007.

Woo-Cumings, Meredith. *The Developmental State* (Ithaca, NY: Cornell University Press, 1999).

Woodward, Bob. *Maestro: Greenspan's Fed and the American Boom* (New York: Touchstone, 2001).

Index

Cambridge Studies in International Relations